sTodpa Language of Lahul in the Himalaya

sTodpa Language of Lahul in the Himalaya

Tobdan

Kaveri Books
New Delhi - 110002

ISBN : 978-93-86463-11-1
Edition 2020

Published by
Kaveri Books
4832/24, Ansari Road, Daryaganj,
New Delhi - 110 002 (India)
Ph. : 011-2328 8140, 2324 5799
E-mail : info@kaveribooks.com
kaveribooks@gmail.com
Website : www.kaveribooks.com

Typesetting at Creative Graphics, Delhi

PRINTED IN INDIA

Preface

sTodpa, a subsidiary of Bhoti, is spoken in the upper part of Bhaga valley in Lahul, in the high Western Himalaya. It is estimated that at present (2019) the language is spoken by about 4000 inhabitants half of which may be presumed to be living outside sTod, but mostly outside Lahul. The area being remote and inaccessible the language remained much saved from the influences of the other close and powerful languages. It remained preserved as such since long past. Therefore it possesses some archaic characteristics. Presently as a result of number of developmental initiatives taken up by the government the area has become much easier to access. The flow of commuters has increased immensely. The Manali-Leh national highway passes right through the whole area. The inhabitants have changed their professions and mode of their living. Culture and language are the worst affected victims of modernisation. The language is at a fast rate of decline.

sTodpa has been studied by some European scholars like H.A. Jaeschke and George D. Roerich. Although Jaeschke has drawn heavily from the language but has not been able to mention the name anywhere in his works.

The existing presentation comes from a non-specialist layman having no professional background but has advantage of being a native speaker. sTodpa is the author's mother tongue. I am deeply indebted to two great scholars on the subject: Prof. Devy and Prof. Koul. Dr. Ganesh N. Devy drew me, laying confidence in me, into the great field of the People's Linguistic Survey of India, even though stranger to the kind of noble task. From the opportunity I earned great energy and confidence and pursued my task with much vigour. I was greatly rewarded by the simple words of advices from Dr. Omkar N. Koul who unhesitatingly accepted my request to go through the first draft of the work. For some reasons, I felt it necessary to peruse the work to bring about some improvement in it.

I am thankful to Shri Rakesh Goel, Kaveri Books, for accepting the book for publication.

Tobdan

Contents

1

Introduction

sTod: The Setting and Environment

Area and the People: The upper inhabited part of Bhaga valley in Lahul, Himachal Pradesh, the length of about 40 kilometers, below Bara Lacha La and above Tingrig (Stingri), on the right side of the river and Čugtā (Pyukar), on the left side, respectively, in Punan, the lower part of Bhaga valley, is known as sTod, literally Upland. This is known as such to the inhabitants and also to those of the other parts of Lahul. Lahul is a bowl of mountains. The three valleys of Chandra, Bhaga and the upper part of the combined river Chandrabhaga are surrounded by high mountain ranges. In the winter it receives heavy snowfall. The area remains cut off from the rest of the world for at least four to five months and even in the summer communication with the neighbouring areas is possible only through the high passes which number around half a dozen, the lowest being 13,000 feet above sea level. Even the passage through the exit of Chandrabhaga from Lahul and entering into Pangi is so narrow as like as closed. Only sheep and men with load could cross the path with difficulty. The usual communication between Lahul and Pangi was through Ghordhar, a pass between Patanam or Miyar Nala, and Saichu, in Pangi.

Lahul remained a meeting point and buffer zone between two great international geographies as well as the cultures of Indo-Aryan in northern India, on the south and that of Central Asia on the north. The international trade route, a branch of the Silk Route, the connecting line between the two great international cultures, touching on the one side with the fertile plains of northern India and on the other with the great trading centres of Yarkand, Kashgar, etc., in Central Asia, passed right through whole of sTod and most part of Lahul.

In the summer number of caravans of laden ponies, large herds of sheep and goats, and perhaps also rarely the hordes of invading armies, passed through the area. Gaddis with their large herds of sheep and goat were the annual visitors to Lahul. They had their *thāč*, resting place, at the top of the villages, where they returned in the evening with their herds after grazing in the day. They spent about three months in Lahul including the period spent in journey for their coming and going. Lahul remained politically attached to Ladak, Chamba and Kullu. Internally Lahul remained generally undisturbed and also less affected by the great disturbances taking place outside, in its long history.

The people were small agriculturists living in a high altitude narrow valley. Only one crop could be grown in a year on the small slopy fields. This could not be done without irrigation. They grew a few kinds of cereals of necessity. In order to augment their income they reared a good number of sheep and goats and cattle. The third sector of their economy was annual small trading trips for wool, salt, etc. between Jangthang and Guge on the north and Kullu, Mandi, Kangra, etc. in the south. The social activities and festivals were much related to them. All these features have now disappeared.

These factors contributed in the preservation and development of the language of the area. These languages nourished in exclusive social groups, a community, and there was limited interaction like marriage, etc. between the communities.

After the independence, the whole environment started changing at a fast speed. Construction of roads and bridges, and introduction of other modern means of communication made the interaction between the communities and with the outside world more frequent, faster, and transport of goods both inwards and outwards speedy. In the new environment there are many kinds of fast moving vehicles, carrying heavy loads and many passengers, and there are offices, hospitals, schools, shops and other kinds of establishments. There are employees, travelers, tourists, labourers, and many kinds of people. They all speak different languages. The old environment of the languages has changed at a great speed to a great degree. People have changed their dress, ornaments, jewellery, labourious hairdo of ladies, tools, implements, and all kinds of items of regular use. They have discarded the old crafts.

Now the sources of new vocabulary, the source of development of the languages, is bazaar, work place, TV, newspaper, etc. None is required to manufacture any word of his own. Development in any activity in the area like agriculture, animal husbandry, etc. all are accompanied by technical terms. The whole kitchen has transformed its set up, utensils and preparations alongwith the raw materials. Thus even if one speaks his own language it is only a skeleton. Many words of their languages have now become disused and are at the verge of disappearance.

The small societies which were tightly regulated by many strict social laws have become liberated at once. Every male child can now establish his own family. This has visibly increased the population and the number of speakers of the small languages. But their quality has weakened. The new generation has grown in an entirely different environment from the one in which their parents had lived. They don't inherit the culture and the language fully. Physically they are handicapped. They possess flat tongues and cannot twist according to the requirement of small archaic languages.

Education has encouraged emigration. As a result the boys and girls marry from different language groups, within Lahul and outside. In the family both the parents speak different languages. They communicate with their children in a third language.

The educated elite class goes out in service and in the village there remain those who could not get work outside. The small languages are in this manner weakening rapidly.

About half a dozen languages are spoken in Lahul belonging to at least two great families of languages. Each language is nourished by the distinct community which possesses distinct traditions and customs.

The ancient small languages differ structurally from their originator, the great language of which they form a part. The small languages have either decimated some organs or they retain some of their original overgrowths. In sTodpa the verbs remain unchanged in all the tenses. The auxiliaries distinguish descriptions by visibility. Different auxiliaries are used with the verbs whether an object is visible, or not visible, or is known by knowledge by the speaker.

The Language: The sTodpa language, a branch of Bhoti language, is known to the linguists, as belonging to the Tibeto-Himalayan branch of the Tibeto-Burman family of languages. The other areas in Lahul speaking language similar to sTodpa, but slightly different, are Patanam (Miyāṛ Nālā), the valley of the tributary of Chandrabhaga which meets it at Udaipur; and some part of Ranglo and Khoksar, i.e. the upper part of Chandra valley. The sTodpas know the lower part of Bhaga valley as Punan and others in Lahul call it Gahar. Chandrabhaga valley is known as Manchad and the Chandra valley is known in three parts as Tinan, the lower part nearer to Tandi and around Gundhla, as Ranglo the middle part, and as Khoksar, the uppermost part, nearer to the Rohtang pass. The languages of these regions are known by the same name respectively.

Methodology: The present work comes from a non-specialist layman, but a native speaker. The aim is to attempt to place some material on the language in preservation. The examples are given mosltly as they come across in the practical use. Some of the sentences were collected from the people spoken on special occasions and gathered during long span of time. Otherwise it might have been difficult to construct such sentences with ordinary efforts. Thus some unnecessary congestions have been created.

Number of Speakers: sTodpa is a colloquial spoken by a few people, one kothi of the fourteen kothis of Lahul. According to the census of 1981 there lived 32,100 inhabitants in district Lahul-Spiti out of which 1732 lived in 342 households in sTod. In 2001 the population of sTod was 2103. At present (2019) the gross number of speakers of the language may be estimated at around 4000 including approximately half of the number as mobile and migrant or living outside the area due to education, employment, occupation, residence, etc. Between the two census figures there has been no significant increase in the population. Among the existing census population there may be number of non-speakers of the language which has not been taken into account in our figure.

Literature: The literature with which the sTodpa society is familiar, is of three kinds. The first and the largest in volume is the written religious literature of Tibetan Buddhism, whose age of advent in the area, may be considered about one thousand years. There are books in the monasteries and with most of the households. Its utilization, however, remains confined to the lamas and that too with a limited purpose. There is no literature of this kind composed by any local scholar. The second kind of literature is of secular nature existing in oral tradition. These are the stories and the various kinds of songs like *bag-glu*, marriage songs, and *gral-glu~ḍal-lu,* songs sung by the laymen during the gatherings, ceremonies and festivals like the New Year, etc. This literature is found written in pieces with some people and it has wide currency in the society. These are samples of the archaic sTodpa literary language. The third kind of the literature is purely local and of folk tradition, but it is again religious. In sTod besides the *Naŋ-pe Čhos*, Buddhism, another kind of religion called *Lha- čhos*, Religion of gods, a primitive folk religion, is also practiced. There are number of folk deities in this religion who are propitiated at some occasions of economic importance like sowing and harvesting and of social importance. There are prayers for these gods. These are small in volume and few in number but they had been in wide use. In the prayers request is made for timely rain, water, good crop, prosperity, health, wealth, safety in the journeys, etc. These prayers are also spoken before taking meal, and at the time of offering *čhaŋ* and *a-rag* (beer and wine) to the guests and at all the important ceremonies. These prayers are purely in folk language and are folk compositions. They are used by the laymen and not by the lamas. The lamas recite prayers on all these occasions from the written religious literature.

All the three forms of the literature are static in sTod. The practitioners stick only to the traditional stock. There has been no new addition known to have been made in the near past. In practice there are some specialists in all these three fields. There is no need to mention about the lamas with respect to the written literature for their role is well known. As regards the folk songs, in every marriage it is tradition that both the parties of the boy and the girl have to engage a *Lur-pon* (*glu-dpon*), Song-Officer, of their own, who leads the party of *ñu-pa,* the bridal party and they sing during the whole three days of the ceremony. As such they are also leaders in singing the *ḍal-lu*. These ceremonial songs are sung in groups therefore there are number of followers to the *Lur-pon*. As regards the third form of literature, which is quite different from those of Buddhism, there are the *Labdag-pa* (*Lha-bdag-pa*), priests, who worship the local deities at least twice a year with full dress. But the two have no antagonism between each other, for there are families where father is *Labdag* and the son is *lama.* This *Labdag* has no other important role. There is no strict ritual for his initiation. He does not experience the possession of spirit. This kind of priest who experiences spirit possession is called *Lha-pha* (possessed of god, i.e. spirit) and there is no *Lha-pha* in sTod. The two kinds of songs, marriage songs and gathering songs, may be taken as representing the old literary form of the language.

Subdivisions of the Language: sTodpa is divided into the following four categories:

1. *Čhos-skad*, Language of the Religion (Buddhism).
2. *Phal-skad,* Language of the common people, Common Language.
3. *Ya-sha-'i skad*, Language of Love or Honorific Language, and
4. *Ṭu-'u-'i skad*, Child Language.

We are not dealing with the first. Our main subject is *phal-skad*, the second kind, the colloquial. The last two sections comprise only small sets of vocabularies and are parts of *phal-skad.*

Salient Features of the Languuage

Relationship between sTodpa and Bhoti language: There is one difference observed prominently in the formation of verbal words in sTodpa and in the literary Bhoti. The verbal words in sTodpa generally begin with the first letter of the row of various classes of alphabets viz. k of k-sde, č of ča-sde, etc. The corresponding word formed in Bhoti begins with the second or third letter of the row of the respective class. Thus against the first letters of the rows of different classes viz. k, č, t, p, ts and ś in sTodpa, the words in Bhoti begin with kh or ga; čh; th or da; pha or ba; tsh; and čh respectively. Examples:

Word in sTodpa	Meaning	Word in Bhoti
skol-če, bkrol-če	*to load, untie*	*'khol-ba, 'khrol-ba*
bkab-če, krum-če	*cover, prune*	*'geb-pa, 'grum-pa*
bču-če, bčag-če	*irrigate, break*	*'čhu-ba, 'čhog-pa*
rtag-če, rtul-če	*grind (in mill)* *grind(manually)*	*'thag-pa, 'thul-ba*
gting-če, gtub-če	*spread, cut*	*'ding-ba, sdub-pa*
dpye-če, dpul-če	*open, offer*	*phyes-ba, 'phul-ba*
tsir-če, btsal-če	*squeeze,search.*	*'tshir-ba, 'tshal-ba*
śi-če, śar-če	*die, rise*	*'čhi-ba, 'čhar-ba*

Formation of New Words: Some words have developed in the peculiar existing geographical situation and cultural environment during the course of long period of existence of the society. Geographically the whole area is a narrow valley. The mountain ranges rise on either side starting nearly close to the *čhu-ta (čhu-mth'a,* water-end), i.e. river, and ending at high peaks. The village settlements are situated on the slopes in between the two points but closer to the river. At the edge of every village on the upper side there is a wide open space called *ma-ka-sam* from where paths lead to *re-'a*, mountain slopes. Each household brings daily in the morning in the first batch the strong bodied sheep, goat and the cattle of the yak species. The village shepherd *lugzi-čhe-'a,* senior shepherd i.e *lug-rdsi* (sheep shepherd), takes them for grazing. The remaining animals are taken by *lugzi čhuŋ-ŋa*, junior shepherd also called *ra-rdsi* (cattle shepherd). There grow in the *re-'a* bushes, nourishing grass, herbs, etc. and there the village cattle are grazed during the summer. In the evening the villagers collect their cattle from there. The turn of the lugzi is now reversed, the junior shepherd comes first. This is a daily meeting place for all the villagers. The second such place is *'murti'*, the water collection point of the village.

In the morning the sun rises behind the rows of sharp edged mountain peaks looking like standing conical chaityas in the east and spreads its pink rays on the mountain peaks on the other side which slowly changing its colour reaches down to touch the river and then covers the whole valley. This sunny part on the mountain face is named *ri-rtsi* (mountain paint). Progress in its movement from the top of the mountain down to the riverline is watched by the villagers very carefully. This phenomenon of movement of the line between the sun and shade in the morning and evening has important role in regulating the routine daily work of the inhabitants including leaving the cattle for grazing and bringing them to home. This has made certain important contributions in the linguistic asset of the area. Some important sentences connected with the term are: *ri-rtsi 'khor-soŋ, ri-rtsi čhu-ta ru sleb-soŋ, ri-rtsi mčhod-soŋ.* These may be translated as: *ri-si* has appeared, *ri-si* has reached the river, *ri-si* has disappeared. This last sentence is an honorific expression.

Some terms have developed in the socio-economic life of the people. For example the work done between the dawn and breakfast is called *'od-las, i.e.* work done in the light. Among the field workers employed on regular basis is, as elsewhere, called *la-bo,* servant. But further terms are of local origin. One who has been kept, may be from the same village or nearby, for the periodically fixed days during the period of heavy work in the summer, say coming on every third day or so, is called *be-mi* (*bas-mi)* sitting man or woman. His turn is termed as *re-mo*, literally line, i.e. turn.

She may be having similar engagements with other households for the other days. The one who is invited on the particular day of requirement on the basis of daily wage is called *li-mi* (*las-mi),* workman. Exchange of labour i.e. a person a day for a person a day, the most common practice of agricultural operations, is called *be* (*bas~be).*

In sTod there has developed certain peculiar terms with social institutions. In the kinship system of sTodpa the brothers and sisters are ranked in the set of four grades by birth and age. The brother or brothers younger than the Ego is addressed as *no*. The eldest, usually the first born, is addressed as *a-čo*. All others between *a-čo* and the Ego are addressed as *čo-čo.* Similarly among the sisters younger than the Ego are addressed as *no-mo*, the first born as *a-či* and all between *a-či* and the Ego are addressed as *a-pu*. These terms are both of address and reference.

In the winter people usually go to Kullu or lower areas who are called *dgun-mjug-pa,* winter migrants. They return at the end of the winter before the starting of the work of ploughing. Those going with the caravan of horses is known as *rta-pa*, horse-man, those going otherwise are known as *mi-raŋ,* man-alone.

Some more Features

The above examples show that some terms developed locally in the typically tough and harsh geographical and socio-economic environment during the long course of existence of the society here. We list here some more features of the language:

i. The language is archaic and unreformed. Verbs don't change with the change of tense, gender and number. There are number of auxiliaries which help a verb in giving the meaning of the desired tenses, (Chs, 8 & 9).

ii. The auxiliary 'is' in the the present has three forms to express three situations: visual, touch, and knowledge.

iii. There are number of particles (Ch. 14) which modify the shades of meaning of the words which fulfill the requirement of vocabulary to a great extent.

iv. In the sentence the subject, wherever necessary, conveys the sense of gender and number. These are not found in the verbs and auxiliaries.

v. The language has a set of vocabulary relating to the children and for dealing with the members of noble class, (Ch. 16).

vi. In the sentences the subject is often not expressed which is understood from the context.

vii. There is a simple way of formation of entirely new words. This is done by describing the sounds, visuals, etc. They are in large number, (Ch. 16), even though they may be weak in conveying the desired meaning.

viii. sTodpa has double form of the dual of the first person, (Ch. 6): *ŋa-ža* and a-'o.

ix. sTodpa has very few borrowed words from other languages.

History of study of the language:

During the British period some European scholars like H.A. Jaeschke and George De Roerich conducted study of the sTodpa language and they have made valuable contributions.

H.A. Jaeschke: The study of sTodpa language alongwith the other languages in Lahul began with the founding of the mission office of the Moravian Church at Kyelang in 1854. In this regard the leading figure was H.A. Jaeschke who came here in 1857 and after remaining here for eleven years returned to Germany in 1868. He was a great linguist and was master of several languages including Sanskrit and Tibetan.

Jaeschke during his stay at Kyelang collected many words from different languages in Lahul and around it including sTodpa, which he calls collectively as West Tibet and incorporated them in his well known work 'Tibetan-English Dictionary' which was first published in 1881. The author gives a list of words separately in a comparative chart and also in the main text. In Lahul this could come substantially from sTod. Jaeschke does not mention the name sTodpa or any other. Before this, Jaeschke also got published a book on the grammar of the language, at Kyelang in 1865. The work, as stated in the title, also treats the spoken languages. These the author has divided into West Tibet and East Tibet. Beyond this we are not able to get detail of any language. The languages of sTod, Zanskar, Ladak and Spiti, if we consider them as Jaeschke's group of languages of West Tibet, vary greatly from each other. The later edition of the work agrees mostly with the religious literary language.

Jaeschke also contributed a sample for the Grierson's great Linguistic Survey of India, which is a piece from the *Dorčhod,* Vajračhedika and does not represent the colloquial language.

Grierson remarks, 'the Lahul dialect has, however, been mentioned and partly described by the late Rev. H.A. Jaeschke, and it will therefore be possible to make some few remarks which it is hoped will be sufficient to show how the dialect should be classed'. Further he says, 'our information about the inflexion of nouns and verbs is exceedingly scanty. We only know that the usual suffix of the verbal noun is *ce*'.'

In the Survey two prominent features have been observed in the language that it has a distinct tone and the compound consonants become simplified. Jaeschke's work is a pioneer work and it gives representation to much wider area. His contributions are by all means invaluable and unforgettable.

Georges de Roerich: Roerich was first scholar to study (1934) the sTodpa language comprehensively together with that of Khoksar in the upper Chandra valley. Roerich, a great scholar and linguist, stayed at Naggar, in Kullu.

He names the language as '*Kolong',* distinguishing it from similar dialects spoken in the areas of Khoksar and Patanam in Lahul. During the rule of the Rajas of Kullu, sTod was administratively known as kothi (a division) Kolong, known after the name of the main village of the area. He, however, does not fail to mention that it is commonly designated by the name of sTod-skad 'the language of the upland'. He further writes that it relates to and is the sub-dialect of the Ladaki spoken in the upper Indus Valley above Sheh, called by A.H. Francke as Rong dialect and that of Zanskar spoken around sPadum.

Roerich writes on the history of the study of the language in the words that: "For some reasons the Tibetan dialect of Lahul in N.W. Himalayas never formed the subject of a separate monograph similar to that on the Ladak dialect by the late Dr. A.H. Francke, although both H.A. Jaeschke and Francke made a prolonged stay in Lahul. The literature on the dialect is very scant. Jaeschke in an article gave a short specimen of the dialect. In his Notes on the Pronunciation of the Tibetan Language (Journal of the Asiatic Society of Bengal, 1865, pp. 91 ff.) he gave a short list of words as pronounced in the Bunan dialect and the Tibetan dialect of upper

Lahul, that in the upper course of the Bhaga river. The Introduction to his Tibetan English Dictionary (London, 1881) contains a list of words in the Lahul dialect on pp. xvi and ff. His Tibetan Grammar (reprinted in 1929) frequently refers to the dialect of Lahul, although in most cases the examples quoted in the text are called West Tibetan, and no differentiation is made between the different dialects of the Western Tibetan group. The great Linguistic Survey of India contains in vol. III devoted to the Tibeto-Burman family of Languages, a brief notice on the Lahul dialect (pp. 69-71) in which it is said that, 'no new materials have been forwarded for the purposes of the Survey. The Lahul dialect has, however, been mentioned and partly described by the late Rev. H.A. Jaeschke," (Roerich,1934:83). Roerich got composed some samples in prose and collected some traditional festival songs as a source material for his work.

About this he writes, 'The first is represented by numerous sentences taken from the everyday speech of the Lahuli hillmen, and the second by several New Year songs and prayers, that represent the literary form of the dialect and belong to an older strata of the language. As in the case of the other Tibetan dialects, the literary form of the Lahul dialect is closely related to the literary Tibetan and is only slightly tinted with colloquialism peculiar to Lahul'.

Roerich further writes, 'The dialects of Central Tibet still exercise a powerful influence on the dialects of Outer Tibet, and each Lahuli hillman, who has visited Central Tibet or made a stay there, represents a channel through which this influence penetrates the local language. Lahuli lamas belonging to the 'Brug-pa bKa'-rgyud sect made frequent trips to Bhutan and Tibet proper, and often spend many years in the study of the Buddhist Doctrine in some of the great centres of learning in the country. The result is that their speech becomes strongly tinted by that of Central Tibet, and exercise a considerable influence on the everyday speech of their countrymen. The Lahul dialect is important for the study of Tibetan linguistics because it represents a transitory stage between the dialects of the Western Tibetan group (Ladak, Zangskar, Balti, Purig) and those of Spiti and sTod mNg'aris-skor-gsum which have a close affinity to the dialects of Central Tibet. The dialect of Lahul preserves many archaic forms of Tibetan speech. Its transitory character has been already noticed in the Linguistic Survey of India, where it is described (Survey, Vol. III, p. 69) 'as a kind of link between Western and Central Tibetan'. This transitory nature of the dialect is clearly demonstrated by the existence of two distinct pronunciations of many words: one corresponding to the Western Tibetan pronunciation, and the other approaching that of the Central Tibetan, (Roerich, 1934: 84).

It may be remarked here that the songs collected by Roerich are old which have been handed down from generation to generation in oral tradition. However, the compositions that he got written were perhaps done by lamas, as at places they appear to have been affected by the religious literary language.

Roerich made some important observations on the language as follows:

i. In colloquial, pronunciation of prefixes and suffixes are not heard, except rarely in the prefixes of the second part of the words. Thus the word most of the time is heard in the same tone in all the three tenses, with a few exceptions. This word is the root of the verb without changing its form of tenses, called *miŋ-rkyaŋ* (only name).

ii. The verb shows the distinctions of tenses and persons by the use of auxiliary 'to be' in different forms that it takes in different tenses and persons. They, however, ordinarily do not show the distinction of sex and number of the subject they qualify.

iii. In the verbs ordinarily the second part is '*ce*', *btaŋ-ce,* which is, when declined, replaced by the auxiliary. But many times it is retained.

iv. The difference in transitive and intransitive verbs is often not heard.

v. Infinitive is formed by adding the particle '*ce*', to the verbal stem. It thus also acquires a substantive value. The subject and the verb which it qualifies, standing close by alone do not convey the meaning, intended to be relayed, clearly, specially in the first person. For example: *ŋa-čha.* Here the format of the sentence is as is placed in other languages, 'I go' in English. But here it also may mean 'go me'. Therefore here the sentence is made clear by adding the set of auxiliaries, or adding the sign of case with the subject, noun or pronoun.

vi. Due to the presence of the strong trend of contraction of the final letter in a word and similarly the final set of auxiliary of a sentence, the auxiliary words in a sentence contract to form one or more words and take several shapes. The changes are based on the final letter of the penultimate word after formation. Their uses differ in person and tense. These are, however, irregular and new forms also appear.

Roerich's contribution to the study of sTodpa language is of immense value. It covers most of the important aspects of the language and is the only and authentic work by any specialist on the subject till the present time. Besides the compositions, the author has also given a glossary of about five hundred words collected from the area.

The Future of sTodpa Language: The situation of living in a compact cultural cluster by the sTodpas is shortlived. They are bound to be uprooted and to disperse in the very near future. sTod has passed through one great physical change. The vehicular road from Manali to Leh has been linked. Great disturbances are likely to occur on the commissioning of two new large developmental projects. The opening of the tunnel under Rohtang is likely to invite heavy flow of crowd into the valley, carrying with it both good and bad elements. Secondly the proposed construction of a big dam over the river Bhaga at the junction of the three rivers of Bhaga and its two tributaries of Yotse and Sumdo is likely to lead to uprooting of the whole population of sTod resulting in pre-mature death of one whole but a tiny culture.

2

Tibetan Script and its Origin

Presently there are three kinds of scripts used in Tibetan writings: dBu-čan, letters with a head at the top, the printing character; dBu-med, the headless character, cursive writing; and Lan-tsa, the sacred and ornamental character. dBu-čan is the easiest among the three types of scripts to learn and is used widely both in printing and writing.

Francke, on the point of origin of the Tibetan script, observes that: 'as regards Tibetan historiography in general there are two distinct schools of it, viz. the Central Tibetan and the West Tibetan school. Thus, the records referring to the introduction of the Tibetan alphabet vary to a certain degree, according to the schools of writers.' 'Those of the first school all agree that king Srong btsan sgampo sent his minister Thonmi to Hindustan, Southern Hindustan or Magadha, to learn reading and writing. The West Tibetan school states that king Srong btsan sgampo sent his minister Thonmi and 16 fellow students to Kashmir, to learn the characters,' (Francke, 1981:266-267).

There is unanimity among all the categories of scholars that Tibetan script was introduced by the minister Thonmi Sambhota who was sent to India by the king Srong-btsan-sgam-po (CE. 617-650) to study and devise a script for Tibetan language. Thonmi went to India in CE 633 and the script might have been finalised after some years thereafter. Beyond this they are divided into two schools as described by Francke above whether Thonmi went towards the north-west to Kashmir or towards the south to Magadha. It depends much on this point whether the script was introduced into Tibet from the north-west or the middle of India.

The difference in opinion originates from the Tibetan authorities themselves. The Fifth Dalai Lama and Gos Lotsava, author of the *Blue Annals*, simply write that Thonmi went to India. Sonam Gyaltšan, author of one of the popular Tibetan semi-historical work, *rGyalrabs gsal-ba'i meloŋ,* writes that Thonmi went towards the south. Bu-ston (Obermiller, 1932:183-184) writes, Tibetan letters were 'given a resemblance to the Kashmirian characters,' from which it may be construed that Thonmi went to Kashmir for study. Rahul Sankrityayan following Buston gives similar description. Nawang Dagpa, a pupil of Tsong-kha-pa (1357-1419), clearly writes that Thonmi went to Kashmir.

Francke states that, "Looking at these two the West Tibetan record strikes me as being the more original of the two. In the first place the country from which the alphabet was brought to Tibet is given here as being Kashmir. This is more in accordance with the result of Dr. Vogel's examination of the alphabet,' (Francke, 1981: 267).

Before we take up the various points separately we here quote the relevant portions pertaining to the origin of Tibetan script from India from two important Tibetan sources. These are: i. *rGyal-rabs bsal-ba'i me-loŋ* (Mirror-like Clear History) by Sonam Gyaltshan (1312-1375), and ii. *mŋaris rgyal-rabs* (History of mŋaris) by Nawang Dagpa, fifteenth-sixteenth century.

rGyal-rabs bsal-ba'i me-loŋ by Sonam Gyaltshan: An extract of the important points on the subject as given by the author are given hereunder. 'For the purpose of enactment of statutes, dispersal of the five divisions of knowledge for the public welfare, sending messages to different places, and for delivering the commandments of the Doctrine among the subjects, there was no writing system in Tibet. Therefore firstly seven chosen intelligent ministers were sent to study to India. But they came back as they met with three kinds of demons of the distant land. Then Thonmi Sambhota, son of Thonmi Anu, a person of persevering nature, sharp intellect and very knowledgeable, was sent with much gold to study to India. He went towards the south. There he came to know about the Brahmin Li-byin, a learned person in the letters of grammar. Thonmi went to him and introduced himself telling that he was a minister of a distant kingdom whose king is very kind. But there was no writing system in his country. He had been sent to study. He offered the presents to the Brahmin and requested him to be his teacher, who agreed readily. He taught him the alphabets. The intelligent Thonmi learnt quickly. There were number of kinds of letters like Nagar, Garata, etc. These were not adopted for Tibetan writing but vowels (perhaps vowel signs) were taken from them. Lan-tsha, the letters of the gods; Vartul (Bha-gru); and the self-born model (lhun-drub tshad-ma) were adopted for Tibetan writing. Out of the fifty Indian alphabets thirty were selected for Tibetan.' Then the author describes at length a number of groups of the letters with varying grammatical functions.

The learned author further writes that, 'Lantsha, the letters like those of the gods, was adopted later on by the learned translators while translating the Sanskrit mantras into Tibetan, after changing the letters like *h* and *'a,* and reversing the letters *n, š* and *th,* and doing the like. Copying it dBu-čan was developed. By imitating the Vartul, the letter of the Nāgas, zur-čan (= edge, tip of corner) i.e. curved letters were formed.

'Moreover, Thonmi Sambhota learned from Pandita Devavidya Simha (Lha-rigs-pa seng-ge) the vyakaranshastra (sgra-bstan-čhos) and others and became learned in the five branches of knowledge. Then he translated several books like Ratnameghasutra, Karandvyūha, etc.' (Gyaltshan: pp. 145-151).

Here the author has taken the Indian teachers referred above as two different persons. Some other sources take them as one and the same person. These two are Li-byin and Lha rigs-pa seng-ge. We observe that the work qualifies the first person as Brahmin and the second as Pandita. Historically, both in Indian and Tibetan traditions, the two terms have been used distinctly. The same pattern is adopted by the other Tibetan authors. The first term signifies the person of a Brahmin class and the second term Pandita, although usually a Brahman, signifies a learned person. The name Li-byin also does not appear to be a personal name and appears to indicate a class. The Tibetan term Li-byin, partly Sanskrit (*li* for Sanskrit *lipi,* script) and partly Tibetan (*byin*, given, for *datta* of Sanskrit), appears to be a translation of the Sanskrit word *Lipidatta,* or the like, which had been in existence in India since much earlier time.

Saratchandra Das translates *Libyin* as *Lipikara* or *Lipidatta,* which may be rendered as a scribe. We also meet with the term *Li-bi-datt* often in Tibetan writings. G.H. Ojha referring to Panini writes *lipi* and *libi*, i.e. to write, as synonyms and translates Lipikara as a scribe (lekhak), (G.H. Ojha, 1917: 6-7). Agrawala writes that Panini by '*lipikara* as well as its variant form *libikara*, denoted a writer.' Agrawala translates *lipikara* here as scribe, (Agrawala, 1953: 311, 410). Libyin might have been an educated Brahmin who might have initially taught Thonmi the alphabets and introduced him to the Sanskrit Language. Saratchandra Das writes,

'In Aryadesh (India) Thonmi studied the Arts, both of Brahmans and the Buddhists, under the Pandita Deva-vid Simha (Lha-rig-pa'i senge), the Brahman Lipikara (Libyin), i.e., Lipi-datta, and other eminent teachers', (Saratchandra Das, 1915: III). Thonmi learnt grammar, literature and other subjects from the learned Pandita Devavitsiṃha or Devavidyasiṃha, (Lha-rigs-pa seŋ-ge).

The author of *rGyalrabs gsal-ba'i melong* according to its colophon was Sonam Gyaltshan who completed it in the year *sa-pho-'brug* , CE 1328. Vostrikov writes that the work is allied to the apocryphal works like *rGyal-po bka'i thang-yig*. But he says that it is different from the apocrypha in the sense that it gives in addition much accurate historical information taken from various authoritative sources, and thus has a place between an apocryphal work and the historical work proper. Vostrikov has examined and analysed the work carefully. Then he concludes that its author was Legs-pa'i še-rab, other than Sonam Gyaltshan, and it was published in the year *sa-khyi,* corresponding to CE 1478, although it was written earlier around the middle of the fifteenth century, (Vostrikov, 1970: 69-75). We, for our purpose, follow here the work according to the terms given in its colophon, like some others. The data given in the work on the present subject is quite extensive and important but it appears to have merged the thoughts from differing quarters like the historical tradition and the popular belief. For example Sonam Gyaltshan gives a very valuable information about the origin of Lan-tsa, which is a historical explanation, but immediately states that dbu-čan was adopted from Lan-tsa, which fact is based on the popular tradition and this fact is not acceptable to the modern scholars. The same fact appears to have influenced Gyaltshan in describing Thonmi to have gone to the middle of India as *lan-tsa* had originated from there.

Nawang Dagpa, the author of mŋaris rgyal-rabs writes on the subject that, "Son of Thonmi Anu, (Thonmi), was sent with a *bre* (roughly half kg., but varies) of gold and sixteen servants to Kashmir to study. He learnt the alphabets from Brahmin Li-byin and grammar from Pandita Deva-Simha. Then adding the sixteen consonants completed the thirty. Collecting four vowels i, u, e and o comparing with the alphabets of Nagar of Kashmir, he completed the (alphabets)," (Nawang Dagpa, 1996: 22-23). Nawang Dagpa was pupil of great Tsong-kha-pa, the founder of the ruling Gelupga sect, and his work of fifteenth century is a valuable historical work. The statement agrees with that found in the Ladaks Gyalrabs which writes, Thonmi went to Kashmir with sixteen fellow students and learned characters from Li-byin and Pandita Sing-ge-sgra (Simhanada) who taught them the language. He chose 30 characters agreeing with the Nagara characters of Kashmir, (Francke, 1026-II: 82). The name of the Pandita in these two and other sources are similar with slight variation. These sources indicate that the script originated from Kashmir and the name of the script is given as Nagar. There were at least two teachers or two classes of teachers of Thonmi. The first was Libyin who introduced him to the Sanskrit characters and language. The second was named Pandita Deva-Simha or a different name from whom he learned the literature.

Origin of Lan-tsa: Lan-tsa is used principally to transcribe the titles of Sanskrit works in original Sanskrit language as they are given before the Tibetan Titles of the books translated into Tibetan. Secondly it is used for writing the sacred mantras in Sanskrit language. Sacred mantras like '*Om Mani padme hum'*, can be seen carved in Lantsa and dBu-čan on rocks, ma-ni wheels and on stone slabs placed on the *ma-ni* walls on the road sides, in Lahul, Spiti, Ladak, Kinnaur, etc.

The opinion current among some Tibetan scholars including the author of the *rGyalrabs gsal-ba'i meloŋ,* about this character, as has been pointed out by some modern scholars, is that Lantsa was the first kind of script that originated in Tibet and dBu-čan evolved from it. Another popular work, *Mani bk'a-bum,* notes that Thonmi after reaching Tibet formed the letters of *dbu-čan* from *lan-tsa* and from *pa-ṭo-la* i.e. vartula, he developed the *dbu-med* characters, (*Mani bk'a-bum*, pp. 399-400).

Some other modern scholars also seem to uphold this belief. Jaeschke writes 'Tibetan alphabet was adapted from the Lantsha form of the Indian letters by Thonmi Sambhota, minister of king Sroŋ-btsan-sgampo', (Jaeschke, 1880:1). Saratchandra Das writes, 'The Bengali, Newari and Tibetan characters clearly resemble, all three having had their origin in Mithila and having been shaped after the model of the form of Devanagari that was current there in the seventh century A.D. The ancient Maithili character bears a striking resemblance to the Lantsha (Ranja of Nepal) or the ornamental Devanagari which was little known in India, (Saratchandra Das, 1915: III note).

Vogel, an eminent archaeologist and epigraphist, has examined the issue very carefully and concludes, saying that, 'besides the ordinary Tibetan character, the lamas have the so called Lantsha which is exclusively used for Sanskrit formulas. The local tradition of Central Tibet holds that the Lantsha is older of the two, and that from it the ordinary Tibetan alphabet has been derived. This has been repeated by European writers, but in view of palaeographical evidences there cannot be the slightest doubt that the tradition has reversed the real fact'.

He further writes, 'The ordinary Tibetan character is the more ancient of the two, and the Lantsha originated several centuries later. Both were derived from Indian scripts, but quite independently of each other. The time of their origin can be approximately fixed, by a comparison with the characters used in Indian Sanskrit inscriptions.'

> 'Our conclusion is that Lantsha was introduced into Tibet about 1000 A.D., and in this instance not from Northern, but from Eastern India. It should be remembered, that in the hill districts of Northern India, and probably in the plains of the Panjab also, Sarada was used, and not Nagari. The Indian alphabet was adopted wholesale and probably unchanged, probably because it was intended to be used for Sanskrit exclusively,' (Vogel in Francke, 1981: 267-271).

This statement is validated by Sonam Gyaltshan who states, as above, precisely like Vogel, that Lantsa, the letters of the gods, was adapted later on by the learned translators while translating, rather transcribing, the Sanskrit mantras into Tibetan. Thus Lantsa evidently originated later than dBu-chan. It was introduced into Tibet by the translators of the Sanskrit books into Tibetan from the Eastern India in around CE 1000.

dBu-čan and dBu-med: Although dBu-čan and dBu-med (*phra-yig*= fine writing, in sTodpa) are two different forms of the same script, one being used for printing and the other for writing letters, yet the two exhibit some difference in their form and style of writing. In the former case each letter is written separately and the vowel signs are also joined separately. The letters, vowel signs and the letters subjoined at the bottom like *r* and *y*, all are simple and devoid of the ornamental flourishing loops. In the form of dBu-med the letters and vowel signs tend to be taking forms of long loops and each letter in a word is connected with the other for the continuous movement of the pen. The vowel signs and other subjoined letters seem to be continuations of the initial letter. dBu-čan is slow to pen and dBu-med has better flow. The dBu-med therefore appears to have evolved naturally from the former as a result of necessity, for basically the letters in both the kinds are the same, unlike that of Lantsa.

dBu-med: Tibetan sources state that dBu-med, the cursive script, originated from Indian Vartul or Kuṭila. As we have seen above Sonam Gyaltshan writes that zur-čan, an archaic term for dBu-med, form of letters was composed by imitating the Vartul, which is like the letters of the Nāgas. In fact the letters are like the curves of the Nāgas, serpents, themselves. Vartul means the same as Kuṭila. Kuṭila is not a conventional name for any kind of script in India. Buhlar substituted the name Kuṭila, adopted by his predecessors, by acute-angled. However the term Kuṭila continued to be in use even thereafter. Conversely Vartul, name of an Indian script, is found preserved in Tibetan sources but is not known as such in Indian history. Both the words mean the same as curved. We may take them as synonyms. Perhaps Kutila or Vartula was not a kind of script but was name of the style for writing in cursive form, as the two terms mean, from which the Tibetan dBu-č**an** transformed into the Tibetan dBu-med. Thus according to the Tibetan sources dBu-med originated by copying the style of Vartul or we can also say from Kuṭila. Vartul possesses two prominent qualities. Firstly the letters have acute angles as has been observed by the Indian palaeographists; secondly its organs are longer and looped, a character highlighted by the Tibetan scholars. While dBu-čan possesses only the former character, dBu-med possesses both the kinds of characters.

Vogel states that the Tibetan alphabet (i.e. dBu-čan) is based on the Indian script, which had developed from the Western Gupta and which used to be designated by the name of Kuṭila. The Tibetan has retained the characteristics of this script, acute angles at the lower ends, small wedges at the tops, and in general a very ornamental and elegant appearance. "Our conclusion is that the Tibetan script is derived from the Northern Indian script, which was used in the 7th century. It is not based on the Sarada, but has certain points of similarity with this script, which suggests that both were derived from the same northern Indian character,' (Vogel in Francke, 1981: 269). Dani writes that Kuṭila originated from the Gupta script which remained in use from the 6th to 9th century CE. He further writes that in the Nirmand (Kullu) inscription of the seventh century CE and the Chamba inscriptions of Panali Nala and Gum, also of the seventh century, all of them clearly show the influence of Kuṭila writing and forms identical with those seen in the Middle Ganges Valley at the same time, (Dani, 1963: 146-147).

dBu-čan: On the origin of the dBu-chan form of the script, Sonam Gyaltshan's description is different. From the fact that Gyaltshan names more than one script, like Nagar, Garat, etc. as above, it may be assumed that Thonmi had got acquainted himself with more than one script, even though Nagar is presumed to be a later interpolation and Garat is an unknown name. Gyaltshan also says that these were not selected for adoption for Tibetan script but Tibetan writing system was developed from Lhun-grub Tshad-ma i.e. the self-evident or created (or miraculously sprung) script. Thonmi might have done much of the exercise sitting with his teachers in Kashmir, as some Tibetan authors also say, but the final shape to the alphabets was given in Lhasa. Buston writes: 'After this alphabet had been definitely formed at the Maru temple at Lhasa, Thonmi composed eight works on writing and grammar, and the king studied them four years abiding in seclusion,' (Obermiller, 1932: 184). Tibetan alphabet consists of two classes of letters: some resembling the Indian characters and the rest which may have been contrived by Thonmi. The table of alphabets agrees in plan with that of the Indian alphabets. Twenty three letters, viz. *k, kh, g, ŋ, č, čh, j, ñ, t, th, d, n, p, ph, b, m, y, r, l, š, s, h, a,* all these letters resemble the Indian alphabets of Sarda. Among the rest, three letters, the alveolar *ts, tsh* and *ds* are formed from the three palatal letters *č*, *čh* and *j* by just putting a small hook over their top on the right. Further, *z* is just the reverse of *j*. Thus actually twenty seven letters agree with the Indian alphabets. The rest three viz. *zh, v* and *'a* are Tibetan originals. Various Tibetan scholars explain in detail how each letter originated. The languages, one from which the script was copied and the other for which it was being adopted, being from two different families, were phonetically also widely different. However in reality the exception was only of the sound of *zh.* The typical sounds of *ts, tsh* and *z* existed in the Sarada alphabets, they exist in the Indo-Aryan languages of the Indian Himalayas. Deambi writes that in the Sarada, or its predecessor, the letters *č, čh* and *j* are pronounced as *ts, tsh* and *z* (Deambi, 1982: 162), even though practically this was of no help to Thonmi.

Thonmi's actual task lay elsewhere. Tibetan language is characterized by the abundance of homonyms which is also one of the causes of its being hard to learn. The Tibetan grammar, a composition of Thonmi, has a unique chapter named Tag-jug (rTags-'jug) which assigns some artificial characters, generally of gender, to the letters while in use in the words. This enables several words of the same sound to be transcribed distinguishingly. This was of great need. The letters also change character by changing the position in a word. Further the list of the alphabets has been enlarged greatly by framing rules for the formation of compound letters. This was essential for making an oral language itself capable of carrying the burden of a great literary asset.

dBu-čan is the principal script which is used in printing. Books are generally found printed or written in this script. Inscriptional evidences of this form of script from c. eighth-ninth centuries CE has been recorded by Richardson, (Richardson, 1985: plate 2, passimo) from Central Tibet. The script had been static since then. We observe the letters retaining the same ancient shapes even today. Slight changes may be observed: the letters in the early samples of dBu-čan appear like square in shape and in the present they appear slightly vertically oblong. Vogel remarks that the letters are like box type and acute angled at the base. This form of the script might have been the first to originate.

As regards the place of origin most of the scholars agree that it originated from Kashmir. Kashmir had been a great centre of learning. The circumstances also point to the same situation. Alberuni, a great scholar from Central Asia of tenth-eleventh century CE, writes that in his time Kashmir and Benaras were two great centres of learning in India. He names several scripts then in use in the western India. Sidhamatrika, which was by some considered as originating from Kashmir for the people of Kashmir used it, was the most generally known alphabet in India

Dani takes Siddhamātṛkā as synonym for Kutila. It may be that Kutila and Siddhamātṛkā are the names of the same script, but the latter name appears to have emerged from a special class of the practitioners, the learned siddhas, who had developed textbooks of their own for the use of their class. Siddham is a famous name in the history of Indian scripts in the eastern countries.

The name of the script current in Kashmir during the period is not definite. Deambi names the script existing in Kashmir between c. BCE 300 to CE 750 as the 'Brahmi alphabet of North-western India' and Upadhyay calls Siddhamatrika, Kutila, acute-angled, etc. (Upadhyay, 1998:21). The script which developed from this is named as Sarda. Accroding to Alberuni, Sarada was name of a people living in Kashmir.

On comparison of Tibetan dBu-čan letters with those of the Western Indian script, the predecessor of Sarada, of the period of 6th-7th century CE, and even from Sarda, we observe that they have close resemblance with each other. Besides the alphabets, we also compare the vowel signs, ligatures and numerals which give similar results.

Francke has also given a very exhaustive comparative chart extending to seven tables, giving the letters of the alphabet, their combinations with the other letters and vowel signs, both for dBu- čan and dBu-med. Each entry is divided into four periods showing the form of the letter as it existed in each period which are: i. Stein's collection of the eight-ninth century CE from Central Asia, ii. c. CE 1000 to 1200, iii. Fifteenth-Sixteenth century and after, and, iv. the Modern period, (Francke, 1911-12: Plate I to VII).

3

Phonology

3.1. **The Alphabets:** sTodpa colloquial, a dialect of Bhoti, uses the Bhoti script which possesses a set of thirty-four alphabets constituting thirty consonants called **ka-li** and four vowels called **a-li** and also as *gsal-byed* and *dbyangs*, respectively.

3.1.1. **Ka-li, Cosonants**. Following are consonants of the alphabet:

ཀ། ཁ ག ང་། ཅ ཆ ཇ ཉ། ཏ ཐ ད ན། པ ཕ བ་ མ།

k kh g ŋ č čh j ñ t th d n, p ph b m

ཙ ཚ ཛ ཝ། ཞ ཟ འ ཡ། ར ལ ཤ ས། ཧ། ཨ།

ts tsh ds v ž z ‘a y r l š s h a

The alphabet **a** appears here as a consonant. Besides another alphabet **‘a** called **a-čhuŋ,** small **a,** with similar sound is also noticed among the consonants. The two have functions as vowels also. The thirty simple letters called *gsal-byed* are placed in seven and half groups called *sde.* Each is named by the first letter of the group viz. *k-sde* which comprises k, kh, g and ŋ. Similarly others are c-sde, t-sde, p-sde, ts-sde, ž-sde and h-sde.

3.1.2. **A-li, Vowels**: The four vowels are:

ཨི། ཨུ། ཨེ། ཨོ།།

i u e o

Here the four vowel signs are placed over the common base of consonant **a.** This base **a** is dropped when the vowel sign is attached with a letter. These vowels have no independent letters which means that they cannot become base of a word and cannot form any word independently.

Use of vowel signs: The four vowel signs are named as *gi-gu*, *žabs-kyu, ‘greñ-bu* and *na-ro*, respectively.

ི ུ ེ ོ གི་གུ།། ཞབས་ཀྱུ།། འགྲེང་བུ།། ན་རོ།།

The signs are fixed to the thirty *gsal-byed*, consonants and their compounds:

མ+ཨི = མི *mi* = man ཁྱ+ ཨི= ཁྱི *khyi* = dog

ཆ + ཨུ = ཆུ *čhu* = water འབ་ + ཨུ = འབུ ‘bu = worm

ད + ཨེ = དེ *de* = that མ + ཨེ = མེ *me* = fire

ས + ཨོ = སོ *so* = tooth ཁ + ཨོ = ཁོ *kho* = he

3.2. Phonological Units

3.2.1. Vowels: There are eight vowel phonemes in sTodpa. These are: i, ī, u, ū, e, o, a, ā.

/*i*/ High front unsounded vowel

mig = eye

tshig = a syllable

‘*i-zam* = this much *gñid* = sleeping *ñi -ma* = The sun

འི་ཟམ། མིག། ཚིག། གཉིད། ཉི་མ།

/ ī / High front unrounded long vowel

mi = man

‘*i* = this

ri = mountain

ki = of

si = by

འི། མི། རི། ཀི། སི།

/e/ Mid front unrounded long vowel

sems	=	mind	*de*	=	that
gŋen	=	kin	*me*	=	fire
dge-ba	=	virtue	*lče*	=	tongue

སེམས། གཉེན། དགེ་བ། དེ། མེ། ལྕེ།

/a/ Low central unrounded short vowel

am-či = a traditional doctor

al-to = a small pitcher

a-loŋ = ear-ring

dar = silk

phad = a large bag of goat wool

ral = goat wool

ཨམ་ཅི། ཨལ་ཏོ། ཨ་ལོང་། དར། ཕད། རལ།

/ *ā*/ Low central unrounded long vowel

ā-'o	=	we
ā-la	=	beautiful
pho-'a'a	=	stomach,

ཨཱ་འོ། ཨཱ་ལ། ཕོ་ལྟཱ།

/o/ Mid back rounded long vowel

'o-le	=	neck	*nor*	=	precious articles
kho	=	he	*og-ma*	=	throat
dgon-pa	=	monastery	*so*	=	teeth
ol-phruŋ	=	necklace	*mčhog*	=	good
ño	=	a wild carrot	*'ol-ñog*	=	A child after birth upto a few weeks.

འོ་ལེ། འོག་མ། འོལ་ཕྲུང་། འོལ་ཉོག། ནོར། དགོན་པ། མཆོག། ཁོ། སོ། ཉོ།

/u/ High back rounded short vowel

'u-khri ~ 'u-ṭhi	=	a large metal pitcher	*bdun*	=	seven
su	=	who	*mgur*	=	a song
'bu	=	insect	*'ul-thag*	=	thrashing field
dgun	=	winter	*sku*	=	body
'u-ṛub-pa	=	larynx			

ཨུ་ཁྲི། ཨུལ་ཐག། ཨུ་རུབ་པ། བདུན། མགུར། དགུན། སུ། འབུ། སྐུ།

/ ū / Mid back rounded long vowel

dr'u - 'u ~ḍū -ū = ball of woolen thread.

d'u- 'u ~ dū-ū	=	bangle.
ṭ'u - 'u ~ ṭū-'ū	=	a child.

ཌུ་ཨུ།   ཊུ་ཨུ།   ཋུ་ཨུ།

Instances of occurance of long vowels is scarce. There is no nasal vowel. A variation in the pronunciation of vowel sound is noticed when the letter to which the vowel is attached is accompanied by a suffix or it is without any suffix. Vowels are voiced short when the letter with the vowel is accompanied by a suffix and it is voiced high when it is not accompanied by a suffix. Thus here *i* in the word *dkyil* sounds like *i* in the English word kill and *i* in the word *ki* like that in the English word key. Similar is the case with other vowels like *a, u, o* and *e.* More examples:

dang	=	and	*da*	=	now	*mkhar*	=	castle
kha	=	snow	*mig*	=	eye	*mi*	=	man
gsum	=	three	*su*	=	who	*bčud*	=	essence
bču	=	ten	*med*	=	don't have	*me*	=	fire
rjes	=	after	*rje*	=	lord	*tshogs*	=	assembly
mtsho	=	sea	*mgon*	=	lord	*mgo*	=	head

དཀྱིལ། ཀི།། དང་། ད། མཁར། ཁ། མིག། མི།། གསུམ། སུ།

བཅུད། བཅུ། མེད། མེ། རྗེས། རྗེ། ཚོགས། མཚོ། མགོན། མགོ།

3.2.2. Consonants

There are thirty two consonant sounds viz.

[p, t,.t, k, kh, ph, th,.th, b, d, ḍ, g, ts, tsh, ds, č, čh, j, s, z, ṣ, š, ž, h, r, l, m, n, ñ, ŋ, v, y]

Examples of use of the phonemes are given as under. Here it may be clarified that as we have seen above, in the construction of a word, although all the thirty consonants can be root letter of a word, the other places around the root letter like the front or back cannot be taken by all the letters.

Stops:

/p/ Voiceless bilabial stop

par	=	print, photo	*dpon*	=	painter	*dpe- ča*	=	book
pa-ra	=	a cross	*dpaŋ-po*	=	witness	*pa-ri*	=	tin box

dpuŋ -pa = arm	*pu-ri* = pipe	*dp'a-bo* = hero
pur-ša = tether	*dpal* = prosperity	

པར། པ་ར། པ་རི། པུ་རི། པུར་ཤ། དཔོན། དཔང་པོ། དཔུང་པ། དཔའ་བོ། དཔལ། དཔེ་ཅ།

/ph/ Voiceless aspirated bilabial stop

Initial			**Medial**		
pha-la	=	ploughshare	*'phel-če*	=	to expand
phaŋ	=	spindle	*'phul-če*	=	to push
phar-ka	=	Other side of river.	*'phrul*	=	ghost
phug	=	cave	*'phur-če*	=	to fly
'phags-pa	=	Arya			

ཕ་ལ། ཕང་། ཕར་ཀ། ཕུག། འཕེལ་ཅེ། འཕུལ་ཅེ། འཕྲུལ། འཕུར་ཅེ། འཕགས་པ།

/b/ Voiced bilabial stop

bag-ma = bride	*'bar-če* = to burn	*'dab-če* = to measure
bal = wool	*'bab-če* = to descend	*thab-ka* = hearth, stove
ba- čhab = cow-urine	*dbaŋ* = power	*baŋ- ŋa* = box for grain
'bod-če = to call	*bo-ra* = sack	*dbu-mdsad* = leader

བག་མ། བལ། བ་ཆབ། བང་ང་། བོ་ར། འབར་ཅེ། འབབ་ཅེ། དབང་། འབོད་ཅེ། དབུ་མཛད། འདབ་ཅེ། ཐབ་ཀ།

t/ Voiceless dental stop

tog-tse = spade	*gtub-če* = to cut
	ston-thog = harvest
	sta-ri = axe
	star-ga = walnut
	gtor-ma = sacrificial dough idol

ཏོག་ཙེ། སྟོན་ཐོག། སྟ་རི། གཏུབ་ཅེ། སྟར་ག། གཏོར་མ།

/th/ Voiceless aspirated dental stop

thu-ru = colt *mthoŋ-če* = to see

thaŋ-ka	=	ground	*mthil*	=	bottom
thur-maŋ	=	spoon	*mthe-bo*	=	thumb
the-ba	=	extra	*'then-če*	=	to draw
thog-tshad	=	a storey	*mthe-tse*	=	sign, mark

ཐུ་རུ། ཐང་ཀ། ཐུར་མང་། ཐེ་བ། ཐོག་ཚད་ མཐོང་ཅེ། མཐིལ། མཐེ་བོ། འཐེན་ཅེ། མཐེ་ཙེ།

/d/ Voiced dental stop

da-ra	=	buttermilk	*bdun*	=	seven
mčhod-pa	=	prayer, worship	*da-ruŋ*	=	more
mdo	=	side	*phyed-ka*	=	half
duŋ	=	shell	*gdung*	=	lineages.
sdad-če	=	to sit	*rdol-thog*	=	stone vessel
md'a	=	arrow	*dal-la*	=	slowly
mdaŋ	=	yesterday			

ད་ར། ད་རུང་། དུང་། རྡོལ་ཐོག། དལ་ལ་། བདུན། མདོ། གདུང་། མདའ། མདང་། མཆོད་པ། ཕྱེད་ཀ། སྡད་ཅེ།

/k/ Voiceless velar stop

kab-ša	=	shoes	*skol-če*	=	to boil
ka-ča	=	news	*dkon-mo*	=	scarce
ko-re	=	cup	*dkar-pho*	=	white
ko-tse	=	a spice plant	*rkod- če*	=	to dig
rkaŋ-pa	=	foot	*skaŋ- če*	=	to fill up

ཀབ་ཤ། ཀ་ཅ། ཀོ་རེ། ཀོ་ཙེ། རྐང་པ། སྐོལ་ཅེ། དཀོན་མོ། དཀར་པོ། རྐོད་ཅེ། སྐང་ཅེ།

/kh/ Voiceless aspirated velar stop

khaŋ-pa	=	house	*mkhas-pha*	=	expert
khu-ru	=	load	*mkhar*	=	castle
kha-ša	=	straw thread	*'khor-če*	=	to spin
kha-so	=	mouth	*'khar-če*	=	to get stuck up
khan-te	=	bitter	*'khor-lo*	=	wheel

ཁང་པ། ཁུ་རུ། ཁ་ཤ། ཁ་སོ། ཁན་ཏེ། མཁས་ཕ། མཁར། འཁོར་ཅེ། འཁར་ཅེ། འཁོར་ལོ།

/g/ Voiced Velar Stop

gom-pa	=	a step	*dgun-ka*	=	winter
phug	=	cave	*goŋ-kal*	=	additional load
mgo	=	head	*mčhog*	=	good
gaŋ-ka	=	ridge	*dgon-pa*	=	monastery
glog	=	electricity	*ga- ča*	=	saddle
gal-pha	=	wound on horse back	*grogs-po*	=	companion

གོམ་པ། གོང་བཀལ། གང་ཀ། ག་ཅ། གལ་ཕ། དགུན་ཀ། མགོ། དགོན་པ།
གྲོགས་པོ། ཕུག། མཆོག། གློག།

Affricates

/ts/ Voiceless alveolar affricate

rtse-po	=	basket,	*gtsaŋ-kan*	=	pauper
tsa-pig	=	slightly	*btson*	=	jail
tsog-če	=	to prick	*btsir-če*	=	to squeeze
tsoŋ-če	=	to sell	*tso-li*	=	a small pitcher

ཙེ་པོ། ཙ་པིག། ཙོག་ཅེ། ཙོང་ཅེ། ཙོ་ལི། གཙང་ཀན། བཙོན། བཙིར་ཅེ།

tsh/ Voiceless aspirated alveolar affricate

tsha-mig	=	pepper	*mtsho*	=	lake
tshoŋ	=	trade	*mtshan*	=	night
tshang-skor	=	nest	mtshams	=	border
tsha-rag	=	haste	*tshag-tshag*	=	insistence

ཚ་མིག། ཚོང་། ཚང་སྐོར། ཚ་རག། ཚག་ཚག། མཚོ། མཚན། མཚམས།

ds/ Voiced Alveolar Affricate

rdsa-ma = pitcher

mdso = a male crossbreed of yak and cow.

mdsad = to do (hon.)

mdsod = store

mdsa-'o = friend

རྫ་མ། མཛོ། མཛད། མཛོད། མཛའ་འོ།

/č/ Voiceless palatal affricate

ča-lag	=	article	*lčaŋ-ma*	=	willow

čuŋ-ka	=	red beaked crow	*gčin*	=	urine
ča-ra	=	messenger	*bčud*	=	essence
čan-da	=	pocket	*bčad-če*	=	to cut
čuŋ-ŋun	=	small, younger	*gčig-po*	=	alone

ཅ་ལག ཅུང་ཀ། ཅ་ར། ཅན་ད། ཅུང་ངུན། ལྕང་མ། གཅིན། བཅུད། བཅད་ཅེ། གཅིག་པོ།

čh/ Voiceless aspirated palatal affricate

čhar-pha	=	rain	*mčhin-pa*	=	liver
čhaŋ-ma	=	beer server	*mčhu-to*	=	beak of a bird
čha-ra	=	blanket of goat hair	*'čham- č*	=	to do religious dance
čho-lo	=	dice game	*mčhod-pa*	=	prayer
čhur-phye	=	dried cheese	*mčhog*	=	excellent

ཆར་ཕ། ཆང་མ། ཆ་ར། ཆོ་ལོ། ཆུར་ཕྱེ། མཆིན་པ། མཆུ་ཏོ། འཆམ་ཅེ། མཆོད་པ། མཆོག།

/j/ Voiced palatal affricate

ja	=	tea	*mjug*	=	end, tail
ju-le	=	a term of salutation	*mjug-ma*	=	The end part
spaŋ -ja	=	a wild tea	*'jam-po*	=	soft.
jo	=	A noble	*'jib- če*	=	to suck
ja-ro	=	residual tea leaves	*mjal-če*	=	to have audience

ཇ། ཇུ་ལེ། སྤང་ཇ། ཇོ། ཇ་རོ། མཇུག། མཇུག་མ། འཇམ་པོ། འཇིབ་ཅེ། མཇལ་ཅེ།

Fricatives

/s/ Voiceless alveolar fricative

sog-po	=	bad	*bsod-nams*	=	merit
lugs-so	=	custom	*siŋ-ge*	=	lion
bsam- če	=	to think	*sems-ba*	=	mind
khyim-sa	=	house waste	*lo-gsar*	=	new year
bsaŋ-zas	=	aromatic mixture for incense	*so-la*	=	coal
gser	=	gold	*saŋ- 'gul*	=	earthquake
gsal-če	=	to offer			

སོག་པོ། སིང་གེ། སྲིམ་ས། སོ་ལ། སང་འགྲུལ། བསོད་ནམས། བསམ་ཅེ། ལོ་གསར། གསེར། གསལ་ཅེ། ལུགས་སོ། སེམས་པ། བསང་ཟས།

/ş / Voiceless retroflex fricative

sprin ~ *şin* = cloud

sran-če ~ şan-če = to bear

skre-ka ~ şe-ka = ladder

srog ~ *şog* = life, the life breath

sruŋ-ma ~ *şuŋ-ma* = guardian deity

སྤྲིན། སྲན་ཅེ། སྐྲེ་ཀ། སྲོག། སྲུང་མ།

/š/ Voiceless palatal fricative

Initial			**Medial**		
šiŋ	=	wood	*gšog-pa*	=	wings
šug-pa	=	juniper	*gšol*	=	plough
šaŋ -ku	=	wolf	*bšad- če*	=	to tell
šes-še	=	to know	*bšig- če*	=	dismantle
šar	=	east	*gšer-če*	=	to ask for

ཤིང་། ཤུག་པ། ཤང་ཀུ། ཤེས་ཤེ། ཤར། གཤོག་པ། གཤོལ་ བཤད་ཅེ། བཤིག་ཅེ། གཤེར་ཅེ།

/z/ Voiced alveolar fricative

za-ra	=	mid day meal	*gzer*	=	nail
zog-ma	=	fake	*bzaŋ-po*	=	good
zam-pa	=	bridge	*gzuŋs*	=	charm
zaŋs-bu	=	kettle	*gzer-pha*	=	a knot
zaŋs	=	copper	*gzugs-pho*	=	body

ཟ་ར། ཟོག་མ། ཟམ་པ། ཟངས་བུ། ཟངས། གཟེར། བཟང་པོ། གཟུངས། གཟེར་ཕ། གཟུགས་ཕོ།

/ /ž/ Voiced palatal fricative

žag	=	a day	*gžuŋ*	=	middle
žo	=	curd	*bžon-ma*	=	a cow in milk
žiŋ-ka	=	field	*gžon-rta*	=	horse for riding

ža-bo = lame — *gžog-če* = to make plain
ža-ra = blind — *bžugs-če* = to sit (hon.)

ཞག། ཞོ། ཞིང་ཀ། ཞ་པོ། ཞ་ར། གཞུང་། བཞོན་མ། བཞོན་ཏ། བཞོག་ཅེ། བཞུགས་ཅེ།

/h/ Voiceless glottal fricative

ha-lo = a wild flower — *ham-pa* = greed
ha-tse = wolf — *han-drang* = a fool
hi-kug = hiccup

ཧ་ལོ། ཧམ་པ། ཧ་ཙེ། ཧན་དྲང་། ཧི་ཀུག།

Trills

/r/ Voiced alveolar trill

ral-pha = rough hair — *šor-če* = to flee
riŋ -mo = long — *'tshar-če* = to grow
rigs = clan — *'khyer- če* = to carry
ran-thag = water mill — *rmur- če* = to chew
rus-pha = bone — *stor- če* = to have lost

རལ་པ། རིང་མོ། རིགས། རན་ཐག། རུས་པ། ཤོར་ཅེ། འཚར་ཅེ། འཁྱེར་ཅེ། རྨུར་ཅེ། སྟོར་ཅེ།

Laterals

/l/ Voiced alveolar lateral

riŋ -mo = long — *'tshar-če* = to grow
lo = year — *tshul* = manner
lug = sheep — *rgyal-če* = to win
lam-ka = road — *yul-pha* = the villagers
ñe-lam = short cut — *gal-to* = a log in the hearth
las-kha = work

ལོ། ལུག། ལམ་ཀ། ཉེ་ལམ། ལས་ཁ། ཚུལ། རྒྱལ་ཅེ། ཡུལ་པ། གལ་ཏོ།

Nasals

m/ Voiced bilabial nasal

mig = eyes — *mar-pho* = red

bčom	=	overpower	*maŋ-po*	=	much
'dsom-če	=	to assemble	*men-tog*	=	flower
dm'a-mo	=	low	*khram-pa*	=	efficient
me-lo	=	ember, burning coal	*kham*	=	liking
me-tshag	=	a spark	*dmag*	=	army
mdsaŋs-ma	=	a lady			

མིག། མང་པོ། མེན་ཏོག། མེ་ལོ། མེ་ཚག། དམར་པོ། དམའ་མོ། དམག།
བཅོམ། འཛོམ་ཅེ། ཁྲམ་པ། ཁམ། མཛངས་མ།

/n/ Voiced alveolar Nasal

naŋ	=	in, room	*gnam-ka*	=	sky
rin	=	price	*no-mo*	=	younger sister
gnod-pa	=	curse	*khan-te*	=	bitter
nas	=	huskless barley	*mn'a-ma*	=	bride
na-so	=	age	*gnan-če*	=	to press
nad-pa	=	patient	*mn'a*	=	oath

ནང་། ནོ་མོ། ནས། ན་སོ། ནད་པ། གནམ་ཀ། གནོད་པ། མནའ་མ། གནན་
ཅེ། མནའ། རིན། ཁན་ཏེ།

/ñ/ Voiced palatal nasal

ñuŋ-ti	=	Kullu (area)	*gñen*	=	relative
ñuŋ-ma	=	turnip	*mñam-po*	=	together with
ñal-če	=	to sleep	*gñid*	=	sleeping
ñug-če	=	to search by feeling	*ña-ga*	=	old weighing scale

ཉུང་ཏི། ཉུང་མ། ཉལ་ཅེ། ཉུག་ཅེ། ཉ་ག། གཉེན། མཉམ་པོ། གཉིད།

/ŋ/ Voiced velar nasal

ŋa-raŋ	=	I myself	*gaŋs*	=	glacier
ŋu-če	=	to weep	*dŋul*	=	silver, rupee
sriŋ (*şiŋ*)-mo	=	sister	*ŋur-pha*	=	snoring
dŋul-čhu	=	perspiration	*phud-šiŋ*	=	fuel wood
ŋo- šes	=	an acquaintance	*rkaŋ-pa*	=	foot
ŋo-tog	=	true, real	*khyog-toŋ*	=	youth

ང་རང་། ངུ་ཅེ། ངུར་ཕ། ངོ་ཤེས། ངོ་ཏོག། གངས། དངུལ། དངུལ་ཆུ།
སྲིང་མོ། ཕུད་ཤིང་། རྐང་པ། ཁྱོག་ཏོང་།

Semi Vowels

/v/ Voiced bilabial semivowel

va = hello!

ཝ།

/y/ Voiced palatal semivowel.

yar = sacred mark of butter
ya-to = companion
ya-so = *The upper teeth*
ya-rkaŋ = one of the pair
yal-če = to fade away, to lose

g-yag = *yak*
g-yar-če = to borrow
g-yos-pha = right side
g-yon-ma = left side
g-y'a = rust

ཡར། ཡ་ཏོ། ཡ་སོ། ཡ་རྐང་། ཡལ་ཅེ། གཡག། གཡར་ཅེ། གཡོས་ཕ། གཡོན་མ། གཡའ།

3.3. Some Explanations

i. **The Consonant *ş*:** In sTodpa the compound consonants formed with *s* and *r*, which may also include other consonants, are pronounced as retroflex fricative ş and the use is quite common but there is no letter to represent this sound.

sring-mo ~şing-mo = sister, *srad-ma ~şad-ma* = peas, *spri-'u~şi-'u*= monkey, *skra ~şa* = *hair. skra-ka* = ladder.

སྲིང་མོ། སྲད་མ། སྤྲི་ཨུ། སྐྲ། སྐྲ་ཀ།

hri: There is another similar sound allied to this which is written as hri and is pronounced as one sound which may be shown as şhi. This letter is found in the prayer: aum badsra guru padma-siddhi hum hri.

ཨོཾ་བཛྲ་གུ་རུ་པདྨ་སི་དྡྷི་ཧཱུྃ་ཧྲཱི།

ii. Syllables *a* and *'a:*

As we have seen above the two syllables **a** and **'a** are included among the consonants. The first is simply normal ***a*** and the second is called **a-čhuŋ,** i.e. small ***a.*** **a-čhuŋ** is said to be only a different form of **a**. This may be true to some extent. But both of them have some independent functions.

A. Syllables *a* and *'a* as consonants:

As a consonant both the alphabets form base of new words and take vowel signs. All the four kinds of vowel signs can be attached with both of them.

a. **Use of *a* as consonant.** *a-ma* = mother. *a-rag* = wine. *a'i-khuŋ* = small hole. *a'u-tshugs* = irritation. *a'e-ma* = Exclamation sign, Oh! *a'en* = small. *aum* = Om!

ཨི །ཨུ། ཨེ། ཨོ། ཨ་མ། ཨ་རག། ཨི་ཁུང་། ཨུ་ཚུགས། ཨེ་མ། ཨེན། ཨོཾ།

b. **Use of *'a* as consonant:** *'i* = This. *'u-thug-pa* = A person who gets irritated soon. *'aŋ* = also. *'o-ma* = milk. *'og* = below. *'og-ma* = Throat.

འི། འུ། འེ། འོ། འུ་ཐུག་པ། འང། འོ་མ། འོག། འོག་མ།

B. Use of *a* and *'a* as Vowel:

i. **Use of *a* as vowel**: No sign of vowel ***a*** is used in Bhoti. Theoretically, as per rules of the grammar, vowel ***a*** is inherent in all the consonants. Without this the letter becomes *srog-med*, soul-less.

This point can be understood from the following example. *kha-ba* and *khab* are two words, both made by combination of two letters *kha* and *ba*. The first word is of two parts and the second is of one part. Now while pronouncing the first word we pronounce the two parts each one fully as *kha-ba*. In the second word while *kha* is pronounced fully the second letter *ba* is heard only partially. This may be explained as a result of the nature of the language being monosyllabic. The stem letter is pronounced fully, the second, the suffix is pronounced only partially, which has lost the power of ***a***.

khab = needle	*kha-ba* = snow	*ra-ba* = fence
rab = good.	*čha-ga* = edge, border.	*čhag* = grain for cattle.

ཁ་བ། ཁབ། ར་བ། རབ། ཆ་ག། ཆག།

ii. Use of *'a* as vowel: The consonant ***'a*** functions itself as vowel a, although it is not considered as vowel and has no vowel sign. The letter can be prefixed, suffixed and subjoined with a letter in the formation of a word.

a. When prefixed it remains silent. *'khur* = to carry. *'grul* = to walk. *'bad* = to endeavour.

འཁུར། འགྲུལ། འབད།

b. When suffixed to a word it lengthens the power of vowel of the stem-syllable. *dg'a* = happy. *bk'a* = Order. *mkh'a* = Sky.

དགའ། བཀའ། མཁའ།

c. When subjoined, i.e. placed below any syllable it works to lengthen the power of the vowel in the syllable. But this function of the letter is obtained only in the transcription of Sanskrit words.

Thus it lengthens the power of the five vowels viz. **a, i, u, e** and **o**. In practice the letter is used to lengthen the sounds of **a, i** and **u.** The two signs of the rare vowels *ai* and *au* for the words like Kailash, Gautam, etc. are obtained by doubling the vowel signs of e and o as they exist in Bhoti.

ཨཱ་མ	= a'a-m	ཕཱིར།	= p'ir	ཀཱིལ	= k'il
གཽཏམ།	= Gautam	ཤཱུ་ལ།	= š'ul		

3.3.3. The following three sets of compound letters are pronounced as ṭ, ṭh, ḍ.

kr, tr, pr = ṭ. khr, thr, phr = ṭh. gr, dr, br = ḍ

Except a few exceptions, these compound letters when surmounted by letters like s, give the same sound of ṭ, ṭh, ḍ.

bkres = hunger	*dpral-pa* = forehead	*khrag* = blood
'phrin = message	*gru* = boat	*dran* = to remember
phrad-če = to meet	*bran* = servant	

ཀྲ ཏྲ པྲ། ཁྲ ཐྲ ཕྲ། གྲ དྲ བྲ །། བཀྲེས། དཔྲལ་པ། ཁྲག། འཕྲིན། གྲུ། དྲན། ཕྲད་པ། བྲན།

3.3.4. Other alphabets: In addition to the above consonants the following four letters are used in reversed form to represent Sanskrit/Hindi sounds.

ཊ ཋ ཌ ཎ། ट ठ ड ण। ṭ ṭh ḍ ṇ.

In sTodpa language some of these sounds are used practically as a result of borrowing of words from Pahari/Hindi. For example: *čha-li ma-ṇa gñis thob.* = Maize-maund-two-found. I got two maunds of maize. *da-ṇa ru ha-ṭi maŋ-po 'dug.* = Manali-at-shop-many-is. There are many shops in Manali. *pha-ṭa la čig gaŋ-'aŋ yoŋ-ŋa ma-nag.* = Wasteland-in-one-which-also (*čig-gaŋ* = nothing)-comes-not-is. Nothing grows in the wild wasteland (*pha-ṭa*, from Pahari = *phāṭ*).

ཚ་ལི་མ་ཎ་གཉིས་ཐོབ།།ད་ཎ་རུ་ཧ་ཊི་མང་པོ་འདུག།།

ཕ་ཊ་ལ་ཅིག་གང་འང་ ཡོང་ང་མ་ནག།།

3.3.5. Although the following sounds don't belong to the language of sTodpa and apparently no imported word with such sound is also found but they are found used in some modern local constructions. The letters are:

gh, dh, bh, jh, ḷ, ḍh. घ ध भ झ ड ढ

གྷ དྷ བྷ ཛྷ ཌ་ ཌྷ་

These letters are not found used in the traditional language but are used in the new contrived words. *gham-dhim zer-de 'brug 'dir-ra-rag.*= *gham-dhim*-say-having-thunder-trembling-is.

The thunderstorm (dragon) is making sound of thundering (trembling) as *gham-dhim. jhim-bhim zer-de 'bag-gun čham-ma rag.* = *jhim-bhim*-say-having-mask-pl. sign-dancing is. The mask-dancers are dancing by making the sound of *jhim-bhim. ḍhim zer-de 'du-bag khrod song.* = *ḍhim* –say-having-matchlock-fire-went. The matchlock was fired with the sound *ḍhim.* *ṭ'u-'u ni ha-ḍag baḍ-dag žig 'dug.* = child-pl. sign-smart-a-is. The boy is smart.

གྷམ་དྷིམ་ཟེར་དེ་འབྲུག་ཌྷིར་ར་རག།།

ཛྷིམ་བྷིམ་ཟེར་དེ་འབག་གུན་འཆམ་མ་རག།།

ཌྷིམ་ཟེར་དེ་དུ་བག་ཁྲོད་སོང་།།

ཏུ་འུ་ནི་ཧཊ༷་དག་བཊ༷་དག་ཞིག་འདུག།།

4

Compound Letters and Words and Their Formation

4.1. Compound Letters: For the construction of words, besides the basic and simple alphabets many compound letters are also used which are formed by combining the simple alphabets. The compound letters have single sound like the basic letters.

4.1.1. Formation of Compound letters: Such compound letters are formed in two ways: by placing a letter over another letter, which then becomes *mgo-čan,* a surmounted letter*;* and by subjoining, i.e. joining a letter at the foot of another letter which then becomes *'dogs-can*, a subjoined letter. In this manner such letters become double piled and even more. They take the vowel signs like the other alphabets. But they don't produce any new sound.

4.1.1.1. mGo-čan: Surmounted letters

Three letters *r, l* and *s* are surmounted over some letters and form compound letters called *mgo-čan*. Each set is known by the letter surmounting the other letters, viz. *r-mgo, l-mgo* and *s-mgo*.

i.. ***r-mgo, r*-headed letters:** Compound letters formed by surmounting *r* are: *rk, rg, rŋ, rñ, rj, rt, rd, rn, rb, rm, rts, rds* and *rl.*

རྐ རྒ རྔ རྙ རྗ རྟ རྡ རྣ རྦ རྨ རྩ རྫ རླ།

In literary language the surmounted letter *r* remains silent in all these compound letters, except one, and only the base letter is pronounced. In sTodpa the surmounted letter *r* is pronounced in some words e.g. *mi-rgod ~mir-god* = a wild man, *ra-rdsi~rar-dsi* = Goat herd. However, the word rdo-rje = thunderbolt, is pronounced in both the forms, literary and colloquy, as *dor-je*.

མི་རྐོད། ར་རྗེ། རྡོ་རྗེ།

ii. ***l-mgo, l*-headed:** The compound letters formed by surmounting *l* are: *lk, lg, lŋ, lč, lj, lt, ld, lp, lb* and *lh*. Here the surmounted letter *l* remains silent except in the last letter where both the letters are pronounced as *lh,* in both the forms.

ལྐ ལྒ ལྔ ལྕ ལྗ ལྟ ལྡ ལྤ ལྦ ལྷ།

iii. ***s-mgo, s*-headed:** The compound letters formed by surmounting *s* are: *sk, sg, sŋ, sñ, st, sd, sn, sp, sb, sm* and *sts*. Here the surmounted letter *s* remains silent in all the compound letters.

སྐ སྒ སྔ སྙ སྟ སྡ སྣ སྤ སྦ སྨ སྩ།

4.1.1.2. 'dogs-can, Subjoined letters. The four letters *y, r, l* and *v* after subjoining with some other letters are called *'dogs-čan*. Each set is known by the letter subjoined to it: *y-btags, r-btags, l-btags and v-btags.*

i. ***y-btags, y*-footed**: Compound letters formed by subjoining the letter *y* are: *ky, khy, gy, py, phy, by* and *my*.

ཀྱ ཁྱ གྱ པྱ ཕྱ བྱ མྱ།

Here the resultant compound letters are pronounced like new letters taking into consideration both the letters. But there occur some variation in pronunciation in some of the letters. Such variations may be found more in the spoken languages which retain some archaic traditions at some places. In the compound letters *ky, khy* and *gy* both the letters are pronounced. The compound letters *py, phy, by* and *my,* in literary language are pronounced as *č, čh, j* and *ñ,* respectively.

In sTodpa language the compound letter *py*, in the word *dpyid-ka* = The Spring season, is pronounced as *pya,* with initial sound of *p*. In other words it is pronounced as *č.* The compound letter *phy* is pronounced with some words in its original form and with others it is pronounced as is done in the literary language. For example the following words are pronounced in their original tone as *f.*

phye(fe)-lha = the god of flour. *phyi-tog* = evening. *phyi-mo* = late. *phyi-ro* = night. *phyi-ta* = outside. *phyed-čad* = half. *phyil-la* = for, case sign, dative, *phyil-kog* = peal, bark. *yhye-mar* = *tsampa*, sugar and ghee mixed.

ཕྱི་ལྷ། ཕྱི་དོག། ཕྱི་མོ། ཕྱི་རོ། ཕྱི་ཏ། ཕྱིད་ཅན། ཕྱིལ་ལ། ཕྱིལ་གོག། ཕྱི་མར།

The following words are pronounced as they are done in the literary language. *phyag* ~ *čhag* = hand (hon.). *phyugs* ~ *čhugs*= cattle. *phyug-po~čhug-po* = rich.

ཕྱག། ཕྱུགས། ཕྱུག་པོ།

In colloquial the combined letter *by* is pronounced in the following words in its original form like *bi, be,* etc. For example: *bye*(*be*)-*ma* = sand. *byi*(*bi*)-*la* = cat. *byir(bir)-kyag* = droppings of rat. *byi*(*bi*)-*ril* = Small balls, like the small potatoes left after separating those of normal size.

བྱེ་མ། བྱི་ལ། བྱིར་ཀྱག། བྱི་རིལ།

In the following words *b* is pronounced as *j. byi*(*ji*)-*pa* = bird. *byil*(*jil*)-*phrug* = a chick of a bird. *byu*(*ju*)-*ru* = coral. *byin*(*jin*)-*rlabs* = A small share of consecrated or sacred eatable distributed to the devotees.

བྱི་པ། བྱིལ་ཕྲུག། བྱིན་རླབས།

ii. ***r-btags, r*-footed**: Compound letters formed by subjoining the letter *r* are: *kr, khr, gr, tr, thr, dr, pr, phr, br, sr, šr* and *hr*.

ཀྲ ཁྲ གྲ ཏྲ ཐྲ དྲ པྲ ཕྲ བྲ སྲ ཤྲ ཧྲ།

In literary language the compound letters *kra, tra* and *pra* are all pronounced as *ṭ* ; *khr*, *thr* and *phr* as *ṭh*; *gr, dr* and *br* as *ḍ*. In sTodpa the letter *kr* in the word *bkra-šis,* as is used in the old songs, is pronounced as *kr*, as *bkra-šis~ krași* = auspicious. Otherwise, normally it is pronounced as *ṭ i.e. ṭa-ši* as in literary language.

བཀྲ་ཤིས།

iii. ***l-btags, l*-footed:** Compound letters formed by subjoining the letter *l* are: *kl, gl, bl, dsl, sl* and *rl.*

ཀླ གླ བླ ཟླ སླ རླ།

The letters joined with *la* are pronounced all as *la* except *dsl* which is pronounced as *da* in both the forms.

iv. ***v-btags, v*-footed**: Compound letters formed by subjoining the letter *v* are: *rtsv* and *tshv.* The subjoined letter v becomes silent in both the compound letter in sTodpa. But it is pronounced in the literary language.

རྩྭ ཚྭ།

A letter can have both *mgo-'dogs* and *smad-'dogs* at the same time like: *skra* = hair, *sgra* = sound, *sprin* = cloud.

སྐྲ། སྒྲ། སྤྲིན།

4.2. Construction of Words and Arrangement of letters

4.2.1. One Word One Sound: When letters combine to form a word they do so according to certain grammatical rules. Phonetically they tend to follow the principle of monosyllabic system. From among the cluster of letters which form a word there is one letter – it may be simple or compound – which forms the base of the word and is articulated fully, others are pronounced with lesser force, or may remain silent. Thus the principle is that one word has one sound, or one principal sound. This base letter may be found at the initial position, in the medial or at the end of the word. But even if a letter remains silent presence of all these in the word is essential. All the thirty consonants can form base of a word, stem letter. But all of them cannot take all the places around the base letter.

4.2.2. Parts of a Word: Each word has a base letter called *miŋ-žhi*. All the thirty *gsal-byed* letters are *miŋ-žhi*. These are classified for the purpose of formation of words as: *sŋon-'jug, rjes-'jug* and *mi-'jug* i.e. prefix, suffix and non-fixable.

miŋ-gži (= name or letter base), Base-syllable: The principal letter of the word is named as *miŋ-gži,* base-syllable. Besides the thirty gsal-byed, there are compound letters which function similarly as base-letter as has been explained above.

Letters and words: Some single syllables of the alphabet are meaningful which form word and are pronounced in normal way as the syllable is pronounced. For example the following syllables are meaningful: *kha* = snow, mouth. *ŋa* = I, *ja* = tea, *ña*= fish, *da* = now, *ma* = original, *la* = mountain pass, *ša* = meat.

ཁ། ང་། ཇ། ཉ། ད ས། ལ།

Similarly a compound letter, also surmounted and subjoined both, can be meaningful, like: *rta* = horse. *bya* = bird. *rna*= ear. *sna* = nose, *sleb-ce* = to reach.

རྟ། བྱ། རྣ། སྣ། སླེབ་ཅེ།

i. *sŋon-'jug*: Prefix. The letter prefixed to *miŋ-gži* is called *sŋon-'jug*, prefix. These are five: *ga, da, ba, ma, 'a.*

ག། ད། བ། མ། འ།

ii. *rjes-'jug*, Suffix: i. Any word may end with only one of the following ten syllables which are called *rjes-'jug* i.e. suffix, viz.

g, ŋ, d, n, b, m, 'a, r, l, s.

ག། ང་། ད། ན། བ། མ། འ། ར། ལ། ས།

All the words ending with the vowels 'i, 'u, e and 'o follow the same rules as apply to the syllable 'a in all kinds of combinations with other words for any kind of formation of words.

All the words of single syllable like ga, ŋa, ja, etc. are presumed to end in vowel, i.e. 'a and follow the same rule as a word ending with 'a.

iii. *yaŋ-'jug*, Extra suffix: The letter placed after the suffix is called *yaŋ-'jug,* extra suffix which are: *d* and *s*. This is not applicable to sTodpa.

ད། ས། མིང་གཞི། སྔོན་འཇུག། རྗེས་འཇུག། ཡང་འཇུག།

Below are given examples of some words showing the places occupied by different letters in the word and the manner of their articulation.

Word Meaning	sŋon-'jug	miŋ-gži	rjes-'jug	yaŋ-'jug
la = pass	-	la	-	-
khab = needle	-	kh	b	-
mgo = head	m	go	-	-
mjug = end	m	ju	g	
thabs= means	-	tha	b	s
gzigs = to see	g	zi	g	s

ལ། ཁབ། མགོ། མཇུག། ཐབས། གཟིགས།

The above system of assignment of different positions to different letters in a word is based on the principle of classification of the alphabets into the four classes of gender: *pho, mo, ma-niŋ* and *šin-tu-mo, i.e.* masculine, feminine, neutral and very-feminine which is not discussed here.

iv. *mi-'jug:* After taking out the ten *sŋon-'jug* and *rjes-'jug* letters, the remainder twenty letters are known as *mi-'jug*, non fixable letters. These letters cannot be added before a word and also they cannot close a word. The letters of the class also cannot combine among themselves for formation of words.

4.3. Articulation of Words: The above arrangement of letters of different classes in a word is the basis for the manner in which they are articulated. We take for example the word *gzigs,* which is made of four letters, containing all the positions of letters in a word. In this word **z**, the second letter, is *miŋ-gži* stem-syllable, the principal syllable of the word which is articulated fully. The first syllable *ga* is prefix and is silent. It is not pronounced. The first of the last two letters **g** is suffix. This syllable is pronounced only partly, it loses the sound of **a**, inherent in it. The last syllable **s** is extra suffix. This may be pronounced very softly or not at all. Thus the whole word is ordinarily heard as **zig** in which **g** is heard only partially. Similarly in all the words *miŋ-gži,* the stem syllable, is pronounced and the others are articulated according to their place in the word, as explained here.

While pronouncing the words of two or more than two parts, each part can be taken as an independent word. For example in the word *gzig-pags* = leopard skin, the two parts of the words *gzig* and *pags* may be taken as two separate words for the purpose of articulation. In these two words *zi* and *pa* are the stem letters.

གཟིག་པགས།

4.3.1. Some variations in Pronunciation: Certain words show slight change in pronunciation in certain situations. The word *za-če* is a noun and means meal and the same word as a verb means to eat. The word is pronounced differently when it is used in the above two different situations. Independently the word will be pronounced in both the situations in the same way as it is pronounced when it is used as noun. But when it is used as verb it is pronounced slightly differently. Here the word is shown used in sentences.

1. *za-če* (noun) *btoŋ.* = Give (me) meal.
2. *za-če* (noun) *za-če* (*zah-če)* (verb) *btoŋ* = Let me eat meal.

The distinction between two meanings of a word can be conveyed and understood only through the distinction made in the pronunciation or the tone. Here the word in sentence number 2 in the latter part is in the form of verb. Here the stem letter '*z*' becomes a little emphatic as '*zah*'. Similar other cases are also found.

4.3.2. Joining of vowel sign: In one word or in a part of a word only one vowel sign is used and it is attached only with the **miŋ-gži,** the stem-letter. Ex. :

čhu	=	water.	*sku*	=	body.	*kun*	=	all.
gži	=	a place.	*sŋon*	=	before.	*mthoŋ*	=	see.
gzigs	=	see.						

ཆུ། སྐུ། ཀུན། གཞི། སྔོན། མཐོང་། གཟིགས།

i. Words of one part: Below are given some words having one part.

ša	=	meat,	*žo*	=	curd,	*khyi*	=	dog,
ras	=	cotton cloth,	*bal*	=	wool,	*lug*	=	sheep,
šing	=	wood,	*mgo*	=	head,	*šig*	=	louse,
mig	=	eye,	*sman*	=	medicine.	*čhu*	=	water.
gos	=	cloth.	*šel*	=	glass	*žiŋ*	=	field.
las	=	work.						

ཤ། ཞོ། ཁྱི། རས། བལ། ལུག། ཤིང་། མགོ། ཤིག། མིག། སྨན། ཆུ། གོས། ཤེལ། ཞིང་ ལས།

Such words join to form new words. Some of these words after joining give new meaning. Below are given words formed by joining two words.

These words retain their original meaning in the new words. *lug-ša* = sheep-meat, sheep's meat. *mig-sman* = eye-medicine, eye ointment. *ras-gos* = cotton cloth- cloth, cotton cloth. *Žiŋ-las* = field - work, work relating to field.

ii. The words below give changed meaning.

khyi-šig = dog - lice, flea. *ras-bal* = cotton cloth-wool, cotton. *čhu-mig* = water – eye, water spring. *mig-šel* = eye-glass, spectacle

ii. **Words of two parts**: Many words are found in two parts as above. Words are found at the most formed of four parts. In the following words usually the first part is meaningful and is the stem of the word. With the second part, the modifier, the word gives its full meaning.

čhar-pha	=	rain	thal-ba	=	soil	thab-ka	=	hearth
thag-pa	=	rope	ñi-ma	=	sun	‘o-ma	=	milk
žiŋ-ka	=	field	las-kha	=	work	rus-pha	=	bone
go-‘a	=	hearth	ñe-mo	=	near	lam-ka	=	path

ཆར་ཕ། ཐལ་བ། ཐབ་ཀ།། ཐག་པ། ཉི་མ། འོ་མ། ཞིང་ཀ།། ལས་ཁ། རུས་ཕ། གོ་འ། ཉེ་མོ། ལམ་ཀ།།

In the following words the root is meaningful and the suffix modifies the meaning of the root word.

bar	=	middle	*bar-pha*	=	the middle one
mdo	=	side	*mdo-ma*	=	the one on the side
‘brug	=	thunder	‘brug-pa.	=	belonging to ‘brug (a sect)
dgu	=	nine	*dgu-pa*	=	the ninth
gži	=	name of a village	*gži-pha*	=	a resident of gži
mth’a	=	distant	*mth’a-pa*	=	One belonging to distant place

མདོ་མ། འབྲུག་པ། དགུ་པ། གཞི་ཕ། མཐའ་པ།

In the following cases the word becomes meaningful only when both the parts are together. Independently no part is meaningful

po-to	=	bush	*be-to*	=	calf	*ba-mo*	=	witch
se-ra	=	hail	*thu-ru*	=	colt	*khu-ru*	=	load
ča-lag	=	article	*ka-ča*	=	news	*ku-lig*	=	lock
so-baŋ	=	comb						

se-ra mgo-la phog-‘a rag = Hail-head-to-hit-is-is.

The hail is hitting the head. *de-de thu-ru daŋ be-to’i-si bzos soŋ.* = That- the one-colt-and-calf-by-ate-went. That has been eaten by the colt and the calf.

ཕོ་ཏོ།། བེ་ཏོ།། བ་མོ།། སེ་ར།། ཐུ་རུ།། ཁུ་རུ།། ཙ་ལག།། ཀ་ཙ།། ཀུ་ལིག།། སོ་བང་།། སེ་ར་མགོ་ལ་ཕོག་འ་རག།། དེ་དེ་ཐུ་རུ་དང་བེ་ཏོ་འི་སི་བཟོས་སོང་།།

4.4. Formation of new words: In the sTodpa language there are large number of words constructed by joining two or more than two words. These may be from among the words of one part or of two. While joining two words each one having two parts, the second part is dropped. Then the root words retain their original meaning. The final word formed after the combination of two words may, besides the literal meaning, also give sometimes a conventional meaning.

4.4.1. Here two noun words are paired

žiŋ- ka+ khaŋ-pa = žiŋ-khaŋ. House and fields, property.

rkaŋ-pa + lag-pa = rkaŋ-lag. Feet and hands, limbs.

ñi-ma + mtshan-mo = ñin-mtshan. Day and night, continuously.

čhen-ma + čhun-ma = čhen-čhun. The elder and the junior (daughters-in-law).

čhen-mo + čhuŋ-ŋa = čhe- čhuŋ. Big and small, all.

ra-ma + lug = ra-lug. Goats and sheep.

skyid-po + sdug-po = skyid-sdug. Happiness and sorrow, shades of life.

sgo + khyi = sgo-khyi. The dog guarding the door, watchdog.

mi + lag-pa = mi-lag. Man and hand. Worker.

žiŋ -khaŋ čhen-mo 'dug. = Property-big-is. He has large property.

mi-lag dkon-mo 'dug. = Workers-scarcity-is. One who has scarcity of workers.

ཞིང་ཁང་།། རྐང་ལག།། ཉིན་མཚན།། ཆེན་ཆུན།། ར་ལུག།། སྐྱིད་སྡུག།། སྒོ་ཁྱི།། མི།ལག་པ།། ཞིང་ཁང་ཆེན་མོ་འདུག།། མི་ལག་དཀོན་མོ་འདུག།།

4.4.2. In the following combination of words the first part of the word assumes the character of genitive case.

pha + nor = father+wealth = *pha-nor*, Father's property, ancestral property.

gser + sku = gold + icon = *gser-sku,* Icon of gold.

lha + tho = god + cairn = *lha-tho,* God's cairn, cairn of a deity.

kha + rud = snow + flood = *kha-rud,* Flood of snow, avalanche.

lčags+sgam = iron+box = Box of iron.

lag+ las = hand + work. = Work of hand. A handicraft.

čhon-la ma-sdad-ta lag-las-re khur sdod. = idle-to-not sitting-hand-work-some-carry-sit. Instead of sitting idle, have some work in your hand (like knitting of socks).

པ་ནོར།། གསེར་སྐུ།། ལྷ་ཕོ།། ཁ་རྡུད།། ཐུགས་སྨམ།། ཆོན་ལ་མ་སྡད་ཏ། ལག་ ལས་རེ་ཁུར་སྡོད།།

4.4.3. Below we see that an adjective joining with a noun word forms a new noun word.

mi + *čhen-mo* = man + great = *mi-čhen,* great man.

čhu + *tshan-te* = water +hot= *čhu-tshan,* hot water.

ñuŋ-ma + *dkar-pho* = turnip + white = *ñuŋ-dkar*, white turnip.

khaŋ-pa + *stoŋ-pa* = house + empty = *khaŋ-stoŋ,* empty house.

lam-ka + *ñe-mo* = path + near = *ñe-lam*, short-cut path.

མི་ཆེན་མོ།། ཆུ་ཚན་ཏེ།། ཉུང་མ་དཀར་ཕོ།། ཁང་པ་སྟོང་པ།། ལམ་ཀ་ཉེ་མོ།།

4.4.4. A verb after joining with noun forms noun.

ber-kha + *rdung-če* = stick + to beat = *ber-rduŋ*, beating of stick.

sgo + *rduŋ-če* = door + beating = *sgo-rduŋ* (gor-duŋ) = beating at door.

las-kha + *čhag-če* = *las-čhag* (*las-šag*), break in work, disturbance in work.

baŋ + *thal-če* = *baŋ-thal*, exceeding race, losing control.

thabs + *čhag-če* = *thabs-čhag* (*thabs-šag*), failed attempt, a work done half heartedly.

lan-ba + *tug-če* = *lan-tug.* To sew a patch, a patchwork.

བེར་ཁ་།། རྡུང་ཅེ།། སྒོ།། ལས་ཁ།། ཆག་ཅེ།། བང་།། ཐལ་ཅེ།། ཐབས།ཆག་ཅེ།། ལན་བ།ཏུག་ཅེ།།

4.4.5. Words with opposite meanings may be joined in pairs in the following manner:

mthon-po + *dm'a-mo* = high + low = *mtho-dm'a,* high and low. Similarly: *riŋ-btuŋ* = long and short. *graŋ-drod.* = cold and warm. *sŋan-rtiŋ* = before and after. *rgyab-mdun* = back and front. *tsha-graŋ* = hot and cold. *gyen-yog* = above and below. Here both parts of the words retain their original meaning.

མཐོ་དམའ།། རིང་བཏུང་།། གྲང་དྲོད།། སྔོན་རྗེང་།། རྒྱབ་མདུན།། ཚན་ཏེ།། གྲང་མོ།། གྱེན་ཡོག།།

graŋ-drod tsug yod na-'aŋ yoŋ-dgos. = cold-warm-how-have-may become-want. Whether it is cold or warm, must come. *čhe-čhuŋ si-rig la šog zer.* = big-small-all-to-come-say. Tell all to come, whether young or old (big or small).

གྲང་དྲོད་ཙུག་ཡོད་ན་འང་ཡོང་དགོས།། ཆེ་ཆུང་སི་རིག་ལ་ཤོག་ཟེར།།

4.5. Words of more than two parts : Words of the kind of more than two parts are mostly explanatory or descriptive. *zer-mkhan-pa* = speak-doer-person, speaker. *šiŋ-bžog-pa* = wood-makes plain-person, carpenter. *lčags-bzo-ba* = ironsmith. *mi-šes-mkhan* = ignorant. *ši-ka-zam-pa* = The traditional bridge made by knitting thick rope of branches of birch wood. *tshom-čhed-mo* = The big hall (in Khangsar Khar). *šes-laŋ med-kan* = Unrecognisable, not understandable.

ཟེར་མཁན་པ།། ཤིང་བཞོག་པ།། ལྕགས་བཟོ་བ།། མི་ཤེས་མཁན།། ཤི་ཀ་ཟམ་པ།། ཚོམ་ཆེད་མོ།། ཤེས་ལང་མེད་ཀན།།

The following long expressions function as single unit of grammar like a subject or adjective.:

[*khaŋ-pa sruŋ-mkhan-pa*] *gčig-gčig ta sdad dgos.* = [House-watch-keeper-one]-one-at least-sit-need. At least one person is needed to stay to keep watch over the house. *'bras* [*lhag-ma lus sdad-mkhan de*] *si-rig ŋe khyi-la btaŋ-ben.* = rice-[remainder-remain-sit]-having-all-I-dog-to-give-did. I gave all the remaining rice to dog.

ཁང་པ་སྲུང་མཁན་པ་གཅིག་གཅིག་ཏ་དགོས།།

འབྲས་ལྷག་མ་ལུས་སྡད་མཁན་དེ་ངེ་སི་རིག་ཁྱི་ལ་བཏང་བེན།།

4.6. Words and particles: Another way of formation of new words is by affixing with a word particles which are many. Here the verb *'grul-če* is joined with some particles which then functions as noun. '*grul-če,*= To walk. *'grul-tshul.*= Manner of walking. *'grul-tshad* = Certain measures of distance for travelling. *'grul-thab.* = Attempt to walk. *'grul-ñin.* =

Willingness to walk. *'grul-khyad* = Necessity to walk. *'grul-laŋ* = The task of walking, *'grul-ba.* = A traveler. *'grul-theb* = A trip. *'grul-mkhan-pa.* = A traveler. *'grul-loŋ* = Leisure/time to walk. *ŋa-la dad-saŋ čha-loŋ med.* = Me-to-now-go-time-not-is. Presently I have no time to go.

འགྲུལ་ཅེ།། འགྲུལ་རྩལ།། འགྲུལ་ཚད།། འགྲུལ་ཐབ།།

འགྲུལ་ཉེན།། འགྲུལ་ཁྱད།། འགྲུལ་ལང་།། འགྲུལ་བ།།

འགྲུལ་ཐེབ།། འགྲུལ་མཁན་པ།། འགྲུལ་ལོང་།།

4.7. Diminutives: i. The following words show the younger ones of the species or smaller of the kind of the animate beings. *ri-'u* = goat kid. *lu-'u,*= lamb. *byil-phrug.*= bird's chicks. *buŋ-phrug.*= kid of a donkey. *khyi-phrug.* = puppy. *pi-phrug* = kitten. *tshag-phrug* = *twin.*

རི་ཨུ། ལུ་ཨུ། བྱིལ་ཕྲུག། བུང་ཕྲུག། ཁྱི་ཕྲུག། པི་ཕྲུག། ཚག་ཕྲུག།།

ii. The following words show the smaller kinds of things of inanimate objects: *rdo-rug.*= pebbles. *šiŋ-rug.*= small wooden pieces. *tsher-rug.* = small pieces of branches of thorny plants. *naŋ-rug* = Filling-stones in the stone wall. *gre-rug* = A tailor's wastes. *šir-rug* = Small invisible pieces of stones in grain flour.

རྡོ་རུག། ཤིང་རུག། ཚེར་རུག། ནང་རུག། གྲེ་རུག། ཤིར་རུག།

Sentences: *'i ŋe khaŋ-pa yin.* =This-my-house-is. This is my house. *ŋa-ža miŋ-ga lŋa yod.* = We-person-five-are. We are five persons. *kho su nag.* = He-who-is. Who is he? *khyod la či dgos.*= You-to-what-need. What do you want? *kho 'i-ru sdad-de 'dug.* = He-here-at-sit-having-is. He is sitting here. *di-riŋ ñi-ma graŋ-mo rag.* = Today-the sun-cold-is. Today it is cold.

འི།ངེ་ཁང་པ་ཡིན།། ང་ཞ།མིང་ག།ལྔ་ཡོད།། ཁོ།སུ།ནག།།

ཁྱོད་ལ།ཅི་དགོས།། ཁོ།འི་རུ།སྡད་དེ་འདུག།། དི་རིང་།ཉི་མ།གྲང་མོ་རག།།

4.8. Syntax: In a sentence the words of different kinds take order as follows: subject, object and verb. Adjectives follow the word they qualify. Adverbs precede the words they qualify.

kho khaŋ-pa-la čha-rug. = He-home-to-go-is. He is going home. *las sla-mo* = work-easy. Easy work. *mi-'un grul-de čha-rug.* = man-pl. sign.-

walk-having-go-is. People are going walking. *kho mgyogs-pha čha-rug.* = He-fast-go-is. He is going fast. *mi -'un khaŋ-pa la grul-de čha-rug.* = man-pl. sign.-home-to-walk-having-go-is. People are going to their home walking.

ཁོ་ཁང་པ་ལ་ཆ་རུག། ལས་སླ་མོ།། མི་ཨུན་འགྲུལ་དེ་ཆ་རུག།

ཁོ་མགྱོགས་ཕ་ཆ་རུག། མི་ཨུན་ཁང་པ་ལ་འགྲུལ་དེ་ཆ་རུག།

4.9. In colloquial it may be observed that many sentences are found without subject. This can be understood from the structure of the sentence which is made clear by the use of different auxiliaries in different context.

In the following sentences subject has not been used. But they can be understood as to whom the sentence is addressed: first, second or the third person. While in the context they become much clearer.

The following sentences relate to the first person:

yod = I have　　*med* = I don't have
soŋ-ben = I went　　*ma-yoŋ* = I did not come
ma-zer = I didn't say　　*tho-re čhen* = I will go tomorrow
mi-čha. = I will not go.　　*čha-kan* = I wish to go
čha-'a-med. I-going-not. = I am not going

The following sentences are addressed to the second person.

ga-ru yod. = Where are you? *či zer-ra yod.* = What are you saying? *či-la ma-yoŋ.* = What-for-not-come. Why did not you come? *nam čha-kan.*= When will you go?

The following sentences are addressed to the third person. *'dug.* = He is. *ga-ru 'dug.* = Where is he? *či zer-rug.* = what-say-is. What does he say? *ga-ru bud-soŋ.* = Where did he go? *'dug pen* = He was there. *čig-gaŋ-'aŋ khur-de mi-nug.* = Some-what-also-carry-having-not=is. = He is carrying nonthing.

ཡོད།།　　མེད།།　　སོང་བེན།།　　མ་ཡོང་།།

མ་ཟེར།　　ཐོ་རེ་ཆེན།།　　མི་ཆ།།　　ཆ་ཀན།།

ཆ་འ་མེད།།　　ག་རུ་ཡོད།།　　ཅི་ཟེར་ར་ཡོད།།　　ཅི་ལ་མ་ཡོང་།།

ནམ་ཆ་ཀན།།　　འདུག།　　ག་རུ་འདུག།　　ཅི་ཟེར་རུག།

ག་རུ་ བུད་སོང་།། འདུག་པེན།། ཅིག་གང་འང་ཁུར་དེ་མི་ནུག།

The letter 's' as rjes-'jug is pronounced after the words ending with the vowel 'o' as 'e' and after the words ending with the vowel 'u' as 'i'.

čhos = *čh*o-e = literature. *tshos* = tsho-e = colour *khyus* = khyu-i = melting. *lus* = *lu-i* = body.

ཆོས། ཚོས། ཁྱུས། ལུས།

5
Noun

5.1. Gender

5.1.1. There are two genders in sTodpa: masculine and feminine. But very few words come under this category of classification. Most of the words remain as genderless. A noun word is found in masculine or feminine form with the suffixes *pho* and *mo* respectively. Words originally in masculine are found in different forms and some with suffixes other than *pho.* The signs for feminine are *mo* and *ma*. However, suffixes *pho* or *mo* do not always function as signs of gender. The use of gender distinction is not very common. The particles *pa* and *ba* are neutral but sometimes they also denote masculine gender.

Example: Below are given some nouns of which some appear attached with gender signs but they are in their natural form.

mčhor-pho	=	handsome	*mčhor-mo*	=	beautiful
rgya-pho	=	king	*rgya-mo*	=	queen
rgad-po	=	old man	rgad-mo	=	old woman
srin-po, Şin-po	=	demon	*srin-mo, Şin-mo*	=	demoness
smyon-ba	=	mad man	*smyon-ma*	=	mad woman
mag-pa	=	groom	*Bab-ma*	=	bride

མཆོར་པོ། མཆོར་མོ། རྒྱ་པོ། རྒྱ་མོ། རྒད་པོ། རྒད་མོ། སྲིན་པོ། སྲིན་མོ། སྨྱོན་པ། སྨྱོན་མ། མག་པ། བག་མ།

5.1.2. The following words are generally used as common gender, but they have feminine equivalents also.

lha = deity — lha-mo = goddess

yon-bdag = landlord — yon-bdag-mo = landlady

mon = a man from Kullu, Chamba etc. — *mon-mo* = A female *mon be-da* = A man of musician class. *be-mo* = A female *be-da.*

ལྷ། ལྷ་མོ། ཡོན་བདག། ཡོན་བདག་མོ། མོན། མོན་མོ། བེ་ད། བེ་མོ།

5.1.3. These words are of common gender: *khyi* = Dog, *bya*= Bird. Gender signs *pho* and *mo* are used rarely and only when necessary. *khyi-pho* = male dog. *khyi-mo* = female dog. *bya-pho* = male bird. *bya-mo* = female bird.

ཁྱི་ཕོ། ཁྱི་མོ། བྱ་ཕོ། བྱ་མོ།

5.1.4. Some nouns have words of common gender and also have separate masculine and feminine forms:

lug	= sheep	*ma-mo*	= an ewe	*khal-pha*	= a castrated male sheep.
ru-bo	= ram	*ba-glaŋ*	= A cattle	*ba-ši*	= cow
glaŋ-to	= bull	*rta*	= horse	*dri-'u*	= mule
rgod-ma	= mare	*gseb*	= male horse		

ལུག། མ་མོ། ཁལ་ཕ་། རུ་བོ། བ་གླང་། བ་ཤི། གླང་ཏོ། རྟ། དྲི་ཨུ། རྒོད་མ། གསེབ།

5.1.5. Certain words have separate forms in masculine and feminine, and don't have word of common gender. *ra-ma* = She-goat. This is also used as common gender. *ra-bo* = Male goat. *bha-ṭo* = Bull goat. *bri-mo* = A female of yak. *g-yag* = Yak (male). *ga-ru* =Young male yak. *gar-mo* = Young female yak. *mdso* = A male cross between yak and cow. *mdso-mo* = Female *mdso. tsha'a-'o* = Nephew, also grandson. *tsha-mo-tsi* = Neice also grand daughter. *khyog-toŋ* = A young man. *na-čuŋ* or *na-čuŋ-ma* = A young woman.

The terms *lug* and *ra-ma* are used generally as common gender.

ར་མ། ར་བོ། བྷ་ཏོ། བྲི་མོ། གཡག། ག་རུ། གར་མོ། མཛོ། མཛོ་མོ། ཚྭ་འོ། ཚ་མོ་ཙེ། ཁྱོག་ཏོང་། ན་ཅུང་མ།

5.1.6. With the following words *mo* does not convey the feminine concept, but is a part of the word. *srad-mo~ṣad-mo* = Thin. *bde-mo* = Handsome. *lhag-mo* = clean. *sriŋ-mo~ṣiŋ-mo.*= Sister. *bred-mo* = Bear.

བདེ་མོ། ལྷག་མོ། སྲིང་མོ། བྲེད་མོ།

5.1.7. Generally the need for distinction of genders arises like in cases as follows:

Masculine	**Feminine**		
gar- ža-pa	*gar-ža-mo*	=	Lahuli man, woman
pi-ti-pa	*pi-ti-mo*	=	Spiti man, woman
zaŋkhar-pa	*zaŋkhar-mo*	=	Zanskar man, woman
ladak-pa	*ladak-mo*	=	Ladakhi man, woman
Man-čhad-pa	Man-čhad-mo	=	Manchad man, woman
Punanpa	Punan-mo	=	Punan man, woman

5.1.8. The following words belong to neuter gender:

phyug-po	=	rich man	*gnod-pa*	=	curse
nad-pa	=	sickman	*la-bo*	=	servant
las-pha	=	worker			

ཕྱུག་པོ། གནོད་པ། ནད་པ། ལ་བོ། ལས་པ།

5.2. Number

5.2.1. There are two numbers: singular and plural. A word in singular form may be changed to plural by adding the particles of plural sign which are: *kun, gun, 'un* and *gya-ma.* Generally there is no strict rule for preference in the use of any of these particles with any word and all the particles may be used with any word like: *mi-kun, mi-gun, mi-'un, mi gya-ma.* = men or all men. All the four expressions convey the same meaning. But this is not applicable in the case of personal pronouns with which we find only the suffix *gya-ma* is used.

མི་ཀུན། མི་གུན། མི་ཨུན། མི་གྱ་མ།

Sentences: *be-to-gun naŋ-ru 'dug.* = calf-pl. sign-room-in-is. The calves are inside. *lug-rdsi-si lug-gun ri-'a-ne khyoŋ 'dug.* = shepherd-by-sheep-pl. sign.-mountain- from-bring-is. The shepherd is bringing the sheep from the waste-land. *ṭu-'u-'un mi-nug.* = child-pl. sign-not-is. The children are not there. *byi-pe ṭu-'u-'un phur-de soŋ-de-mi-nug.* = bird-of-child-pl. sign-fly-have-went-having-not-is. The chicks of the bird have flown away and are not there.

བེ་ཏོ་གུན་ནང་རུ་འདུག། ལུག་རྫི་སི་ལུག་གུན་རི་འ་ནེ་ཁྱོང་འདུག།

བྱི་པེ་ཊུ་ཨུ་ཨུན་ཕུར་དེ་སོང་དེ་མི་ནུག།

5.2.2. Besides the signs given above, there are some words which function as plural sign when joined with a word in singular form, which all mean 'all' viz.: *thams-čad, tshaŋ-ma, si-rig* and *ča-be.* Thus *mi-thams-čad, mi-tshaŋ-ma, mi-si-rig, mi-ča-be.* All these expressions mean, 'all men'. *ča-be* means the whole.

མི་ཐམས་ཅད།། མི་ཚང་མ།། མི་སི་རིག།། མི་ཅ་བེ།།

5.2.3. The personal pronouns have plural forms, as shown in the chapter on Pronoun.

5.2.4. The sense of plural can also be obtained by repeating the word and inserting the conjunctive particle *daŋ* (= and) in between them. Like: *khyi daŋ khyi* = dog and dog, i.e. many dogs. *mi daŋ mi* = Man and man, many men. *'bu daŋ 'bu* = Worm and worm, many worms. *mi-daŋ-mi thaŋ-ka teb khaŋ 'dug.* = man-and-man ground-full filled-is. The ground is full with people. *tshugs-sa ru khyi-daŋ-khyi 'dsoms 'dug.* = Courtyard-in-dog-and-dog-gather-is. Many dogs have gathered in the courtyard. *'i-ni riŋ-mo daŋ riŋ-mo 'dug.* = This-rather-long-and-long-is. This is quite long. *'i-ni či-'aŋ riŋ-mo 'dug.* = This-rather-quite-long-is. This is quite long. *tsam 'thad 'thad riŋ-mo 'dug.* = Sufficient-long-is. It is sufficiently long.

ཁྲི་དང་ཁྲི།། མི་དང་མི།། འབུ་དང་འབུ།། མི་དང་མི་ཐང་ཀ་ཏེབ་ཁང་འདུག།།
ཚུགས་ས་རུ་ཁྲི་དང་ཁྲི་འཛོམས་འདུག།། འི་ནི་རིང་མོ་དང་རིང་མོ་འདུག།།
འི་ནི་ཅི་འང་རིང་མོ་འདུག།། ཙམ་འཐད་འཐད་རིང་མོ་འདུག།།

5.2.5. Similarly the particle *'e* also gives the same meaning. *lug 'e lug.*= Sheep, and only sheep, many many sheep. *khaŋ-pa 'e khaŋ-pa.* = Houses and only houses. *thal-ba 'e-thal-ba.* = Soil and only soil, nothing but soil. *tsher-maŋ 'e tsher-maŋ 'khad 'dug.* = Thorn-only-thorn-stuck-having-is. It is fully stuck up with thorns.

ལུག་འེ་ལུག།། ཁང་པ་འེ་ཁང་པ།། ཐལ་བ་འེ་ཐལ་བ།། ཚེར་མང་འེ་ཚེར་མང་འཁད་འདུག།།

5.2.6. Natural pairs of parts of the body are treated in this manner: *ŋe mig-la či-žig rag.* = My-eye-to-what-some-is. There is something in my eye or eyes. *ŋe rnam-čog ya-gčig la zug 'thon-de rag.* = my-ear-(*ya* = one of the pair)-one-to-pain-having-is. I have pain arisen in one of my ears.

pa-pu ya-rkaŋ la me-yaŋ rdol-de rag. = Sock-one (of pair)-foot-to-hole-burst-having-is. There is a hole created in one of the pairs of my socks. *ŋe rkaŋ-lag gun kyag-kug bčos ñan-laŋ me-rag.* = I cannot move (stretch and curve) my limbs (feet and arms).

ང་མིག་ལ་ཅི་ཞིག་རག།། ང་རྣམ་ཅོག་ཡ་གཅིག་ལ་ཟུག་འཐོན་དེ་རག།། ང་པ་པུ་ཡ་རྐང་ལ་མེ་ཡང་རྡོལ་དེ་རག།། ང་རྐང་ལག་གུན་ཀྱག་ཀུག་བཅོས་ཉན་ལང་མེ་རག།།

Sentences: i. *mi riŋ-mo gya-ma rgyab-la sdad-de 'dug.*= Man-long-pl. sign-back-at-sit-having-is. Long men are sitting behind. *yon-bdag-mo gun da-'u lab-ben 'dug.* = Landlord-fem. sign-pl. sign-talk-talking-is. The landladies are gossiping. *mi thams-čad yoŋ-ŋo la yoŋ 'dug.* = Man-all-this side-to-come-is. All men are coming to this side. *yul-pha ča-be 'dsoms 'dug.* = Villager-all-gather-is. All the villagers have assembled. *grul-mkhan-pa si-rig 'i-ne čha-rug.* = Walker-all-this-from-go-is. All those who are going on foot are going from here. *bag-thon la čha-mkhan-pa gun čha-rug.* = Marriage-to-goer-pl. sign-go-is. Those who were to go to marriage are going.

མི་རིང་མོ་གྱ་མ་རྒྱབ་ལ་སྡད་དེ་འདུག།། ཡོན་བདག་མོ་གུན་ད་འུ་ལབ་བེན་འདུག།། མི་ཐམས་ཅད་ཡོང་ངོ་ལ་ཡོང་འདུག།། ཡུལ་ཕ་ཙ་བེ།འཛོམས་འདུག།། གྲུལ་མཁན་པ་སི་རིག་འི་ནེ་ཆ་རུག།། བག་ཐོན་ལ་ཆ་མཁན་པ་གྱུ་མ་ཆ་རུག།།

5.3. Declensional Postpositions

5.3.1. No change occurs in the stem root when declining a word. Case signs are simply suffixed. Various case signs used are given as under:

Case	Case signs
1. Nominative	--
2. Accusative	*la*
3. Agentive	*'i, 'e.si, 'i-si*
4. Dative	*la, 'e, phyil-la*
5. Ablative	*ne,ne-si, kha-ne, kha-ne-si*
6. Genitive	*'e, 'i*
7. Locative	*ru,la*
8. Vocative	*v'e, vz'a, le*

5.3.2. Exampzle: *khaŋ-pa,* House.

		Singular	**Plural**
1.	Nominative	*khaŋ-pa*	*khaŋ-pa 'un*
2.	Accusative	*khaŋ-pa la*	*khaŋ-pa 'un-la*
3.	Agentive	*khaŋ- pe*	*khaŋ-pa 'un si*
4.	Dative	*khaŋ-pa la*	*khaŋ-pa 'un-la*
5.	Ablative	*khaŋ-pa-ne*	*khaŋ-pa 'un ne*
6.	Genitive	*khaŋ-pe*	*khaŋ-pa 'un ne*
7.	Locative	*khaŋ-pa-ru*	*khaŋ-pa 'un ru*

ལ། འི། འི་སི། སི། ཕྱིལ་ལ། ནེ། ནེ་སི། ཁ་ནེ། ཁ་ནེ་སི། འི། ར། རུ།
ལྷ། ལྷེ། ལེ།

5.3.3. Joining the case signs: There are some differences in the case signs used in the colloquy from that in literary practice.

i. The case signs of Agentive and Genitive cases in the colloquial are short and simple viz. *si* and *'i*, respectively. In the literary form these are: a. Agentive: kyis, gis, gyis, 'is, yis. b. Genetive: kyi, gi, gyi, 'i, yi.

ཀྱིས། གིས། གྱིས། འིས། ཡིས། སི། ཀྱི། གི། གྱི། འི། ཡི། འི་འི།

ii. Below are given examples of use of the case signs in colloquy in the seven different cases.

1. Nominative: *rdor-rje čha-rug.* = Dorje-go-is. Dorje goes/is going. *sgrol-ma sil-lug.* = Dolma-read-is. Dolma reads/is reading.
2. Accusative: *khaŋ-pa la čha-rug.* = Home-to-go-is. Is going to home. *kho-la zer.* = He-to-ask. Ask him/her.
3. Agentive: *čhu-'i-si khyer soŋ.* = Water-by-take-went. Water (the river) has taken away. *khaŋ-pe las-khe-si.* = House-of-work-of-by. By the reason of the work at home. *khaŋ-pa čhed-mo-'un –si bkag-de 'dug.* = House-big-pl. sign-by-obstructed-having-is. The big buildings have obstructed.
4. Dative: *ŋa-la yod.* = I-to-have. I have. *kho-ba tshaŋ-ma la 'dug.* = they-all-to-is. All of them have.
5. Ablative: *khaŋ-pa ne bud soŋ.* = Home-from-go-went. He went from home. *kho-be-kha-ne khyer soŋ.* = They-of-from-take-went. He took from them.

6. Genitive: *ŋe khaŋ-pa.* = My-house. My house. *mi-'un-ne khaŋ-pa.* = People-pl. sign-of-house. Houses of the people.
7. Locative: *de-ru 'dug.* = That-in-is. It is there. *kho khaŋ-pa ru 'dug.* = He is at home.
8. *va-chi-bcho-'a yod.* = Oh-what-doing-is. Oh! What are you doing?

རྡོ་རྗེ་ཆ་རུག།། སྒྲོལ་མ་སིལ་ལུག།། ཁང་པ་ལ་ཆ་རུག།། ཁོ་ལ་ཟེར།
ཆུ་འི་སི་ཁྲིར་སོང་།། ཁང་པེ་ལས་ཁེ་སི།། ཁང་པ་ཆེད་མོ་ཙུན་སི་བཀག་
དེ་འདུག།། ང་ལ་ཡོད།། ཁོ་བ་ཚང་མ་ལ་འདུག།། ཁང་པ་ནེ་བུད་སོང་།།
ཁོ་བེ་ཁ་ནེ་ཁྲིར་སོང་།། ངེ་ཁང་པ།། མི་ཙུན་ནེ་ཁང་པ།། དེ་རུ་འདུག།།
ཁོ་ཁང་པ་རུ་འདུག།། ཝ། ཅི་བཙོ་འ་ཡོད།།

Some times the case signs get contracted and sometimes they disappear. Thus they become like: *čhaŋ-ŋe dri-ma.*= *čhaŋ-ri.* Smell of beer. *śiŋ-ŋe khaŋ-pa.*= *śiŋ-khaŋ.* Wooden house. *lam-me rgyags.* = *lam-rgyags.* Provisions for a journey.

ཆང་ངེ་དྲི་མ།། ཆང་རི།། ཤིང་ངེ་ཁང་པ།། ཤིང་ཁང་།། ལམ་མེ་རྒྱགས།།
ལམ་རྒྱགས།།

5.4. Below are given examples of the use of some case signs of other forms:

i. Dative. *khyo-'e phyil-la khyo-ma khyoŋ-de yod.* = you-of-for-present-bring-having-is. I have brought gift for you.
ii. Ablative. *ŋa-la kho-'e kha-ne dŋul lŋa thob-če yod.* = I-to-he-from-rupee-five-receive-having-is. I have to receive rupees five from him.
iii. In the locative case *naŋ-la* (= into) has been added. *čhu'i naŋ-la ña thob-čen.* = Water-of-in-in-fish-find-is. = Fish is found in water. Sentences:

    a. *'i rtsigs-pa rdo-rje-si rtisgs-soŋ.* = This-wall-Dorje-by-construct-was. This wall was constructed by Dorje. *ŋe khaŋ-pa khyo-'e-de saŋ čuŋ-ŋun yod.* = My-house-your-the one-from-small-is. My house is smaller than yours. *gčig-si-gčig la phul-de nan btaŋ 'dug.*

= One-by-one-to-push-having-trample-give-is. One is pushing the other and are trampling over.

b. *thag-pa su'i kha ne khyoŋ-če.* = Rope-who-from-from-to bring. From whom should I bring rope? *'i-ne phyi-ta la ltos.* = This-from-outside-to-see. Look out from here. *mi-'un ltad-mo lta-'a la čha-rug.*= Man-pl. sign-show-looking-for-go-is. People are going to see the show. *mi-'un-ne ṭ'u-'u-la ma-dran.* = Man-pl. sign-of-child-to-not-vie. Don't vie with the children of other people (other children). *khyog-toŋ 'un-si mthsan-mtshan-la la 'gal btaŋ-dog.* = Youngmen-pl. sign-by-night-night-to-pass-cross-give-have. The youngmen have crossed the pass during the night itself.

འི་རྩིག་པ་རྡོ་རྗེ་སི་རྩིགས་སོང་།། ངེ་ཁང་པ་ཁྲོ་འི་དེ་སང་ཙུང་ངུན་ཡོད།།
གཅིག་སི་གཅིག་ལ་ཕུལ་དེ་ནན་བཏང་འདུག།། ཐག་པ་སུ་འི་ཁ་ནེ་ཁྱོང་ཅེ།།
འི་ནེ་ཕྱི་ཏ་ལ་ ལྟོས།། མི་ཨུན་ལྟད་མོ་ལྟ་འ་ལ་ཆ་རུག།། མི་ཨུན་ནེ་ཏུ་
ཨུ་ལ་མ་དྲན།། ཁྱོག་ཏོང་ཨུན་སི་མཚན་མཚན་ལ་ལ་འགལ་བཏང་དོག།།

c. *'yog'* = 'down.' *yog-la* = Downwards. *Yog-yog-la* = Downwards. *yog yog-la* = To down below. *yog-yog yog-la* = Down and downwards. *yog 'e yog-la* =To the extreme down. *yog ne yog-la* = From down to further down. *yog ne si-'aŋ yog la.* = Down to still further down. *dbyar-ka dbyar-ka kho lug rtso-'a la čha-'a nag, dgun-ka dgun-ka bal skal-la la sdad-ta nag.* = During the summer he goes to graze sheep and during the winter he stays to spin wool.

ཡོག་ལ།། ཡོག་ཡོག་ལ།། ཡོག།ཡོག་ལ།། ཡོག་ཡོག།ཡོག་ལ།། ཡོག་འེ།
ཡོག་ལ།། ཡོག་ནེ།ཡོག་ལ།། ཡོག་ནེ་སི་འང་།ཡོག་ལ།། དབྱར་ཀ་དབྱར་ཀ་ཁོ་
ལུག་རྩོ་འ་ལ་ཆ་འ་ནག། དགུན་ཀ་དགུན་ཀ་བལ་"བཀལ་ལ་ལ་སྡད་ཏ་ནག།།

d. rtsig-pa la ši-'u ma-čar. = Wall-to-paper-not-stick. Don't stick paper on the wall. *kho-čuŋ-ŋun-ne-si-phal-la 'i-ya-las-kha bčo-'a yod.* = He-small- from (*ne-si*) –from (*phal-la*) -this very same-work-doing-is. He has been doing this work since his childhood.

རྩིག་པ་ལ་ཤི་ཨུ་མ་བཙར།། ཁོ་ཙུང་ངུན་ནེ་སི་ཕལ་ལ་འི་ཡ་ལས་ཁ་བཙོ་འ་ཡོད།།

6
Pronoun

6.1. Personal Pronouns: The three personal pronouns of the first, second and third persons are given as under:

Singular			**Plural**		
ŋa	=	I	ŋa-ža	=	we,
khyod	=	thou	*khyo-ža*	=	you
kho	=	he	kho-ba	=	they.

In pronoun there is no distinction of gender. We observe that all the personal pronouns have their plural forms. These plural forms again take the plural signs. *ŋa-ža gya-ma. a-‘o gya-ma. khyo-ža gya-ma. kho-ba gya-ma.*

ང་ཞ་གྱ་མ། ཨཱ་འོ་གྱ་མ། ཁྱོ་ཞ་གྱ་མ་། ཁོ་བ་གྱ་མ།།

6.2. In the first person there is another form *a ‘a- ‘o* which means we. The two pronouns *ŋa-ža* and *a ‘a- ‘o* both mean ‘we’. The first term *ŋa-ža* stands for the first person plural. The second term *a ‘a- ‘o* includes the first and the second person both.

‘i žiŋ-ka ‘a-‘o-‘e nag. = This-field-we-of-is. This is our (I and thou) field. *‘a-‘o-‘e žiŋ-ka ‘i saŋ čhed-mo yod, ‘a-le.* = We-of-field-this-from-big-is, is'nt it. Our (I and thou) field is larger than this, isn't it? *di-riŋ ‘a-‘o-‘e goŋ-sal-la thug-pa žig bkol-‘en.* = Today-we-of-dinner-for-thug pa-a-boil-will. Today we will boil (prepare) *thug-pa* (gruel) for dinner.

ཞིང་ཀ་ཨཱ་འོ་འེ་ནག།། ཨཱ་འོ་འེ་ཞིང་ཀ་འི་སང་ཆེད་མོ་ཡོད།ཨ་ལེ།། དེ་རིང་
ཨཱ་འོ་འེ་གོང་སལ་ལ་ཐུག་པ་ཞིག་བཀོལ་འེན།།

6.2.1. This term *a’a-‘o* is sometimes used only for the second person. Then it becomes a polite way of expression. It is done with the intention to give respect to the second person. Thus if it is desired to say, ‘you don't have this book,’ instead of saying *khyod-la ‘i dpe-ča med’* [you-to-this-book-not is] we say *a’a-‘o la ‘i dpe-ča med* [we-to-this-book-not-is].

ཁྱོད་ལ་འི་དཔེ་ཙ་མེད།། ཨཱ་འོ་ལ་འི་དཔེ་ཙ་མེད།།

Some other forms of use of the term *a'a-'o* are: *a'a-'o gñis-kod* = We-two-both. We two. *a'a-'o-raŋ.* = We ourselves. *a'a-'o raŋ-gya-ma* = We all ourselves. *a'a-'o raŋ-ka.* = We ourselves. In these expressions 'we' means 'I and thou' or 'we and you'.

ཨཱ་འོ་གཉིས་ཀོད།། ཨཱ་འོ་རང་།། ཨཱ་འོ་རང་གྱ་མ།། ཨཱ་འོ་རང་ཀ།།

6.3. In the second and third persons there are two more terms in honorific form. These are *ño-raŋ* =Thou; *ño-ža* = You, plural; and *khoŋ* = He; and *khoŋ gya-ma* = They. *der-gyag-la ŋa-ža gya-ma 'khor yoŋ-'en.* = That time-by-we-pl.sign.-round -come-will. Meanwhile we will come taking a round.

ང་། ཁྱོད། ཁོ། ང་ཞ། ཁྱོ་ཞ། ཁོ་བ། ང་ཞ་གྱ་མ། ཉོ་རང་། ཉོ་ཞ། ཁོང་། ཁོང་གྱ་མ།། དེར་གྱག་ལ་ང་ཞ་གྱ་མ་འཁོར་ཡོང་འེན།།

6.4. Declesion of pronominals.

6.4.1. *ŋa* = I

1. Nominative	ŋa	ŋa-ža
2. Accusative	ŋa la	ŋa-ža-la
3. Agentive	ŋe, ŋe-si	ŋa-že, ŋa-že-si
4. Dative	ŋa-la, ŋe-phyil-la	ŋa-ža-la, ŋa-že phyil-la
5. Ablative	ŋe-kha-ne	ŋa-že-kha-ne-si
6. Genitive	ŋe	ŋa-že
7. Locative	ŋa-la	ŋa-ža-la

6.4.2. khyod = you

1. Nominative	khyod	khyo-ža
2. Accusative	khyod-la	khyo-ža-la
3. Agentive	khyo-'e, khyo-'e-si	khyo-že, khyo-že-si
4. Dative	khyod-la, khyo-'e phyil-la	khyo-ža-la
5. Ablative	khyo-'e-kha-ne	khyo-že-kha-ne
6. Genitive	khyo-'e	khyo-že
7. Locative	khyod-la	khyo-ža-la

'a-'o raŋ laŋ-čhen. = We ourselves-stand-go-will. Let us go. *kho-raŋ ki a-ba daŋ khyad mi-nug.* = He himself-of-father-and-difference-not-is. He is very similar to his father. *ŋa-raŋ ke ča-lag ŋa-raŋ-ke khur-ren.* = I myself-of-article-I myself-by-carry-will. I will carry my articles myself. *rgyal-sa ru sleb-de si-rig raŋ-ka so-so-'e khaŋ-pa la bud-soŋ.* = Kullu-at-reach-having-all-own-separate-of-home-to-went-was. After reaching Kullu town everyone went to his home. *kho ma-yoŋ-na 'a-'o-'e čig-gaŋ 'aŋ bčos 'khyud-ta ma-nag.* = He-not-come-if-we-by-some-which-also-do-able-to-not-is. If he does not come, we will be able to do nothing.

ཨཱ་འོ་རང་ལང་ཆེན།། ཁོ་རང་གི་ཨ་བ་དང་ཁྱད་མི་ནུག།། ང་རང་གི་ཅ་ལག་ང་རང་གི་ཁུར་རེན།། རྒྱལ་ས་རུ་སླེབ་དེ་སི་རིག་རང་ཀ་སོ་སོ་འེ་ཁང་པ་ལ་བུད་སོང་།། ཁོ་མ་ཡོང་ན་ཨཱ་འོ་འེ་ཅིག་གང་འང་བཅོས་འཁྱུད་ཏ་མ་ནག།

6.5. Demonstrative pronouns

These are: *'i.* = This. *'i gya-ma.* = These. *'i-de.* = This one. *'i-de gya-ma.*= These. *de.* = That. *de-de.* = That one. *de gya-ma.* = Those. *de-de gya-ma.* = Those. *ha-'i.* = That. *ha-'i gya-ma.* = Those. *ha-'i-de.* = That one. *ha-'i de gya-ma.* = Those. *'o-de.* = That one. *'o-de-de.* = Exactly that one. *'i-za-na* = During this time. *'i-zam.* = This much. *ga-zam.* = How much.

འི། འི་གྱ་མ། འི་དེ། འི་དེ་གྱ་མ། དེ། དེ་དེ། དེ་གྱ་མ། དེ་དེ་གྱ་མ། ཧ་འི། ཧ་འི་གྱ་མ། ཧ་འི་དེ། ཧ་འི་དེ་གྱ་མ། འོ་དེ། འོ་དེ་དེ། འི་ཟ་ན། འི་ཟམ། ག་ཟམ།

Sentences: *ŋa 'i-ru yod.* = I-here-at-am. I am here (at this place). *ŋa 'i 'a ru yod.* = I-this-itself-at-am. I am here itself. *ŋa 'i-'un la yod.* = I-this-pl. sign-at –am. I am here at these places. (I am here around). *ŋa 'i-'a 'un la yod.* = I-here-itself-pl. sign-at-am. I am around here. *'o-de-de-ka ŋa-la dgos-še rag-pen.* = That-the-very-I-to-wanting-having-was. I wanted the very same. *de-ta su-'i si 'aŋ bčo-'e khyud-ta nag.* = That-particularly-who-by-by-also-do-able-is. Anybody can do that. *'i-zug bčo-'e khyoŋ -'en bsam-de ŋe bsam-me ma-bsam.* = This-like- will do-bring-will-think-haing-by me-thought-not-thought. I did not think that he would do like this. *ha-'i men-tog tsiŋ-tsiŋ-de tsug bde-mo 'dug.* = That-flower-small-that-how-beautiful-is. How beautiful is that tiny flower?

ང་འི་རུ་ཡོད།། ང་འི་འ་རུ་ཡོད།། ང་འི་ཨུན་ལ་ཡོད།། ང་འི་འ་ཨུན་ལ་ཡོད།།

ནོ་དེ་དེ་ཀ།ང་ལ་དགོས་ཞེ།རག་པེན།། དེ་ཏ།སུ་འི་སི་འང་།བཙོས་འབྲུད་ཏ་ནག།།
འི་ཟུག་བཙོ་འི་ཁྲོང་འཛིན།བསམ་དེ།ངེ་བསམ་མེ་མ་བསམ།། ཏ་འི།མེན་
ཏོག་ཅེང་ཅེང་དེ། ཚུག་བདེ་མོ་འདུག།།

6.6. Articles

There are two kinds of articles: i. Definite and ii. Indefinite.

6.6.1. Definite Article: There is one definite article *de* equivalent to the English *the*. *de* also means that, a pronoun, and sometimes the two terms come in use together. Thus:

de de = That (pr.) –de (article). That one. *de mi de* = That (pr.) man-the. That very man. *de khaŋ-pa de su'e nag.* = That (pr.)-house-the (article)-whose-is. Whose house is that?

དེ་དེ།། དེ་མི་དེ།། དེ་ཁང་པ་དེ་སུ་འེ་ནག།།

6.6.2. Indefinite Articles: There are three indefinite articles: *čig, žig, šig*, which are equivalent to English a and an. According to the grammatical rules *čig* comes after the words ending in *ga, da, ba; žig* comes after the words ending in *ŋa, na, ma, 'a, ra, la;* and *šig* comes after the words ending with *sa.* In colloquy these rules are found not being followed completely.

6.6.2.1. ***čig:*** There are found few examples of use of this article as compared to the other two. *lem-čig* = Just now. *yaŋ-čig* = the other one. *srib (Şib)-čig.* = A moment. *kho-'e lag-ne lem-čig-la bčos btaŋ-soŋ.* = His-hand-with-just now-by-do-give-went. He did within just a moment. *yaŋ-čig-de kho-'e a-čo nag.* = Other-one-the-his-eldest brother-is. The other one is his eldest brother. *rdsa-ma srib* (şib) *čig-čig la khaŋ yoŋ soŋ.* = The pitcher was filled within a moment. *kha-čig yoŋ-ŋo la šor kha-čig phoŋ-ŋo la šor, mi-'un-la šor-sa ma-thob-de ̣tan mthoŋ 'dug-pen.* = Some people were running to this side and some to that side, there being no place to run, the people were facing great difficulty. Here the terms *lem-čig* and *yaŋ-čig* do not follow the rule.

ལེམ་ཅིག།། ཡང་ཅིག།། སྲིབ་ཅིག།། ཁོ་འེ་ལག་ནེ་ལེམ་ཅིག་ལ་བཅོས་བཏང་
སོང་།། ཡང་ཅིག་དེ་ཁོ་འེ་ཨ་ཅོ་ནག།།རྫ་མ་སྲིབ་ཅིག་ཅིག་ལ་ཁང་ཡོང་སོང་།། ཁ་ཅིག་

ཡོང་ངོ་ལ་ཤོར།ཁ་ཅིག་ཡོང་ངོ་ལ་ཤོར།མི་ཙུན་ལ་ཤོར་ས་མ་ཐོབ་དེ།ཏན་མཐོང་འདུག་པེན།།

6.6.2.2. ***žig:*** *ga-čen-žig.* = In good quantity; after sometime. *mi-žig.* = Some person. *tsad-ki-žig.* = A little. *maŋ-ñuŋ-žig.* = Some more or less. *šiŋ ga-čen-žig khur-šog.* = Bring fire-wood in good quantity. *ga-čen-žig la kho-'aŋ sleb khyoŋ-soŋ.* = After sometime hc also arrived.

ག་ཅེན་ཞིག། མི་ཞིག། ཚད་ཀི་ཞིག། མང་ཉུང་ཞིག། ཤིང་ག་ཅེན་ཞིག་ཁུར་ཤོག།། ག་ཅེན་ཞིག་ལ་ཁོ་འང་སླེབ་ཁྱོང་སོང་།།

This article ***žig,*** is found, used with all kinds of words ending with any kind of vowel and consonant.

6.6.2.3. ***šig:*** Examples of use of the term are: *da-lo šig.* = During these years. *na-niŋ šig.* = During the previous years. *naŋ-par-šig.* = During the coming years. *mdaŋ-šig.* = During the yesterdays. *tho-re-šig.* = During the days to come. *naŋ-mo-šig.* = During the days to come. *di-žag-šig.* = During the previous days. *nam-šig.* = During sometime. *ga-šig-čig.* = Somewhere. *a-tsig-šig.* = Some moment.

ད་ལོ་ཤིག། ན་ནིང་ཤིག། ནང་པར་ཤིག། མདང་ཤིག། ཐོ་རེ་ཤིག། ནང་མོ་ཤིག། དི་ཞག་ཤིག། ནམ་ཤིག། ག་ཤིག་ཅིག། ཨ་ཙིག་ཤིག།

mdaŋ-šig kho yoŋ-ŋa yod-ten.= He used to come during the previous days. *nam-šig, žig-na kho yoŋ-ŋa rag-pen.* = He was coming sometime back. Here the articles ***žig*** and *šig* are used together.

མདང་ཤིག། ཁོ་ཡོང་ང་།ཡོད་ཏེན།། ནམ་ཤིག།ཞིག་ན།ཁོ།ཡོང་ང་།རག་པེན།།

7

Adjectives

7.1. Adjectives follow the nouns they qualify, viz. *mi riŋ-mo.* = Man long, Long man. *ran-thag mgyogs-pha.* = Fast watermill. *lam-ka thag-riŋ.* = Distant path. *žiŋ-ka čhed-mo.* = Big field. *nor mod-po.* = Abundant wealth. *khaŋ-pa bde-mo.* = Beautiful house. *ba-glaŋ rgyag-pha.* = Healthy cattle. *rkun-ma sog-po.* = Bad thief. *rta dkar-pho.* = White horse.

མི།རིང་མོ།། རན་ཐག།མགྱོགས་ཕ།། ལམ་ཀ།ཐག་རིང་།། ཞིང་ཀ།ཆེད་མོ།། ནོར།མོད་པོ།། ཁང་པ།བདེ་མོ།། བ་གླང་།རྒྱག་ཕ།། རྐུན་མ།སོག་པོ།། རྟ།དཀར་ཕོ།།

Sentences: *mi re-re daŋ ḋngul re-re yoŋ-če rag.* = Man-one-one-and-rupee-one-one-coming-is. In the share of each person will come one rupee. *'i men-tog dmar-pho daŋ bde-mo 'dug.* = This-flower-red-and-beautiful-is. This flower is red and beautiful. *men-tog čhed-mo 'aŋ 'dug dmar-pho 'aŋ 'dug.* = Flower-big-also-is-red-also-is. The flower is big as well as red. *men-tog tshaŋ-ma dkar-pho 'dug.* = Flower-all-white-is. All the flowers are white. *ko-re čhag-po naŋ la thug-pa rlan-te ma-blug.* = Cup-broken-in-to-thug-pa-thin-not-pour. Don't pour thin *thug-pa* (gruel) in the broken cup. *naŋ dog-mo la mi maŋ-po 'dsom yoŋ-soŋ.* = Room-narrow-to-man-many-gather-come-went. The room was narrow/small but the people gathered in large number.

མི།རེ་རེ།དང་།དངུལ།རེ་རེ་ཡོང་ཅེ་རག།། འི་མེན་ཏོག།དམར་ཕོ།དང་།བདེ་མོ།འདུག།། མེན་ཏོག་ཆེད་མོ་འང་འདུག་དམར་ཕོ་འང་འདུག།། མེན་ཏོག་ཚང་མ་དཀར་ཕོ་འདུག།། ཀོ་རེ་ཆག་པོ་ནང་ལ་ཐུག་པ་རླན་ཏེ་མ་བླུག།།ནང་དོག་མོ་ལ་མི་མང་པོ་འཛོམ་ཡོང་སོང་།།

7.2. When a term is accompanied by an adjective other extensions like the signs of plural take their place after the adjective.

Sentences: i. *men-tog ser-pho gya-ma.* = Flowers-yellow- pl. sign. The yellow flowers. Here the plural sign *gya-ma* for *men-tog* (flower) has been placed after the adjective *gser-pho*. *men-tog ser-pho daŋ dmar-pho gun.*= Flowers-yellow-and-red-pl. sign. The yellow and red flowers. *mi phyug-po gya-me žiŋ-ka.* = Man-rich-pl.sign-of-field. Fields of the rich people. *men-tog ser-pho kun bde-mo 'dug.* = Flowers-yellow-pl. sign-beautiful-is. Yellow flowers are beautiful. *lug rid-pa gya-ma ri-'a-la khyer-soŋ.* = The weak sheep have been taken to the pasture land for grazing.

མེན་ཏོག་སེར་ཕོ་གྱ་མ།། མེན་ཏོག་སེར་ཕོ་དང་དམར་ཕོ་གུན།། མི་ཕྱུག་པོ་གྱ་མེ་ཞིང་ཀ།། མེན་ཏོག་སེར་ཕོ་ཀུན་བདེ་མོ་འདུག།། ལུག་རིད་པ་གྱ་མ་རི་འ་ལ་ཁྱེར་སོང་།།

ii. In such cases the case sign is attached after the plural sign. *khal-pha nag-pho-'e-si ri-'u-'un-la rduŋ 'dug.* = Sheep-black-by-by-goat lambs- to-hit-is. The black sheep hits the goat lambs. *gos-lag dkar-pho 'un-si tshos 'zum-mug.* = Clothe-white-pl. sign-by-colour-catch-is. The white clothes catch colour. *dpe-ča rñiŋ-pa 'un-la 'bu zhug 'dug.* = Book-old-pl. sign-to-worm-enter-is. Worms have attacked the old books.

ཁལ་ཕ་ནག་ཕོ་འེ་སི་རི་ཨུ་ཨུན་ལ་རྡུང་འདུག།། གོས་ལག་དཀར་ཕོ་ཨུན་སི་ཚོས་འཛུམ་ སུག།། དཔེ་ཅ་རྙིང་པ་ཨུན་ལ་འབུ་ཞུག་འདུག།།

7.3. In the following sentences adjectives are repeated. Repetition of the adjectival term makes it emphatic. *če-'a skam-po skam-po gya-ma naŋ-la bčug bor.* = Put the dry cow-dungs in. *lam-ke dkan dkan ne grul, gzur la ma 'grul.* = Walk on the upper side of the road and not on the edge.

Here it functions in superlative degree. *men-tog dmar-pho dmar-pho de su la btaŋ-laŋ yin.* = To whom is to be given this reddest flower? *thug-pa tshan-te tshan-te 'thuŋ-de kha-so la čhul-gyaŋ 'thon de rag.* = Having taken very hot *thug-pa,* I have blister in my mouth. *las-kha khag-čan khag-čan gun ŋe bčo-'e bten .*= I will do the urgent works. *khu-ru yaŋ-mo yaŋ-mo de ŋa khur-de yod.* = I am carrying the lightest load.

ཅེ་འ་སྐམ་པོ་སྐམ་པོ་གྱ་མ་ནང་ལ་བཅུག་བོར།། ལམ་ཀེ་དཀན་དཀན་ནེ་གྲུལ། གཟུར་ནེ་ མ་གྲུལ།། མེན་ཏོག་དམར་ཕོ་དམར་ཕོ་དེ་སུ་ལ་བཏང་ལང་ཡིན།།

ཐུག་པ་ཚན་ཏེ་ཚན་ཏེ་འཐུང་དེ་ཁ་སོ་ལ་ཆུལ་གྱུང་འཐོན་དེ་རག། ལས་ཁ་ཁག་ཅན་ཁག་ཅན་གུན་ངེ་བཙོ་འེ་བཏེན།། ཁྲུ་རྟུ་ཡང་མོ་ཡང་མོ་དེ་ང་ཁྲུར་དེ་ཡོད།།

7.4. Comparative

7.4.1. Comparison between two objects or positions can be shown by placing the particle '*saŋ*' between them.

Examples: *don-grub saŋ bsod-nams la rtsva mod-po 'dug.* = Dondub-from-Sonam-to-hay-much-is. Sonam owns more grass than Dondub. *mdaŋ saŋ di-riŋ ñi-ma drod-mo rag.* = Yesterday-from-today-sun-warm-is. Today it is warmer than it was yesterday. *'i saŋ rgyal-la či dgos.* = This-from-good-what-need. What do you need better than this? *men-tog dkar-pho de saŋ dmar-pho-de bde-mo 'dug.* = Flower-white-the-from-red-beautiful-is. The red flower is more beautiful than the white one.

དོན་གྲུབ་སང་བསོད་ནམས་ལ་རྩྭ་མོད་པོ་འདུག། མདང་སང་དེ་རིང་ཉི་མ་དྲོད་མོ་རག། འི་སང་རྒྱལ་ལ་ཅི་དགོས།།མེན་ཏོག་དཀར་ཕོ་དེ་སང་དམར་ཕོ་དེ་མང་པོ་བདེ་མོ་འདུག།

7.4.2. **Superlative:** Superlative position can be formed by adding the particle *šog* to the adjectival word. Thus: *če-šog.* = The eldest or the greatest. *čhuŋ- šog.* = The smallest/youngest. *ŋe.tu-'u čhe-šog de khaŋ-pa ru sdad-ta yod; bar-pha de bla-ma bčo-'a yod; čhuŋ-šog de rta mñam-po 'grul-la nag.* = My-son-eldest-the-home-at-sits-is, middle-the-lama-does-is, youngest-horse-with-walks-is. My eldest son lives at home; the middle one is lama and the youngest one travels with the ponies.

ཆེ་ཤོག།ཆུང་ཤོག། ངེ་ཏུ་འུ་ཆེ་ཤོག་དེ་ཁང་པ་རུ་སྡད་ཏ་ཡོད།། བར་ཕ་དེ་བླ་མ་བཙོ་འ་ཡོད།། ཆུང་ཤོག་དེ་རྟ་མཉམ་པོ་འགྲུལ་ལ་ནག།

7.4.3. This objective of comparison in degree can also be achieved by using the term '*saŋ*', combined with other adjectival terms like: *thams-čad, tshaŋ-ma* and *si-rig*, all of which mean 'all'. Thus: *thams-čad saŋ sog-po.* = Worst of all. *tshaŋ-ma saŋ riŋ-mo.* = The longest of all. *si-rig saŋ rgyal-la.* = The best of all. *'i lu-'u se-'o de ŋe thams-čad saŋ bče-pa yin.* = I love best this ash coloured lamb.

ཐམས་ཅད་སང་སོག་པོ།། ཚང་མ་སང་རིང་མོ།། སི་རིག་སང་ཀྱལ་ལ།། འི་ལུ་ཞུ་སེ་འོ་དེ་ཊེ་ཐམས་ཅད་སང་བཅེ་པ་ཡིན།།

7.4.4. There are some other ways of showing this feature of comparison.

The adjectival word is repeated and the particle *'ka'* is placed between them. *ñuŋ-ŋun ka ñuŋ-ŋun tsam čhen.* = The least, how much will be required? *maŋ-po ka maŋ-po da-ruŋ khu-ru gñis yoŋ-ŋen.* = At the most there will be two loads more.

ཉུང་ངུན་ཀ་ཉུང་ངུན་ཙམ་ཆེན།། མང་པོ་ཀ་མང་པོ་ད་རུང་ཁུ་རུ་གཉིས་ཡོང་ངེན།།

This word '*saŋ'* also gives the meaning of 'instead': *kho la zer-ra saŋ khyo-raŋ ke bčos btoŋ.* = He-to-say-from-you-yourself-by-do-give. Instead of asking him, do it yourself.

ཁོ་ལ་ཟེར་ར་སང་།ཁྱོ་རང་ཀེ་བཙོས་བཏོང་།།

We can get the notion of superlative degree by repeating the adjective. *h-yi khaŋ-pa bde-mo bde-mo de su-yi nag.* = The house which is the most beautiful, whose is it?

ཧ་ཡི་ཁང་པ་བདེ་མོ་བདེ་མོ་དེ་སུ་ཡི་ནག།།

7.5. Numerals: The Numerals in cardinal and ordinal orders are shown below.

7.5.1. Cardinal Numbers

7.5.1.1. Numbers from one to ten are pronounced as it is done in the literary language. gčig, gñis, gsum, bži, lŋa, drug, bdun, brgyad, dgu, bču. 1, 2, 3, 4, 5, 6, 7, 8, 9, 10.

གཅིག། གཉིས། གསུམ། བཞི། ལྔ། དྲུག། བདུན། བརྒྱད། དགུ། བཅུ།

7.5.1.2. Pronunciation of the numbers from eleven onwards upto ninety-nine get changed greatly. Below these numbers are given from eleven to twenty. They have been written as they are pronounced. *čug-šig, čuŋ-ñi, čug-sum, čub-ži, čo-ŋa, ču-rug, čub-dun, čob-gyad, čur-gu, ñi-šu.* 11, 12, 13, 14, 15, 16, 17, 18, 19, 20.

ཙུག་ཤིག། ཙུང་ཉི། ཙུག་སུམ། ཙུབ་ཞི། ཙོ་ང་། ཙུ་རུག། ཙུབ་དུན། ཙོབ་གྱད། ཙུར་གུ། ཉི་ཤུ།

7.5.1.3. While counting the numbers from twenty-one to ninety-nine, the first number of the decade like *ñi-šu sag-šig* (twenty-one), *sum-ču sog-šig* (thirty-one), *gub-ču-gog-šig*, (ninety-one), etc. are pronounced fully. Thereafter the adjective showing the decade like *ñi-šu* (twenty), *sum-ču* (thirty), *gub-ču* (ninety), etc. are dropped and the remaining part is pronounced like *sag-ñi* 22, *sog-ñi* 32, *gor-gu* 99, etc. till the ninth figure like *sar-gu* - 29, *sor-gu* - 39, etc. and then the next decadal number is pronounced fully like *sum-ču* (30), *žib-ču* (40), *brgya* (100), etc.

ñi-šu-sag-šig, sag-ñi, sag-sum, sab-zhi, se-ŋa, sa-rug, sab-dun, sab-gyad, sar-gu, sum-ču. 21, 22, 23, 24, 25, 26, 27, 28, 29, 30.

ཉི་ཤུ་སག་ཤིག། སག་ཉི། སག་སུམ། སབ་ཞི། སེ་ང་། ས་རུག། སབ་དུན། སབ་གྱད། སར་གུ། སུམ་ཙུ།

sum-ču sog-šig, sog-ñis, sog-sum, sab-ži, so-ŋa, sa-rug, sab-dun, sab-gyad, sar-gu, žib-ču. 31, 32, 33, 34, 35, 36, 37, 38, 39, 40.

སུམ་ཙུ་སོག་ཤིག། སོག་ཉི། སོག་སུམ། སབ་ཞི། སོ་ང་། ས་རུག། སབ་དུན། སབ་གྱད། སར་གུ། ཞིབ་ཙུ།

žib-ču žag-šig, žag-ñis, žag-sum, žab-ži, že-ŋa, ža-rug, žab-dun, žab-gyad, žar-gu, ŋab-ču. 41, 42, 43, 44, 45, 46, 47, 48, 49, 50,

ཞིབ་ཙུ་ཞག་ཤིག། ཞག་ཉི། ཞག་སུམ། ཞབ་ཞི། ཞེ་ང་། ཞ་རུག། ཞབ་དུན། ཞབ་གྱད། ཞར་གུ། ངབ་ཙུ།

ŋab-ču ŋag-šig, ŋag-ñi, ŋag-sum, ŋab-zhi, ŋe-ŋa, ŋa-rug, ŋab-dun, ŋab-gyad, ŋar-gu, drug-ču. 51, 52, 53, 54, 55, 56, 57, 58, 59, 60.

ངབ་ཙུ་ངག་ཤིག། ངག་ཉི། ངག་སུམ། ངབ་ཞི། ངེ་ང་། ང་རུག། ངབ་དུན། ངབ་གྱད། ངར་གུ། དྲུག་ཙུ།

drug-ču rag-šig, rag-ñis, rag-sum, rab-ži, re-ŋa, ra-rug, rab-dun, rab-gyad, rar-gu, dun-ču. 61, 62, 63, 64, 65, 66, 67, 68, 69, 70.

དྲུག་ཅུ་རག་ཤིག། རག་ཉི། རག་སུམ། རབ་ཞི། རེ་ང་། ར་དྲུག། རབ་དུན། རབ་རྒྱད། རར་དགུ། དུན་ཅུ།

dun-ču don-šig, don-ñi, don-sum, don- ži, don-ŋa, don-dug, don-dun, don-gyad, don-gu, gya-ču. 71, 72, 73, 74, 75, 76, 77, 78, 79, 80.

དུན་ཅུ་དོན་ཤིག། དོན་ཉི། དོན་སུམ། དོན་ཞི།དོན་ང་། དོན་དྲུག། དོན་དུན། དོན་རྒྱད། དོན་དགུ། རྒྱ་ཅུ།

gya-ču gyag-šig, gyag-ñis, gyag- sum, gyab-ži, gye-ŋa, gya-rug, gyab-dun, gyab-gyad, gyar-gu, gub-ču. 81, 82, 83, 84, 85, 86, 87, 88, 89, 90.

རྒྱ་ཅུ་རྒྱག་ཤིག། རྒྱག་ཉི། རྒྱག་སུམ། རྒྱབ་ཞི། རྒྱེ་ང་། རྒྱ་དྲུག། རྒྱབ་དུན། རྒྱབ་རྒྱད། རྒྱར་དགུ། གུབ་ཅུ།

gub-ču gog-šig, gog-ñis, gog-sum, gob-ži, go-ŋa, go-rug, gob-dun, gob-gyad, gor-gu, gya. 91, 92, 93, 94, 95, 96, 97, 98, 99, 100.

གུབ་ཅུ་གོག་ཤིག། གོག་ཉི། གོག་སུམ། གོབ་ཞི། གོ་ང་། གོ་དྲུག། གོབ་དུན། གོབ་རྒྱད། གོར་དགུ། རྒྱ།།

1,000; *stoŋ gčig* = One thousand; 10,000; *khri* = ten thousand. 1,00,000; *bum*= one lakh.

སྟོང་གཅིག་། ཁྲི། བུམ།

7.5.1.4. Some odd numbers: 101, gya-dang-gčig. 110, gya daŋ ču. 200, nyib-gya. 1637, stoŋ-čig daŋ drug-bgya gsum-bču sab-bdun.

བརྒྱ་དང་གཅིག།། བརྒྱ་དང་བཅུ།། སྟོང་གཅིག་དང་དྲུག་བརྒྱ་སུམ་ཅུ་སབ་བདུན།།

7.6.1. Fractions

i. *phyed* = half. *phyed daŋ gñis.* = One and half. *phyed daŋ gsum.*= Two and half. *dgod-če* = partitioning, dividing.

ཕྱེད།། ཕྱེད་དང་གཉིས།། ཕྱེད་དང་གསུམ།། དགོད་ཅེ།།.

ii. *gñis daŋ phyed.* = Two and half. *bži-daŋ-phyed.* = Four and half. *phyed-phyed.* = Half half. *phyed-ka gñis.* = Two halves. *phyed-te-phyed.* = Half of half.

གཉིས་དང་ཕྱེད།། བཞི་དང་ཕྱེད།། ཕྱེད་ཕྱེད།། ཕྱེད་ཀ་གཉིས།། ཕྱེད་དེ་ཕྱེད།།

Here the difference between the two expressions like *phyed-daŋ-gñis* and *gñis-daŋ-phyed* is notable.

7.6.2. Multiplicatives: Multiplicatives are formed by adding the particle *ldab* = number of times, with the number. Thus *gñis-ldab* (*gñil-dab*) = twice. *gsum-ldab* = three times. *bži-ldab* (*bžil-dab)* = four times, etc.

གཉིས་ལྡབ།། གསུམ་ལྡབ།། བཞི་ལྡབ།།

7.6.3. Aggregatives: Aggregatives are formed by adding the particle *bsag* = to add. *gñis-bsag,*= two layers. *gsum-bsag* = three layers. *gñis kha-la gsum bsag-na lŋa čha-'a nag.* = Two-over-to-three-add-if-five-goes-is. By adding three over two it becomes five. *khab re-re-la gŋul-re-re bčo-rug*. = Needle-one-one-to-rupee-one-one-do-is. One needle costs one rupee.

གཉིས་བསག།། གསུམ་བསག།། གཉིས་ཁ་ལ་གསུམ་བསག་ན་ལྔ་ཆ་འ་ནག།།
ཁབ་རེ་རེ་ལ་དངུལ་རེ་རེ་བཅོ་རུག།།

7.7. Ordinal Numbers: Ordinal numbers are counted as *daŋ-po* or *go-ma.* = The first. After that the suffix *pa* is added with every number like *gñis-pa*= Second. *gsum-pa* =T hird, etc.

དང་པོ། མགོ་མ། གཉིས་པ་། གསུམ་པ་།

7.8. Some conventions: Below are given somc old conventional practices connected with counting, weighing and measuring.

7.8.1. While starting measuring something one adds the word *soŋ* with each measur*e,* meaning 'gone' with every number like: g*čig soŋ.*= One gone or complete. *gñis soŋ* = Two gone, etc.

7.8.2. After the figures of tens, like ten, twenty, etc. sometimes the word *tham-pa* is added like *bču-tham-pa.* Ten (complete?). *ñi-šu tham-pa.*= Twenty, etc.

7.8.3. In one convention, when starting measuring grains in a *ḍe, (bre),* a measuring pot of the volume of about a half kilogram, one starts counting as *gaŋ* (one full), *do, gsum* i.e. one, two, three. g*aŋ* literally means full. *da ko-re gaŋ-re do-re da-ruŋ mthuŋ btoŋ ni.* = Now-cup-one-a-two-a-more-drink-give-ni (emphatic). Now have each of you at least one or two cups more.

གཅིག་སོང་། གཉིས་སོང་། ཐམ་པ་། འབྲི། གང་། དོ།གསུམ། བཅུ་ཐམ་པ་།
ཉི་ཤུ་ཐམ་པ་། ད་གོ་རེ་གང་རེ་དོ་རེ་ད་རུང་མཐུང་བཏོང་ནི།

Examples: *khag-ma gsum.* = Three places. *re-pa gñis-pa.*= One or two, very sparsely, very few. *rim-pa-la.* = Stepwise. *khyi-gčig mi-gčig mi-nug.* = There is not even a man and a dog, i.e. there is not a soul. *gčig rgyab ne gčig.* = One after another. *lan brgya laŋ-ŋa nag, lan brgya sdad-ta nag.* = He stands up and sits down hundred times; he stands up and sits down again and again. *'i ra-ma 'un lo lŋa-re (*or *lŋa-lŋa-re) soŋ-mkhan yin-če 'dug.* = These goats appear to be of around five years old each. *'i ra-ma de lo ŋa žig soŋ-mkhan yin-če 'dug.* = This goat appears to be of around five years of age. *sman žag-taŋ sŋa-tog phyi-tog thur-maŋ gaŋ-re zo.* = Take one spoonful of medicine everyday in the evening and morning.

ཁག་མ་གསུམ།། རེ་པ་གཉིས་པ།། རིམ་པ་ལ།། ཁྱི་གཅིག་མི་གཅིག་མི་ནུག།
གཅིག་རྒྱབ་ནེ་གཅིག། ལན་བརྒྱ་ལང་ང་ནག།ལན་བརྒྱ་སྡད་ད་ནག།། འི་ར་མ་
ཨུན་ལོ་ལྔ་རེ་སོང་མཁན་ཡིན་ཅེ་འདུག། འི་ར་མ་དེ་ལོ་ལྔ་ཞིག་སོང་མཁན་ཡིན་
ཅེ་འདུག།། སྨན་ཞག་ཏང་སྔ་ཏོག་ཕྱི་ཏོག་ཐུར་མང་གང་རེ་ཟོ།།

bdun-phrag.= A week. *bdun-tshig.* = A ritual performed at the end of seven weeks. *gchig čhag-de ñi-šu.*= One less twenty, nineteen. *gčig ma-tshaŋ-ŋa ñi-šu.* = One not completing twenty, nineteen.

བདུན་ཕྲག།།བདུན་ཚིག།། གཅིག་ཆག་དེ་ཉི་ཤུ།། གཅིག་མ་ཚང་ང་ཉི་ཤུ།།

rkyaŋ-bag = Single layer. *gñil-bag.* = Two fold. *gñil-thab* = Two times. *dpag-mtshad gñis* = two measures (the distance between one resting place with load or otherwise and the next). *lam-taŋ* = all along the way. *žag-taŋ* = Every day. *ñin-tshe-re* = whole day long. *lo-daŋ*= Every year. *čab-ča-re* = Always. *gom-pa-gaŋ*= One step. *sor-gčig* =Measure of one finger. *mthe-bo gčig* = Measure of one thumb. *tho gaŋ.* = One span. *khru* = One cubit. *rkaŋ-pa gaŋ* = Thickness (of snow) equal to that the foot can merge, about five centimeters. *pa-ra* = One handful, single palm. *ku-ru* = One handful, both palms held open and close together. *thu-'a gaŋ* = One lapful of a cloak. *paŋ-pa gaŋ* = One armful. *khal* = Twenty *de*. *kha-ri* = Twenty *khal*.

རྐྱང་བག། གཉེལ་བག། གཉེལ་ཐབ། དཔག་ཚད་གཉིས། ལམ་ཏང་། ཞག་ཏང་། ཉེན་ཆེ་རེ། ལོ་དང་། ཅབ་ཅ་རེ། གོམ་པ་གང་། སོར་གཅིག། མཐེ་བོ་གཅིག། ཐོ་གང་། ཁྲུ། རྐང་པ་གང་། པ་ར། ཀུ་རུ། ཐུ་འ་གང། པང་པ་གང་། ཁལ། ཁ་རི།

7.9. Suffixes: The following are two suffixes *ka* and *kod* which are joined with the words representing numbers.

i. ***ka.*** This letter *ka* with any numeral means 'only'. *gsum-ka.* = Only three. *lŋa-ka-lŋa.* or *lŋa-lŋa-ka.* = Only five each. *gsum-ka-gsum.* = Merely three.

ii. ***kod:*** This word *kod* joined with a word representing small numbers, means including or all. *gñis-kod tsog-se 'dug.* = Both are similar. *gsum-kod phyogs-šig-la čha rug-pen.* = All the three were going together.

གསུམ་ཀ། ལྔ་ལྔ་ཀ། གསུམ་ཀ་གསུམ། གཉིས་ཀོད་ཙོག་སེ་འདུག།. གསུམ་ཀོད་ཕྱོགས་ཤིག་ལ་ཆ་རུག་པེན།

7.10. There is a popular metaphorical saying which carries the use of the concept of comparision to five degrees. It says: *čhun-ma, čhun-ñis, čhun-sum, čhun-ñag.* The whole sentence means: the junior daughter-in-law, the second, the third, and the last or the junior most daughter-in-law. In a household the first daughter-in-law is dcsignated as *na-ma,* which also means bride. The second and all others of the same class and of the same generation are designated as *chhun-ma*, younger daughter-in-law, or daughters-in-law. Na-ma has a great prestige for she will assume the place of *gyug-mo,* mother-in-law, holding the position of *yondag-mo* (yon-bdag-mo), landlady. She holds the keys of the stores of the household. *na-ma,* a yondag-mo in waiting, is both a term of reference and address. The terms *gyug-mo* and *čhun -ma* are the terms of reference.

In a household, it is presumed that the daughters-in-law receive respect and all kinds of treatment according to their rank. Consequently the youngest or the junior most *čhun-ma* receives, particularly in some houses, the least respect or benefits, or she is treated in the worst way. She will have no interference in the kitchen and household matters. She mostly remains out of the house, in the fields, will have to work more. This would be the condition of the *čhun-nyag,* the junior most *na-ma*, as she is designated here. In practice this saying is a simile for any woman who is passing through a condition of bad treatment in a family.

ཆུན་མ་ཆུན་ཉེས།ཆུན་སུམ།ཆུན་ཉག།།

7.11. The game of Čho-lo: Čho-lo is a very popular indoor game current in all the areas along the high Himalayas as in sTod. Men play it mostly in the winter when outside the door the land all around is covered with thick white layer of snow. In the game two dice are used. One face of both the dice have drawn a cross which is called *pa-ra.* On the other five faces holes numbering from two to five are drawn on each face. The aggregate of numbers of the two opposite sides is always seven. Thus when two dice are thrown by a player the number of the holes and crosses may count any number from two to twelve. It is noteworthy that these numbers in this game are counted in a different manner than it is done in general. It is more important to say that this number is counted in the same way throughout Lahul. Their relationship with any culture cannot be known. It does not agree with Tibetan. The numbers are given as under:

pa-ra	=	two.	*su-gu*	=	three.	*tsig or pi-tse*	=	four.
kar	=	five.	*ṭu-gu*	=	six.	*rih*	=	seven.
šad	=	eight.	*gur*	=	nine.	*čhu*	=	ten.
thog	=	eleven.	*čāh*	=	twelve.			

pa-ra is a cross like x. Oridinarily it means cross representing one, but in the game of **čho**-lo there being two crosses, it also means two.

There is a small couplet about the game: *šar gyi šad bzaŋ-po, nub kyi gur bzaŋ-po.* = The eight of the east and the nine of the west are good.

པ་ར།། སུ་གུ།། ཙིག། ཡང་ན་པི་ཙེ།། ཀར།། ཊུ་གུ།། རྷི།། ཤད།། གུར།། ཆུ།། ཐོག།། ཙྷ།། ཤར་གྱི་ཤད་བཟང་པོ།། ནུབ་ཀྱི་གུར་བཟང་པོ།།

8

Verb : Auxiliaries

8.1. Auxiliaries: Verbs don't change with the change of tenses except in a few cases. This function of tenses in a sentence is performed by the auxiliaries and helping verbs. There are number of such terms. Thus before we take up the verbs and tenses we may get familiarized with these auxiliaries.

Auxiliaries may be classified into two categories: i. Auxiliaries used in the literary works and also in colloquy which are: *yod, yin* and *'dug*; and ii. Those belonging purely to the colloquy: *rag, nag, nug, kag, khag, čag, šag, še-ka, tro (to,) dro (ḍo)*, and *dog*. The method of use in the colloquy of both the types of the terms appears to be archaic. The auxiliaries of negation viz. *med, man,* etc. have been given in a coming chapter (Ch.10).

ཡོད། ཡིན། འདུག། རག། ནག། ནུག། ཀག། ཁག། ཅག།། ཤག། ཤེ་ཀ།

ཏྲོ། དྲོ། མེད། མན། དོག།

8.1.1. Auxiliaries of the first kind: The three principal and the commonly used auxiliaries *yod, yin* and *'dug* come at the end of sentences and all mean 'is' in the present tense, if they are not accompanied by any other helping verb. They are, however, not substitutes of one another.

i. ***yod:*** The term *yod* functions like is, are, has and have. But it is used mostly in the possessive sense, like has and have. It is used with all the three persons in the present tense but in different situations.

a. *ŋa yod.* = I am. But for the second and third persons here the term used is *'dug*. Thus *khyod 'dug.* = Thou art. *kho – 'dug.* = He is. Here if we say, *kho yod.* = He is, (the subject 'he' is not visible).

Now we use the term in possessive sense. *ŋa la dpe-ča yod.* = I have a book. Here 'dug is not used. For the second and third persons both the terms can be used but with different senses. *khyod la dpe-ča 'dug.* = You have a book. Here the book is in view of the speaker. *khyod la dpe-ča yod.* = You have a book. Here the speaker cannot see the book but he knows by knowledge. Similarly for the first and third person.

khyod/kho čha-'a yod. = It means that thou/he is in the habit of going. It does not convey the sense of 'thou/he is going.'

khyod-la pu-la yod-ta. = Do you have straw-shoes? In the following cases the subject is beyond the view of the speaker. *kho yod.* = He is present. ('I' am telling 'you' that, although not in our view, but it is in my knowledge, that presently 'he is there'.). It is used with other helping verbs *kag, tro, etc.*

b. Use with verbs: *ŋa čha-'a yod.*= I go/am going. *ŋa sil-la yod.* = I study/am reading *khyod/kho čha-'a yod.* = You/He goes. This suggests that the action takes place as a habit, and also in future tense.

c. With the helping verbs it is used in the past and future tenses also. *kho/khyod/ŋa yod ten.* (past). = He/you/I was (there). In the interrogative form it is used in the second and third persons. *khyod ga-ru čha-'a yod.* = Where are you going? *kho ga-ru čha rug.* = Where is he going?

Of the three helping verbs as shown above two also belong to the class of verb, viz. *yin-če. yod-če.*

ཁྱོད་ལ་པུ་ལ་ཡོད་ཏ།། ང་ཆ་འ་ཡོད།། ང་སིལ་ལ་ཡོད།། ཁོ་ཆ་འ་ཡོད།།

ཁྱོད་ག་རུ་ཆ་འ་ཡོད།། ཁོ་ག་རུ་ཆ་རུག།

8.1.2. ***yin*:** The term *yin* (also *'in*) is used in the present tense with all the three persons and it gives the sense of assertion. Thus *ŋa/khyod/ kho yin.* = It is me/thou/he. *khyod draŋ-po yin.* = You are true. It is found used with the verbs rarely. *ŋa čha-če yin.* = I have to go. *yin* is used with the helping verbs: *yin-khag, yin-nag, yin dro.* Here it functions like a verb.

ང་ཡིན།འིན།། ཁྱོད་ཡིན།། ཁོ་ཡིན།། ཁྱོད་དྲང་པོ་ཡིན།། ང་ཆ་ཅེ་ཡིན།།

8.1.3. ***'dug:*** The term *'dug* shows that an object is present and is in view of the speaker. *'i-ru khyi-žig 'dug.*= There is a dog here. *dpe-ča 'i-ru 'dug* = The book is here. *ŋe mig-śel khyod yod-sa ru 'dug-'a.* = My-spectacle-you-is-place-at-is-question. Is my spectacle near you? It is used with second and third persons and not with the first person. *khyod/kho 'dug.* = Thou/he is.

འི་རུ་བྲི་ཞིག་འདུག། དཔེ་ཅ་འདི་རུ་འདུག། ང་མིག་ཤེལ་བྲོད་ཡོད་ས་རུ་འདུག་ལ།།

8.2. Verbs function mostly by dropping their additive particle *če*. When the auxiliary *'dug* is used with the verbs in their full form no change occurs to it. But when it is used with the verbs after their having dropped the additive particle the auxiliary changes with the verbs in this form ending with the ten different *rjes-'jug* viz. *g, ŋ, d, n, b, m, 'a, r, l, s* in the following manner: *ldag-'dug* = Licks/Is licking. *'khoŋ-'dug* = shrinks. *'gred-tug* = Slips. *phan-nug* = Benefits. *bab-bug* = Comes down. *skam-mug* = Dries up. *lta-rug* = Looks. *'dar-rug* = Trembles. '*khol-lug* = Boils. *khyus-sug* = Melts.

The words ending with *rjes-'jug g* and *ŋ* take the auxiliary *'dug* in its primary form and no change occurs. *ldag-'dug*, *'khoŋ-'dug*. With the verbs ending without *rjes-'jug* like *lta, čha,* and those ending with any of the four vowels, and those ending with *r,* the auxiliary changes to *rug*: *lta-rug, 'dar-rug*. In the verbs ending with the rjes-'jug *l, b, m*, *n* and *s*, the rjes-'jug gets reduplicated and then the terminal *'ug,* part of *'dug,* is added with it. Thus: '*khol-lug; bab-bug*, *skam-mug*, *phan-nug*. While pronouncing they are heard only like *ba-bug*, *ska-mug*, *khyus-sug (khyui-sug),* etc. The verbs ending with *d* change in the manner: *'gred-'ug ~ 'gre-tug.*

ལྡག་འདུག། ཁོང་འདུག། འགྲེད་ཏུག། ཕན་ནུག། བབ་བུག། སྐམ་མུག།
ལྟ་རུག། འདར་རུག། འཁོལ་ལུག། ཁྱུས་སུག།

8.3. Auxiliaries of colloquy: These are: *rag, nag, nug, kag, khag, čag, šag, še-ka, dog, tro (to,)* and *dro (ḍo)***.**

རག། ནག། ནུག། ཀག། ཁག། ཅག། ཤག། ཤེ་ཀ། དོག། ཏྲོ།། དྲོ།།

The general arrangement of the various auxiliaries of the class, in relation to verbs, appear to be that the term *rag* relates to actions taking place close to but out of view of the speaker; *nag* to actions taking place in view; *kag* to the actions taking place out of view of the speaker; *khag* relates to the actions accomplished and *čag* to an action intended to be accomplished.

su-žig yoŋ-ŋa rag. = (I feel) Somebody is coming. *'i ŋe ko-re nag.* – This is my bowl (personal eating bowl). *kho gos-lag sdeb-ba yod-kag.* = (out of view) He is changing clothes. *kho di-žag sleb-khag.* = He reached day before yesterday. *kham-žig yoŋ na bčo-čag.* = If a desire arises, I will do.

སུ་ཞིག་ཡོང་ང་རག།། འི་ངེ་ཀོ་རེ་ནག།། ཁོ་གོས་ལག་སྡེབ་བ་ཡོད་ཀག།།
ཁོ་དི་ཞག་སླེབ་ཁག།། ཁམ་ཞིག་ཡོང་ན་བཅོ་ཅག།།

8.3.1. *rag*

i. The term *rag* is used for the intangible things, abstract facts, and ii. with the verbs for the actions taking place out of view but close to the speaker which come to his knowledge by feeling, sense, taste, smell, etc. i. *ŋa-la zug rag.* = I-to-pain-is. I am feeling pain. *ŋa-la ltog-ri rag.* = I-to-hunger-is. I am feeling hungry. *ŋa-la skyug-če yoŋ-če rag.* = I-to-vomiting-coming-is. I feel like vomiting. *'brug ldir-ra rag.* = Dragon (cloud)-thundering-is. The dragon is roaring. (= the cloud is thundering.). *me-la drod me-rag.* = There is no warmth in the fire.

ii. In the present tense with the third person it describes actions taking place out of view of the speaker: *kho čha-'a rag.* = He goes or is going. *kho-ba rtse-'a rag.*= They are dancing. *tru-'u ŋu-'a rag.* = The child is weeping. The actions are taking place behind the view.

ང་ལ་ཟུག་རག།། ང་ལ་ལྟོག་རི་རག།། ང་ལ་སྐྱུག་ཅེ་ཡོང་ཅེ་རག།། འབྲུག་ལྡིར་ར་
རག།། མེ་ལ་དྲོད་མེ་རག།། ཁོ་ཆ་འ་རག།། ཁོ་བ་རྩེ་འ་རག།། ཏྲུ་འུ་
ངུ་འ་རག།།

iii. It is used in the past with the helping verbs. *kho čha-'a rag-pen.* = He was going. Here the action is taken in the past but is out of view of the reporter.

ཁོ་ཆ་འ་རག་པེན།།

iv. The following examples explain the difference in the use of the three auxiliaries *yod, rag* and *'dug,* which all mean 'is': *ŋe čan-da la dŋul gñis yod/rag/'dug.* All the three sentences with three different auxiliaries mean the same as: There are two rupees in my pocket. But there is difference in the use of all these three.

1. (by knowledge) I possess two rupees.
2. (by feeling) I have two rupees.
3. (by seeing.) I have two rupees. In the first sentence the speaker says with knowledge that he has two rupees in his pocket. In the second instance it is known by feeling. In the third it is known by actually seeing the object.

ངེ་ཅན་ད་ལ་དངུལ་གཉིས་ཡོད།། རག།། འདུག།

8.3.1.1. Change in the Verbs: When the auxiliary *rag* is used with verbs, letter *'a* is added to the verbs ending with the vowels. With the verbs ending with the other nine consonants the end letter is reduplicated and the auxiliary *rag* remains unchanged. Similar is the case with other two auxiliaries of *nag* and *kag*. Ex.

čha-če = to go	*čha-'a rag*	*čha-'a nag*	*čha-'a kag*
sdad-če = to sit	*sdad-ta rag*	*sdad-ta nag*	*sdad-ta kag*
'grul-če = to walk	*'grul-la' rag*	*grul-la nag*	*'grul-la kag.*

rug: The regular auxiliary indicative of the present tense for the second and third persons is *rug*. Khyod/kho *čha-rug.* = Thou/ he is going.

8.3.2. *nag*

i. It means 'is'. It is used for the objects lying before and the actions taking place in view of the speaker. i. It identifies an object *'i či nag.* = What is this? '*i glaŋ-pho-čhe nag.* = This is an elephant. *tho-re tshe-śu nag.* = Tomorrow it is the festival of tshe-śu. *'i las-kha sog-po nag.* = This is a bad work.

འི་ཅི་ནག།། འི་གླང་པོ་ཆེ་ནག།། ཐོ་རེ་ཚེ་ཤུ་ནག།། འི་ལས་ཁ་སོག་པོ་ནག།།

ii. Here the term functions as an indicative of indefinite future. *ŋe bčo-'a nag.* = It will be done by me. Similarly, *'gag-ga nag.* = It gets choked/May get choked. *mthoŋ-ŋa-nag.* = May be visible. *'khrid-ta nag.* = May lead. *lčeb-ba nag* = May embrace. *'gom-ma-nag* = May cross over, step over a thing.

དེ་བཙོ་འ་ནག།། འགག་ག་ནག།། མཐོང་ང་ནག།། འཁྲིད་ཏ་ནག།། ལྡེབ་བ་" ནག།། འགོམ་མ་ནག།།

iii. The following sentences indicate a habit or process. *kho-tsher-ra nag.* = He gets worried/may get worried. *kho 'khyor-ra nag.* = He staggers. (It is his nature).

ཁོ་ཚེར་ར་ནག།། ཁོ་འཁྱོར་ར་ནག།།

Distinction in the use between *'dug* and *nag*. *'kho-'e gser tsoŋ 'dug.* = He is selling gold. *kho-'e gser tsoŋ-ŋa nag.* = He sells gold. The first sentence here indicates the present action. The second sentence indicates a habit or a process. This is his business to sell gold.

ཁོ་འེ་གསེར་ཙོང་འདུག།། ཁོ་འེ་གསེར་ཙོང་ང་ནག།།

iv. Similar examples of habitual actions or processes can be given as: *'kho žag-taŋ las-kha-la čha-'a nag.* = He goes to work daily. *gŋul gčig la ku-śu gu-ra gñis thob-ba nag.* = Two numbers (*gu-ra*= grain) of apple is available for a rupee. *kho-'e čig-gaŋ 'aŋ zer-ra ma-nag.* = He does not say anything. *'i khyi rmug-ga ma-nag.* = This dog does not bite.

ཁོ་ཞག་ཏང་ལས་ཁ་ལ་ཆ་འ་ནག།། དངུལ་གཅིག་ལ་ཀུ་ཤུ་གུ་ར་གཉིས་ ཐོབ་བ་ནག།། ཁོ་འེ་ཅིག་གང་འང་ཟེར་ར་མ་ནག།། འི་ཁྱི་རྨུག་ག་མ་ནག།།

8.3.3. *nug.* This appears to have close relation both in form and meaning with *nag* and *'dug.* It means 'is' but is found used only with the negative prefix '*mi*' (= not) and is used in the present tense. Thus: *kho 'i-ru mi-nug.* = He is not here. *kho čha-rug-ga čha-'a mi-nug.* = Is he going or not? *khyod de-ru mi-nug-pen.* = You were not there.

ཁོ་འི་རུ་མི་ནུག།། ཁོ་ཆ་རུག་གཀཆ་འ་མི་ནུག།། ཁྱོད་དེ་རུ་མི་ནུག་པེན།།

8.3.4. *kag*: It is found used only with the auxiliaries *yod* and *med.*

i. It is used for the objects lying beyond the view and the actions taking place out of view in the present tense. *dad-sang kho de-ru med-kag.* = Presently he is not there. (Subject out of view). *de ne si kho 'e khaŋ-pa ha-lam thag-riŋ yod-kag.* = From there his house is considerably distant.

དད་སང་ཁོ་དེ་རུ་མེད་ཀག། དེ་ནེ་སི་ཁོ་འེ་ཁང་པ་ཧ་ལམ་ཐག་རིང་ཡོད་ཀག།

ii. **Use with verbs:** The action is taking place out of view and at a distance. *kho tsher-ra kag.* = He is/may be worrying. *mdaŋ di-riŋ kho khaŋ-pa bčo-'a kag.* = These days he is constructing house.

ཁོ་ཚེར་ར་ཀག། མདང་དི་རིང་ཁོ་ཁང་པ་བཙོ་འ་ཀག།

The use of the term *yod* with *kag* becomes optional when the term *kag* is used with verbs because while pronouncing the sentence *yod* becomes contracted and silent. Kho yod kag. = He is (should be) there. *kho tho-re yoŋ-ŋa yod-kag/kag.* = He is coming tomorrow.

ཁོ་ཐོ་རེ་ཡོང་ང་ཡོད་ཀག།ཀག།

This may be explained further. *kho-la tshor-rug.* = It is being heard to him. *kho-la tshor-ra kag.* = It is heard by him. *kho-la tshor-ra yod-tro.* = It may be heard by him. Actions in the first two sentences are definite: the first takes place in view of the speaker and the second beyond. The third is probable.

ཁོ་ལ་ཚོར་རུག། ཁོ་ལ་ཚོར་ར་ཀག། ཁོ་ལ་ཚོར་ར་ཡོད་ཏྲོ།།

8.3.5. *khag:* This term denotes an action accomplished beyond the view of the speaker. Therefore it looks like in the past tense. It is used with all the three persons.

i. **Past tense:** *ŋa/khyod/kho soŋ khag.* = I/thou/he went. *kho mdaŋ yoŋ-khag.* = He came yesterday. *kho tham-phog gčig soŋ-de yoŋ-khag.* He-turn-one-go-having-come-having. = He having gone once, came back. *kho-'e ḍa-ba ni si-rig zin-khag.* = He spent all his money. *kho'e rñiŋ-pa khaŋ-pa tsoŋ-de so-ma ños khag.* = He having sold his old house, purchased a new one.

ང་།ཁྱོད།ཁོ་སོང་ཁག། ཁོ་མདང་ཡོང་ཁག། ཁོ་ཐམ་ཕོག།གཅིག་སོང་དེ་ཡོང་ཁག། ཁོ་འེ་ཊ་བ་ནི་སི་རིག་ཟིན་ཁག། ཁོ་འེ་ཁང་པ་རྙིང་པ་ཙོང་དེ་སོ་མ་ཉོས་ཁག།

ii. **Future tense:** The term is also used in indefinite future tense. *kho-'e bčo-na bčo-khag.* = If he wants to do, he may do. *a'a-'o laŋ čhen, kho rgyab-ne yoŋ-khag.* = We will go, he may come from behind.

a'a-'o sleb-sleb la kho 'khor-ren ko-ra btaŋ-ŋen sdad-khag. = Till we reach, he may stay rambling and circumambulating.

ཁོ་འི་བཙོ་ན་བཙོ་ཁག།། ཨཱ་འོ་ལང་ཆེན་ཁོ་རྒྱབ་ནེ་ཡོང་ན་ཡོང་ཁག། ཨཱ་འོ་སླེབ་
སླེབ་ལ་ཁོ་ཁོར་རེན་ཀོ་ར་བཏང་ངེན་སྡད་ཁག།།

The following sentences distinguish between the past and the future forms by the form of the verbs in the present and future. *soŋ-khag* = Has gone. *čha-khag* = May go. *bčos-khag* = He did. *bčo-khag.* = May do. The following expressions can be explained in both the tenses. *zer-khag* = Said/ May say. *dgar-khag.* = Imprisoned/May imprison. *'grul khag* = Walked/ May walk. For the proper past tense the sentences would be: *ŋa soŋ ben.* = I went. *khyod/kho bud soŋ.* = Thou/he went.

སོང་ཁག།། ཆ་ཁག།། བཅོས་ཁག།། བཅོ་ཁག།། ཟེར་ཁག།། འགར་ཁག།།
གྲུལ་ཁག།། ང་སོང་བེན།། ཁྱོད།ཁོ་བུད་སོང་།།

kho la ŋa yoŋ-če tshor khag./… tshor ra nag./ …tshor ra yod kag./ … tshor rug. = He heard me coming (past)./ hears me (he can)./is hearing (out of view)./ is hearing (in view).

ཁོ་ལ་ང་ཡོང་ཅེ་ཚོར་ཁག།། ཚོར་ར་ནག།། ཚོར་ར་ཡོད་ཀག།། ཚོར་རུག།།

8.3.6. *čag*:

i. It denotes an action intended to be accomplished. As it is to take place at a distance it appears like in future. It is used with all the three persons. *da lem čhom-čag.* = We will start moving just now. *čha dsa na ñuŋ-ti žug de čha čag.* = While going we will go through Kullu. *yoŋ dsa-na spi-ti skor de yoŋ čag.* = While coming we will come by taking round of Spiti. *khyo'e ma-bčo na ŋe bčo-čag.* = If you don't do, I will have to do. *ŋa yoŋ-čag. khyod čha čag.* = I will have to come. You will have to go.

ད་ལེམ་ཆོམ་ཅག། ཆ་ཛ་ན་ཉུང་ཏི་ཞུག་དེ་ཆ་ཅག།། ཡོང་ཛ་ན་སྤི་ཏི་
སྐོར་དེ་ཡོང་ཅག།། ཁྱོ་འེ་མ་བཅོ་ན་ངེ་བཅོ་ཅག།།

ii. **Past:** It is used in the past tense. *khur-de či bčo-kan. su-žig la btaŋ yoŋ-čag.* = What will you do by carrying it with you, you should have given it to somebody. *yoŋ dsa-na khyo-'e ñuŋ-ti ne ku-šu khyoŋ-*

čag. = While coming you should have brought apple from Kullu. Sentences in the regular future and past would be*: da lem čhom-en.* = We will start moving just now. *bor yoŋ-ben* = We left it there. *kho de-ʻa-ru bor yoŋ-čag.* = You should have left him there.

ཁུར་དེ་ཙེ་བཙོ་ཀན།སུ་ཞིག་ལ་བཏང་ཡོང་ཙག། ཡོང་ཇ་ན་ཁྲོ་འི་ཞུང་ཧེ་ནེ་ཀུ་སུ་ཁྲོང་ཙག། བོར་ཡོང་བེན།། ཁོ་དེ་འ་རུ་བོར་ཡོང་ཙག།

iii. Below are given examples of the use of some auxiliaries in the present tense which distinguish them from each other in their use. *ʻi ŋe dpe-ča yin.* = This is my book. *dpe-ča thug-mo ʻdug.* = The book is thick. *dpe-ča lčin-te rag.* = (I feel that) the book is heavy. *ʻi ŋe dpe-ča nag.* = This is my book. *dpe-če rin dŋul gsum nag.* = The price of the book is three rupees. *ʻi khro-pa dpe-ča ñis ŋa-la da-ruŋ yod.* = I have two more books like this.

འི་ངེ་དཔེ་ཙ་ཡིན།། དཔེ་ཙ་ཐུག་མོ་འདུག།། དཔེ་ཙ་ལྕིན་ཏེ་རག།།

འི་ངེ་དཔེ་ཙ་ནག།། དཔེ་ཙེ་རིན་དངུལ་གསུམ་ནག།། འི་ཁྲོ་པ་དཔེ་ཙ་ང་ལ་ད་རུང་གཉིས་ཡོད།།

The two sentences, as given above: *ʻi ŋe dpe-ča yin* and *ʻi ŋe dpe-ča nag,* both mean ʻThis is my book'. The first sentence shows ownership and the second one distinguishes book among other books or things.

iv. Some of the auxiliaries given above can be shown below distinguishing from each other. It is also observed that changes in the meanings of the sentences are brought about by the change of auxiliaries without changing the form of the verb. *kho-ʻe ŋa yoŋ-če mthoŋ soŋ.* = (I saw that) He saw me coming. *kho-la ŋa yoŋ-če mthoŋ dog.* = (I know that) He saw me coming. *kho-la ŋa yoŋ-če mthoŋ ʻdug.* = He is seeing me coming. *kho-la ŋa yoŋ-če mthoŋ khag.* = (I know that) He saw me coming. *kho-la ŋa yoŋ-če mthoŋ-ŋa yod-kag.* = (I know that) He is seeing me coming. *kho-la ŋa yoŋ-če mthoŋ-ŋa nag.* = He can/may see me coming,

ཁོ་འི་ང་ཡོང་ཙེ་མཐོང་སོང་།། ཁོ་ལ་ང་ཡོང་ཙེ་མཐོང་དོག།། ཁོ་ལ་ང་ཡོང་ཙེ་མཐོང་འདུག།། ཁོ་ལ་ང་ཡོང་ཙེ་མཐོང་ཁག།། ཁོ་ལ་ང་ཡོང་ཙེ་མཐོང་ང་ཡོད་ཀག།། ཁོ་ལ་ང་ཡོང་ཙེ་མཐོང་ང་ནག།།

8.3.7. ***čen:*** This auxiliary is used in describing the past scenes like the method used by the folk story-tellers and can be translated as 'there used to be'. *sŋon la 'i-ru khaŋ-pa žig yoŋ-čen. a-bi-žig-'aŋ yoŋ-čen. kho sruŋ bśad-če daŋ glu taŋ-če la min-'dra mkhas-pha yoŋ-čen.* = Earlier there used to be a house here. There also lived an old lady. She used to be very proficient in telling stories and singing songs.

Then it describes the nature of a thing. Ex.: *mdaŋ di-ring ñuŋ-ti ru ku-śu yoŋ-čen.* = These days apple is available in Kulu. *Kar-iŋ gdan-la mog-śa maŋ-po thob-čen.* = Mushroom is found in the slope of Karing in good quantity. *mo-ṭar med-de ŋa-zha 'grul-de čha-čen.* = Motor-not-having-we-walk-having-go-are. There being no motor, we used to go on foot. *'i-ru ni mtshan la 'phrul bčo-čen.* = In the night there appear ghosts here.

སྔོན་ལ་འི་རུ་ཁང་ཙུང་ཞིག་ཡོང་ཅེན།། ཨ་བི་ཞིག་འང་ཡོང་ཅེན།། ཁོ་སྲུང་བཤད་ཅེ་དང་གླུ་བཏང་ཅེ་ལ་མིན་འདྲ་མཁས་པ་ཡོང་ཅེན། མདང་དི་རིང་ཉུང་ཏི་རུ་ཀུ་ཤུ་ཡོང་ཅེན།། ཀ་རིང་གདན་ལ་མོག་ཤ་མང་པོ་ཐོབ་ཅེན།། མོ་ཊར་མེད་དེ་ང་ཞ་འགྲུལ་དེ་ཆ་ཅེན།། འི་རུ་ནི་མཚན་ལ་འཕྲུལ་བཅོ་ཅེན།།

8.3.8. ***šag:*** It is used after the verbs ending in *ra* and *sa* in place of *čag.* It means 'may'. *ŋe khyod-la či zer-šag/zer-čag.* What can I say to you? *khyod de-ru su-'e šes-šag.* = Who will recognize you there?

ངེ་ཁྱོད་ལ་ཅི་ཟེར་ཤག།ཅག།། ཁྱོད་དེ་རུ་སུ་འེ་ཤེས་ཤག།།

8.3.9. ***dog*:** This term is used in the sense of an action already completed, but in the near past. *kho soŋ dog.* = (I see that) He has gone. *las-kha bčos tshar-dog.* = (I see that) The work has been finished. *ŋa sleb-sleb la kho soŋ tshar dog.* = By the time I reached he had already gone.

ཁོ་སོང་དོག།། ལས་ཁ་བཅོས་ཚར་དོག།། ང་སླེབ་སླེབ་ལ་ཁོ་སོང་ཚར་དོག།།

8.3.10. ***še-ka*:** The term *še-ka* means 'may' and is probable, and is used in third person in future tense. *kho čha-še-ka.* = He may go. *kho yoŋ-še-ka.* = He may come. *kho-ba sdad-še-ka* =They may stay.

ཁོ་ཆ་ཤེ་ཀ།། ཁོ་ཡོང་ཤེ་ཀ།། ཁོ་བ་སྡད་ཤེ་ཀ།།

8.3.11. ***tro* (*to*) and *dro* (*ḍo*):** These two particles mean 'may'. The term *tro* is used with *yod* and *med* and *dro* with *yin* and *man*. *kho de-ru yod* *tro.* = He may be there. *kho yin dro.*= It may be him. *kho de-ru med-tro.* = He may not be there. *kho man dro.* = It might not have been him. *'i-zam-la ŋa la rgal-tshar-de yod tro.* = This- so much-to-I-pass-cross-finish-having-have-may. By this time I would have crossed the pass.

ཁོ་དེ་རུ་ཡོད་ཏྲོ།། ཁོ་ཡིན་དྲོ།། ཁོ་དེ་རུ་མེད་ཏྲོ།། ཁོ་མན་དྲོ།། འི་ཟམ་ལ་ང་ལ་
རྒལ་ཚར་དེ་ཡོད་ཏྲོ།།

8.3.12. ***śig:*** The term *śig* means 'should.' It functions with all kinds of verbs in the same form. *'khur- śig.* = 'Should have carried.'. *čha- śig.* = Should have gone. *yoŋ- śig* = Should have come. *las-kha med-na 'khrug-śad khur-de 'grul- śig.* = If he has no work, he should roam about carrying quarrel-making vessel. (An idle man creating quarrels wherever he goes.).

འཁུར་ཤིག།། ཆ་ཤིག།། ཡོང་ཤིག།། ལས་ཁ་མེད་ན་འཁྲུག་ཤད་ཁུར་དེ་འགྲུལ་
ཤིག།།

9

Verb : Tenses

In the language of sTodpa verb is a disyllabic word consisting of a monosyllabic meaningful verbal root and an additive particle *će*. However, the verbs ending in the 'jes'jug *ra* and *sa* possess additive *śe*. In its simple form a verb is verbal noun. For example *'grul-će* = walking or to walk, *sil-će* = reading. *'khur-će* = carrying. *sdad-će* = sitting. *tshor-śe, bor-śe, tshos-śe, śes-śe, khros-śe, stor-śe, zer-śe. khyo-'e min la chi zer-śen.* = What is your name? *ćaŋ śes-śe mi-nug.* = Cannot be known.

འགྲུལ་ཅེ། །སིལ་ཅེ།། འཁུར་ཅེ།། སྡད་ཅེ།། ཚོར་ཤེ། བོར་ཤེ། ཚོས་ཤེ། ཤེས་ཤེ། ཁྲོས་ཤེ། སྟོར་ཤེ། ཟེར་ཤེ། ཁྱོ་འེ་མིན་ལ་ཅི་ཟེར་ཤེན།། ཅང་ཤེས་ཤེ་མི་ནུག།

9.1. When a verb is used in the sentence no change takes place in the verb due to change in tenses, gender and number. Ex:

Feminine and Masculine: Singular

ŋa ćha-'a yod.	=	I go/ am going.
khyod ćha-rug.	=	Thou goest/is going.
kho ćha-rug	=	He goes/ is going.
bo-mo ćha-rug.	=	Girl or woman goes/is going.
bu-tsa ćha-rug.	=	Boy or man goes/is going.

Feminine and Masculine: Plural

ŋa-ža ćha'a yod.	=	We go/ are going.
khyo-ža ćha-rug	=	You go/are going.
kho-ba ćha-rug.	=	They go/are going
bo-mo –'un ćha-rug.	=	Girls or Women go/are going
bu-tsa-'un ćha-rug.	=	Boys or men go/are going.

Here *čha,* root of the verb *čha-če,* remains unchanged in all the cases even after changes having taken place in gender and number.

ང་ཆ་འ་ཡོད།། ཁྱོད་ཆ་རུག།། ཁོ་ཆ་རུག།། བོ་མོ་ཆ་རུག།། བུ་ཙ་ཆ་རུག།།

ང་ཞ་ཆ་འ་ཡོད།། ཁྱོ་ཞ་ཆ་རུག།། ཁོ་བ་ཆ་རུག།། བོ་མོ་ཙན་ཆ་རུག།། བུ་ཙ་ཙན་

ཆ་རུག།།

kho 'grul-soŋ. = He walked.
kho 'grul-lug. = He walks.
kho 'grul-la nag. = He will walk.

ཁོ་འགྲུལ་སོང་།། ཁོ་འགྲུལ་ལུག།། ཁོ་འགྲུལ་ལ་ནག།།

Tenses: Verbs don't change with the change of the tense. The function of change in the tenses is performed by the numerous auxiliaries. However, there are two verbs: *čha-če* = to go, and *bčo-če* = to do, which have other forms. The verb *čha-če* has past form *soŋ* and also another word for it in the past is in use. The other verb *bčo-če* has its past form and future. *bud soŋ. = (He) went. soŋ ben.* = (I) went. *bčos-ben.* = (I) did. *bčos-'en.* = (I) will do.

བུད་སོང་།། སོང་བེན།། བཙོས་བེན།། བཙོས་འེན།།

9.2. Verbs function in two manners: (i) without dropping the additive particle *če* and (ii) by dropping the particle. *čha-čen. Čhen. čha-če yin. čha-laŋ yin.* = (I)Will go.

ཆ་ཅེ་ན། ཆེན། ཆ་ཅེ་ཡིན། ཆ་ལང་ཡིན།

9.2.1.

i. A verb functions with the additive particle *če* in its primary form. But in this form it has limited functions. Example: *čhu 'khol-če 'dug.* = Water-boiling-is. Water is about to boil. *rdo-'a 'gril-če 'dug.* = Stone-falling-is. The stone is about to fall, (is in unstable position.). *kho tshe-riŋ yin-če 'dug.* = He-Tshering-is-may-is. He appears to be Tshering. *da-lo dgun-ka graŋ-mo maŋ-po yoŋ-če 'dug.* = This year-winter-cold-much-come-may-is. It appears that this year winter will be severer. *zam-pa čhu'i si khyer-če 'dug.* = Bridge-water-by-by-carry-may-is. The bridge is likely to be carried away by water, the river.

In the above examples the verb in its original form of verbal noun indicates an action likely to take place.

ii. Often two verbs function in combination in their primary form. *kho yoŋ-če khyud-če mi-nug.* = He-coming-able-not-is. He is not able to come. *kho-la čha-če btaŋ-če man.* = He-to going giving not. We will not allow him to go. The first verb verbal noun is subject and the second is part of the predicate.

ཆུ་འཁོལ་ཅེ་འདུག།། རྫོ་འ་འགྲིལ་ཅེ་འདུག།། ཁོ་ཚོ་རིང་ཡིན་ཅེ་འདུག།། ད་ལོ་དགུན་ཀ་གྲང་མོ་མང་པོ་ཡོང་ཅེ་འདུག།། ཟམ་པ་ཆུ་འི་སི་ཁྱེར་ཅེ་འདུག།། ཁོ་ཡོང་ཅེ་ཁྱུད་ཅེ་མི་ནུག།། ཁོ་ལ་ཆ་ཅེ་བཏང་ཅེ་མན།།

iii. Sometimes when two verbs function in combination the first verb drops its additive part but the other one remains unchanged. Ex. *btaŋ bor- če.* (*bor- če* = to leave) = To give away. *btaŋ btaŋ-če.* = To give away. Here the first verb functions as verb and is the principal verb and the second verb lays emphasis to the first.

iv. In the following sentences the first verb in both the forms, with and without additive particle, give the same meaning. '*grul-če khyud-če mi-nug* or '*grul khyud-če mi-nug.*= It is not possible to walk. *sdad/ sdad-če ñan-če 'dug.*= It is possible to sit. *bčo/bčo-če ñan-če 'dug.*= It is possible to do.

9.2.2. A verb functions with the help of auxiliaries and helping verbs with full meaning by dropping its additive particle. Words: *yoŋ-če* = to come, *lta-če* = to see, *čha-če* = to go. Sentences: *kho yoŋ-'dug.* = He-come-is. He comes or is coming. *khyod lta-rug.* = You-look-is. You are looking. *ŋa khyod lta-'a-la yoŋ-khag.* = I-you-seeing-for come-auxiliary. = I came to see you. *čha-če ka yod-na či-la yoŋ-ben.* = going-if-have-if-why-for-come-past. If you had to go, why did you come?

ཁོ་ཡོང་འདུག།།ཁྱོད་ལྟ་རུག།།ང་ཁྱོད་ལྟ་འ་ལ་ཡོང་ཁག།།ཆ་ཅེ་ཀ་ཡོད་ན་ཅི་ལ་ཡོང་བེན།།

The combined function of two verbs together in some forms can be explained as under. In the first column simple verb is given with its meaning. In the second column the principal verb *grul-če* has dropped its additive particle. It has a supporting verb *btaŋ-če* which means 'to give'. Now the phrase *grul-btaŋ-če* =walk-give, means to walk spontaneously. In the third form both the verbs in full form become causative. To let the other one walk, to let talk, and to let jump.

grul-če = to walk	*grul-btaŋ-če*	*grul-če btaŋ-če.*
lab-če = to talk.	*lab-btaŋ-če.*	*lab-če btaŋ-če.*
mčhoŋ-če = to jump.	*mčhoŋ btaŋ-če*	*mčhoŋ-če btaŋ-če.*

Ex: *čig-gaŋ 'aŋ med-ta la laŋ btaŋ-če.* = Any-which-too not-to stand-give. To stand up for no cause. *kho'e tshaŋ-ma yod-sa ru zer btaŋ soŋ.* = He-by all-in front-at-speak give went. He said before everyone. *kho'e bśigs soŋ kho-raŋ ka la bčo-če btaŋ čen.* = He damaged it, we will let him repair it himself. *su-la-'aŋ btaŋ-če btaŋ-če-man.* = who-to-too- giving giving-not. We will not let it to be given to anybody.

9.3. Tenses: While inflecting the verbs drop the additive particle *če* and case signs are joined with the verbal stem which remains unchanged.

9.3.1 Present Tense

i. In the present form the present indicative and the continuous are exhibited by the same expression.

ii. The actions are distinguished in two forms: i. Happening in view of the speaker, and ii. Happening out of view of the speaker which includes the actions known through knowledge, etc.

Present Indicative and continuous: Ex.: Verb: ***čha-če,*** to go.

	Singular	**Plural**
1.	*ŋa čha-'a yod.* = I go./ I am going.	*ŋa-ža čha-'a yod* =We go./ We are going.
2.	*khyod čha-rug.* = Thou goest.	*khyo-ža čha-rug.* = You go./You are going.
3.	1. (Visible) *kho čha-rug.* =He goes./ He is going.	*kho-ba čha-rug.* = They go/ They are going.
3.	2. (Invisible) *kho čha-'a rag* = He goes./He is going.	*kho-ba čha-'a rag.* = They go./They are going.

3. 3. *kho čha-'a yod-če rag* - =(Invisible, indefinite) He goes./He is going. — *kho-ba čha-'a yod-če rag.* = They go./They are going.

Here we observe that the auxiliaries don't change with the change of person.

ང་ཆ་འ་ཡོད།། ང་ཞ་ཆ་འ་ཡོད།། ཁྱོད་ཆ་རུག།། ཁྱོ་ཞ་ཆ་རུག།། ཁོ་ཆ་རུག།། ཁོ་བ་ཆ་རུག།། ཁོ་ཆ་འ་རག།། ཁོ་བ་ཆ་འ་རག།། ཁོ་ཆ་འ་ཡོད་ཅེ་རག།། ཁོ་བ་ཆ་འ་ཡོད་ཅེ་རག།།

In the above instances in the second and third persons the auxiliary *rug* indicates an action taking place in view of the speaker. In the case of the second person there is one situation. In the case of the third person two situations have been given. 1. In the first case the action takes place in view of the speaker. 2. In the second case the action takes place behind the view of the speaker.

For the verb *yoŋ-če,* 'to come' and *'grul-če,* 'to walk', the auxiliaries used in the second and third person are different from that for *čha-če* as above. Thus ***yoŋ-če:***

1. *ŋa yoŋ-ŋa yod.* = I am coming. — *ŋa-ža yoŋ-ŋa yod.* = We are coming.
2. *khyod yoŋ 'dug.* = Thou comest. — *khyo-ža yoŋ-'dug.* = = You are coming.
3. 1. (Visible) *kho yoŋ 'dug.* = He is coming. — *kho-ba yoŋ 'dug.* They are coming.
3. 2. (Invisible) *kho yoŋ-ŋa rag.* = He is coming. — *kho-ba yoŋ-ŋa rag.* =They are coming.
3. 3. *kho yoŋ-ŋa yod-če rag.* = (Invisible, indefinite) He comes/ is coming. — *kho-ba yoŋ-ŋa yod-če rag.* =They come./ are coming.

ང་ཡོང་ང་ཡོད།། ང་ཞ་ཡོང་ང་ཡོད།། ཁྱོད་ཡོང་འདུག།། ཁྱོ་ཞ་ཡོང་འདུག།། ཁོ་ཡོང་འདུག།། ཁོ་བ་ཡོང་འདུག།། ཁོ་ཡོང་ང་རག།། ཁོ་བ་ཡོང་ང་རག།། ཁོ་ཡོང་ང་ཡོད་ཅེ་རག།། ཁོ་བ་ཡོང་ང་ཡོད་ཅེ་རག།།

Verb *'**grul-če*** = to walk.

	Singular	Plural
1.	*ŋa 'grul-la yod.* = I am walking.	*ŋa-ža 'grul-la yod.* = We are walking.
2.	*khyod 'grul-lug.* = Thou walkest.	*khyo-ža 'grul-lug.* = You are walking.
3.	1. *kho 'grul-lug.* = He is walking.	*kho-ba 'grul-lug.* = They are walking.
3.	2. *kho 'grul-la rag.* = He is walking.	*kho-ba 'grul-la rag.* = They are walking.
3.	3. *kho 'grul-la yod- če rag.* = He is walking.	*kho-ba 'grul-la yod-če rag.* = They are walking.

ང་འགྲུལ་ལ་ཡོད།། ང་ཞ་འགྲུལ་ལ་ཡོད།། ཁྱོད་འགྲུལ་ལུག།། ཁྱོ་ཞ་འགྲུལ་ལུག།།
ཁོ་འགྲུལ་ལུག།། ཁོ་བ་འགྲུལ་ལུག།། ཁོ་འགྲུལ་ལ་རག།། ཁོ་བ་འགྲུལ་ལ་རག།།
ཁོ་འགྲུལ་ལ་ཡོད་ཅེ་རག།། ཁོ་བ་འགྲུལ་ལ་ཡོད་ཅེ་རག།།

Examples of actions taking place in view of the speaker. i. The following are examples of use of the verbs *ñal-če,* sleeping, and *tsher-če,* to worry, in the present tense. *ñal-če 'dug.*= He is about to sleep. *ñal-če bčo-rug.*= He is preparing to sleep. *ñal-lug.* = He is doing the act of sleeping. *ñal-dog.* = He has slept./He has completed the action of sleeping. *ñal-de 'dug.* = He is lying sleeping.

ཉལ་ཅེ་འདུག།། ཉལ་ཅེ་བཅོ་རུག།། ཉལ་ལུག།། ཉལ་དོག།། ཉལ་དེ་འདུག།།

ii. *kho tsher-rug.* = He is worrying. *kho-la tshi-ri 'dug.* = He has worry./ He is worried. *kho tshi-ri bčo-rug.*= He is doing worry./ He is worrying. In the three sentences the verb *tsher-če* has been used in the first as verb and in the other two as noun with auxiliary verb to attain the same result.

ཁོ་ཚེར་རུག།། ཁོ་ལ་ཚི་རི་འདུག།། ཁོ་ཚི་རི་བཅོ་རུག།།

iii. Here is given example of verb *'bri-če* = to write, in different forms of present continuous: *kho 'bri-rug.*= He writes or is writing. *kho 'bri-'en 'dug.* = He has been writing. *kho 'bri 'bri-'a-'dug.* = He has been writing continuously. *kho 'bri-'en bčo-rug.*= He is writing (intermittently). *kho bri-'en bčo-rug, sil-len bčo-rug.* = He is writing and then reading, (doing alternately). *kho 'bri-'en 'bri-'en sil-'ug.* = He is reading, while writing. (He is doing both the acts together).

ཁོ་འབྲི་རུག།། ཁོ་འབྲི་འེན་འདུག།། ཁོ་འབྲི་འབྲི་འ་འདུག།། ཁོ་འབྲི་འེན་བཅོ་རུག།། ཁོ་འབྲི་འེན་བཅོ་རུག། སིལ་ལེན་བཅོ་རུག།། ཁོ་འབྲི་འེན་འབྲི་འེན་སིལ་ཨུག།།

čen: This auxiliary is used in number of ways. These sentences show simple narration. *ṭu-'u-'un kha-ra la thad-čen.* = Children-sweets-to-please-are. Children like sweets. *gar-ža ru a-ṛu maŋ-po yoŋ-čen.* = Lahul-in-potato-much-come-are. In Lahul there grows much potato.

ཏུ་ཨུ་ཨུན་ཁ་ར་ལ་ཐད་ཅེན།། གར་ཞ་རུ་ཨ་ཊུ་མང་པོ་ཡོང་ཅེན།།

9.3.2. Past Tense: In the simple past tense the auxiliary *ben*, *ban, pen* and *ten* are joined with the stem verb in the case of first person. The use of auxiliary *ben* is more common. *yoŋ-ben* = I came. *sdad-ben/sdad-pen* = I sat. *yod-pen./ yod-ten.* = I was there. *ten* comes after the verb ending with *d.*

In the case of second and third persons the word *soŋ*, past form of the verb *čha-če,* is used as an auxiliary or some other auxiliaries, like *pen.* Thus: *kho-be bčos soŋ.* = They did. *de-ru mi-žig 'dug-pen.* = There was a man. There are other forms in the past tense. Here the stem word *bčo* of the verb *bčo-če,* has changed to *bčos,* past form, but it takes auxiliary like all other verbs. Thus: *bčos-ben.* = I did. *bčos-soŋ.*= He did.

ཡོང་བེན།། སྡད་བེན།། ཡོད་པེན།། དེ་རུ་མི་ཞིག་འདུག་པེན།། བཅོས་བེན།། བཅོས་སོང་།།

9.3.2.1. Past Perfect. This denotes an accomplished action.

Verb: čha-če = to go.

	Singular	**Plural**
i.	*ŋa soŋ ben.* = I went.	*ŋa-ža soŋ-ben.* = We went.
ii.	*khyod bud-soŋ.* = Thou went.	*khyo-ža bud-soŋ.* = You went.
iii.	*kho bud-soŋ.* = He went.	*kho-ba bud-soŋ.* = They went.

ང་སོང་པེན།། ང་ཞ་སོང་པེན།། ཁྱོད་བུད་སོང་།། ཁྱོ་ཞ་བུད་སོང་།། ཁོ་བུད་སོང་།། ཁོ་བ་བུད་སོང་།།

Here in the first person the verb is in the form of past tense and the auxiliary is also in the same form. In the second and third persons another form *bud* of the verb *čha-če* has been used and the verb *soŋ* in the past form functions as auxiliary.

9.3.2.2. Past Continuous

	Singular	**Plural**
1.	*ŋa čha-'a yod-ten.* = I was going.	*ŋa-ža čha-'a yod-ten.* = We were going.
2.	1. *khyod čha rug-pen.* = Thou was going.	*khyo-ža čha–rug-pen.* =You were going.
2.	2. *khyod čha-'a rag-pen.* =Thou was going.	*khyo-ža čha-'a rag-pen.* = You were going.
3.	1. *kho čha- rug-pen.* = He was going	*kho-ba čha-rug-pen.*= = They were going.
3.	2. *kho čha-'a rag-pen.* = He was going.	*kho-ba čha-'a rag-pen.* = They were going.
3.	2. *kho čha-'a yod-če rag-pen.* = He was going.	*kho-ba čha-'a yod-če rag-pen.* = They were going.

Here in the past tense the division in the invisible and the visible actions is seen in the second person also.

ང་ཆ་འ་ཡོད་ཏེན།། ང་ཞ་ཆ་འ་ཡོད་ཏེན།། ཁྱོད་ཆ་རུག་པེན།། ཁྱོ་ཞ་ཆ་རུག་པེན།། ཁྱོད་ཆ་འ་རག་པེན།། ཁྱོ་ཞ་ཆ་འ་རག་པེན།། ཁོ་ཆ་རུག་པེན།། ཁོ་བ་ཆ་རུག་པེན།། ཁོ་ཆ་འ་རག་པེན།། ཁོ་བ་ཆ་འ་རག་པེན།། ཁོ་ཆ་འ་ཡོད་ཅེ་རག་པེན།། ཁོ་བ་ཆ་འ་ཡོད་ཅེ་རག་པེན།།

Here it may be noted that the verb has two auxiliaries simultaneously. The last particle *'pen'* is indicative of the past. In fact if this is removed what remains is a sentence in the present tense. Thus the whole sentence of the present tense has been changed to past by merely joining the particle '*pen*' of the past tense at the end of the sentence.

9.3.2.3. Perfect participal is formed by joining the particle *de* = having. *ŋa kho-ba-la las-kha skad-de soŋ-ben.* = I-they-to-work-give-having-went-sign of past. I went after entrusting the work to them. *kho-raŋ-ke las-kha tshar-de rtiŋ-la kho khaŋ-pa la bud-soŋ.* = He-himself-of-work-finish-having-after-at-he-home-to-went-sign of past. He went to home after having finished his own work *las-kha bčos de bčos-de 'aŋ tshar-laŋ mi-nug.* ≐ Work-do-having-do-having-yet-finish-to be-not-is. The work is not coming to finish even after having worked so much. *di-žag ni mgo-la zug si śi-če rag-pen.* = The other day I was feeling like dying with headache.

ང་ཁོ་བ་ལ་ལས་ཁ་སྐད་དེ་སོང་བེན།། ཁོ་རང་གི་ལས་ཁ་ཚར་དེ་རྟིང་ལ་ཁོ་ཁང་པ་ལ་བུད་སོང་།། ལས་ཁ་བཅོས་དེ་བཅོས་དེ་འང་ཚར་ལང་མི་ནུག།། དི་ཞག་ནི་མགོ་ལ་ཟུག་སི་ཤི་ཅེ་རག་པེན།།

The verb *tshar-če* = to complete, is often found used with another verb. This denotes that the action has been completed. *ŋe bčos tshar.* = I have finished doing. *ŋe khu-ru phaŋ-tshar.* = I-load-throw-finished. I have finished putting down the load.

ངེ་བཅོས་ཚར།། ངེ་ཁུ་རུ་ཕང་ཚར།།

9.3.3. Future Tense. The auxiliaries used in the future tense are *'en, čen, kan, laŋ, nag, kag, khag, čag, śe-ka, dro* and *tro*. Of these '*en* is used for indicating the future tense. The three terms *śe-ka, dro* and *tro* are probables. The rest are used in more than one tense. In this manner the future form is clear in the first person. In respect of the other two persons it is not very clear.

'en: In the future tense, the auxiliary *'en* is used for all the three persons. Thus: *ŋa čha-'en* = I will go. But here the two parts, the verb and the auxiliary, of the word get joined and is contracted to *čhen* and the word is heard only in this form. Thus *ŋa-čhen.* = I will go. Similarly *btaŋ-'en* = *bten*. Will give, I will give. Here instead of *lta-'en* it becomes *ltos-'en, lto-en.* = I will see. *ŋa-že bčo-'en.* = We will do. Ex. *khyod/khyo-ža/kho/kho-ba čhen.* = Thou/you/he /they will go. *snaŋ-ŋa bčos ṭu-'u mi-khrod la btor čhen.* = Care-do-boy-man-among-in-lost-go-will. Take care child may get lost in the crowd. 'grul-len, zer-ren, etc. *či-čhen* = What may happen? *tsug-čhen* = How it may be? *čhe-čhen* = It may exceed.

ང་ཆ་འེན།། ང་ཆེན།། བདང་འེན།། བཏེན།། ལྡོ་འེན།། ང་ཞེ་བཙོ་འེན།། སྔང་ང་བཙོས་ཏུ་ཙུ་མི་ཁྲོད་ལ་བསྡོར་ཆེན།། ཅི་ཆེན།། ཙུག་ཆེན།། ཆེ་ཆེན།།

Verbs ending in ten different terminals function with the auxiliary *'en* as follows: *log-'en* = Will return. *laŋ - ŋen* = Will get up. *sdad-ten* = Will sit. *sñan-nen* = Will hear. *lab-'en* = Will talk. *rtsem-men* = Will sew. *zer-ren* = Will say. *sil-len* = Will read. *śes-sen* = Will know. They follow the same rule as explained above. The simple rule is that the auxiliary is simply joined or the ultimate letter of the verb is reduplicated and then the 'en is joined.

ལོག་འེན།། ལང་ངེན།། སྡད་ཏེན།། སྙན་ནེན།། ལབ་འེན།། རྩེམ་མེན།། ཟེར་རེན།། སིལ་ལེན།། ཤེས་སེན།།

Here it may be noted that *'en* is a sign of future tense and the verb *bstad-če* in future becomes *bsdad-ten* = will sit. However, two verbs which also function as helping verbs in similar position have the form in past tense thus:

yod – yod-ten = I was.

med – med-ten = I was not.

i. ***čen:*** *či čha-čen. khyo-raŋ bčos-'en bčos.* = What will happen (does not matter), you keep on doing. *tho-re kho-ba sŋa-mo ne čha-čen-lo.* = Tomorrow-they-morning-from-go-will-said. They say that tomorrow they will go early in the morning. *ŋa-ža miŋ-ga gñis čha-čen. tho-re ñuŋ-ti-ru sdad-čen.*= We will go two persons. Tomorrow we will stay in Kullu. *čha-čen daŋ čha-čen zer-de nam čha-čen.* = Go-will-and-go-will-say-having-when-go-will. Saying going and going, when will he go?

ཅི་ཆ་ཅེན།།ཁྱོ་རང་བཅོས་འེན་བཅོས།། ཐོ་རེ་ཁོ་བ་སྔ་མོ་ནེ་ཆ་ཅེན་ལོ།། ང་ཞ་མིང་ག་གཉིས་ཆ་ཅེན།། ཐོ་རེ་ཉུང་ཏི་རུ་སྡད་ཅེན།།ཆ་ཅེན་དང་ཆ་ཅེན་ཟེར་དེ་ནམ་ཆ་ཅེན།།

The three expressions *gril-'en, 'gril-čen* and *'gril-čhen* mean respectively: may fall (future), there is chance of falling, and may fall (future). *gril-'en, ltos-de grul.* = (You) may fall, walk looking (forward). *(Walk carefully). 'i-ru ni bab 'gril-čen ltos de grul.* = Stones fall here (from the slope), walk carefully. *ti-bi gril čhen zum-de bor.*= The cap may fall down, keep it holding.

གྲིལ་འཛིན་ལྷོས་དེ་གྲུལ།། འི་རྟུ་ཉེ་བབ་གྲིལ་ཅེན་ལྷོས་དེ་གྲུལ།། ཧེ་བི་གྲིལ་ཆེན་བྱམ་དེ་བོར།།

ii. ***nag*****:** The auxiliary *nag* is used with all the three persons in both the numbers. A verb gets lengthened by adding the particle *'a* before the particle *nag. khyod čha-'a nag.* = You will go. *kho-ba čha-'a nag.* = They will go and also means 'They may go'. Following are forms of the sentences in simple future tense. *tho-re tshe-šu nag.* = Tomorrow- *tshe-šu -is.* Tomorrow it is the festival of *tshe-šu. ŋa čha-a' nag.* = I may/will go. *khyo-'e bčo-'a nag.* = You may/will do.

ཁྱོད་ཆ་འ་ནག།། ཁོ་བ་ཆ་འ་ནག།། ཐོ་རེ་ཚེ་ཤུ་ནག།། ང་ཆ་འ་ནག།། ཁྱོ་འེ་བཙོ་འ་ནག།།

iii. **kag:** *kho-ba si-rig yoŋ-ŋa yod-kag.* = They are coming all. *tho-re kho čha-'a kag.* = He will be going tomorrow.

ཁོ་བ་སི་རིག་ཡོང་ང་ཡོད་ཀག།། ཐོ་རེ་ཁོ་ཆ་འ་ཀག།།

iv. **khag:** It is equivalent to 'may' and is used generally with the third person. *kho čha na čha-khag.* = If he wants to go he may go. *kho-ba raŋ-ke bčo-khag.* = They may do themselves. *kho-ba raŋ-ke bčos-khag*. = They did themselves.

ཁོ་ཆ་ན་ཆ་ཁག།། ཁོ་བ་རང་ཀེ་བཙོ་ཁག།། ཁོ་བ་རང་ཀེ་བཙོས་ཁག།།

v. ***kan***. It is found used in the first person singular. *ŋa čha-kan.*= I want to go. I will go. But with the second and third persons it is used in interrogative form. *yoŋ kan na.* = Do you want to come? *kho-ba yoŋ -ŋa yod kan na.* = Whether they are coming? *khyod čha-kan-na sdad kan.* = Whether you want to go or stay.

ང་ཆ་ཀན།། ཡོང་ཀན་ན།། ཁོ་བ་ཡོང་ང་ཡོད་ཀན་ན།། ཁྱོད་ཆ་ཀན་ན་སྡད་ཀན།།

vi. ***laŋ*****:** *tho-re ŋa/ŋa-ža čha-laŋ yin.* = Tomorrow-I/we-go-need-is. I have to go tomorrow. In the same way it can be used with second and third persons in singular and plural. *ŋa/khyod/kho/ŋa-ža/khyo-ža/kho-ba čha-laŋ yin* = I/thou/he/we/you/they have to go.

ཐོ་རེ་ང་ཆ་ལང་ཡིན།

vii. čag: It is generally found used with the first person singular. *ŋa čha-'čag.* = I will go or I have to go (if nobody is ready to go).

sdad-go byung-na tho-re sal-sal ru sdad-čag. = If required, we will stay at Salsal.

ང་ཚ་ཅག། སྡད་གོ་བྱུང་ན་ཐོ་རེ་སལ་སལ་རུ་སྡད་ཅག།

viii. ***śe-ka:*** It indicates a probable action and is used with the third person singular. *kho čha-śe-ka.* = He-go-may. He may go. *kho di-riŋ sdad-śe ka.* = He may stay toeay.

ཁོ་ཆ་ཤེ་ཀ།། ཁོ་དི་རིང་སྡད་ཤེ་ཀ།།

dro, tro: They indicate the action in the present tense taking place out of view. *kho yin-dro/man-dro.* = It may be/may not be him. *kho yod-tro med-tro.* = He may be/may not be there.

ཁོ་ཡིན་དྲོ།མན་དྲོ།། ཁོ་ཡོད་ཏྲོ།མེད་ཏྲོ།།

9.4. **Verbs, Transitive and Intransitive:** Verbs are different in the transitive and intransitive forms. Ex:

Transitive			**Intransitive**		
bkar-če.	=	To obstruct.	*'khar-če.*	=	To get obstructed.
skaŋ-če.	=	to fill.	*khaŋ-če.*	=	To get filled up.
stug-če.	=	To burn.	*sdug-če.*	=	To get burned,
spir-če.	=	To disperse.	*bir-če.*	=	To get dispersed,
rtsod-če.	=	To cook.	*tshos-še*	=	To get ripened.

བཀར་ཅེ། སྐང་ཅེ། སྟུག་ཅེ། སྤིར་ཅེ། རྩོད་ཅེ།། འཁར་ཅེ། ཁང་ཅེ། སྡུག་ཅེ། བིར་ཅེ། ཚོས་ཤེ།

ŋe kya-pha la nas skaŋ ben. = I filled the sack with barley. *kho-'e men-tog spir-dog.*= He has dispersed (to press the dry flower to separate seed from leaves) the flower.

ངེ་ཀྱ་ཕ་ལ་ནས་སྐང་བེན། ཁོ་འེ་མེན་ཏོག་སྤིར་དོག།

Intransitive: *nas-si kya-pha khaŋ soŋ.* = The sack has become filled with barley. *men-tog bir dog.* = The flower has scattered.

ནས་སི་ཀྱ་ཕ་ཁང་སོང་།།མེན་ཏོག་བིར་དོག།

9.5. **Causative:** The following are verbs joined with some other verbs. In this manner they show change in their form. *grub-če* = To be finished. *'grub-če btaŋ-če.* = To let finish. *'grub čha-če btaŋ-če.* = To let to be finished. *khaŋ čha-če* = To get filled up. *khaŋ-če btaŋ-če.* = To let fill up. *khaŋ čha-če btaŋ-če.* = To let to be filled up.

འགྲུབ་ཅེ།། འགྲུབ་ཅེ་བཏང་ཅེ།། འགྲུབ་ཆ་ཅེ་བཏང་ཅེ།། ཁང་ཆ་ཅེ།། ཁང་ཅེ་བཏང་ཅེ།། ཁང་ཆ་ཅེ་བཏང་ཅེ།།

kho-'e khor-lo bskor-rug. = He is turning the wheel. *kho-'e 'khor-lo bskor-če btaŋ 'dug.*= He is letting (him) to turn the wheel. *'khor-lo 'khor-rug.*= The wheel is revolving. *'khor-lo 'khor-če btaŋ 'dug.*= He is allowing the wheel to get revolved. *ŋe ku-lig dpye-'a yod.* = By me –lock-opening-is. I am opening the lock. Ku-lig dbye-'a mi-nug. = Lock-opening-no-is. The lock is not opening. *bu-ṭa 'gyel-lug.* = The tree is falling aside. *kho-'e bu-ṭa skyel-lug.* = He is pulling down the tree.

ཁོ་འེ་འཁོར་ལོ་སྐོར་རུག།། ཁོ་འེ་འཁོར་ལོ་སྐོར་ཅེ་བཏང་འདུག།། འཁོར་ལོ་འཁོར་རུག།། འཁོར་ལོ་འཁོར་ཅེ་བཏང་འདུག།། ངེ་ཀུ་ལིག་དབྱེ་འ་ཡོད།། ཀུ་ལིག་དབྱེ་འ་མི་ནུག།། བུ་ཊ་འགྱེལ་ལུག།། ཁོ་འེ་བུ་ཊ་སྐྱེལ་ལུག།།

9.6. The verb *soŋ*: The word *soŋ* is past and imperative form of the verb *čha-če,* to go. It is used in the following manner. i. It is used as verb in the past tense and takes with it a terminal. Thus: *ŋa soŋ-ben.* = I went. *kho de-ru či-la soŋ-khag* = Why did he go there? *da-ruŋ kho ma-soŋ dog.* = Still he has not gone. *khyod su mñam-po soŋ ben.* = With whom did you go?

ཁོ་དེ་རུ་ཅི་ལ་སོང་ཁག།། ད་རུང་ཁོ་མ་སོང་དོག།། ཁྱོད་སུ་མཉམ་པོ་སོང་བེན།།

ii. It is used as an imperative: *soŋ.* = Go. *khyod soŋ.* = Thou go. *khyod lem-ka soŋ.* = Thou go immediately.

iii. It functions as helping verb in the past tense. *kho bud-soŋ.*= He went. *las-kha 'grig-soŋ.*= The work has been finished. *ñi-ma šar soŋ* = The sun has risen. *loŋ-šog/soŋ.* = Come up/go away.

ཁྱོད་སོང་།། ཁྱོད་ལེམ་ཀ་སོང་།། ཁོ་བུད་སོང་།། ལས་ཁ་འགྲིག་སོང་།། ཉི་མ་ཤར་སོང་།། ལོང་ཤོག།ལོང་སོང་།།

iv. *ŋa čha-če soŋ.* = I have to go. (If nobody goes.). *khyo-'e bčo-če soŋ* = You have to do. (If some other does not do.).

ང་ཆ་ཅེ་སོང་།། ཁྲོ་འི་བཙོ་ཅེ་སོང་།།

9.7. Verbs ***yoŋ*** and ***soŋ*:** The two verbs *yoŋ* and *soŋ*, to come and to go, are often used together. The verb *soŋ* is here used as an auxiliary to the verb *yoŋ*. *yoŋ-soŋ*. = He came. *ma-yoŋ-soŋ*. = Not- come-go. He has not come. *kho soŋ de yoŋ soŋ*. = He-went-having- come-go. He came back after going. *yoŋ-de soŋ dog*. = Come- having-went-have. He has gone after coming. *yoŋ-ka ma-yoŋ soŋ*. = Come-even-not-come-went. He did not come at all. *yoŋ-če yoŋ-soŋ sdad ma-sdad soŋ*. = Coming-come-went-stay-not-stay-went. Although he came, but he did not stay.

མ་ཡོང་སོང་།། ཁོ་སོང་དེ་ཡོང་སོང་།། ཡོང་དེ་སོང་དོག།། ཡོང་ཀ་མ་ཡོང་སོང་།། ཡོང་ཅེ་ཡོང་སོང་།སྡད་མ་སྡད་སོང་།།

9.8. **Frequentative use of verbs:** 1. Sometimes verbs are repeated and then they give slightly different meaning. *be-to spo-ma laŋ-če laŋ-če bčo rug, laŋ khyud-ta mi-nug*. = The presently born calf is trying to get up, but is not able to stand up. *ŋa laŋ laŋ-ŋa sdad-de čhad soŋ*. = I am tired by keeping standing continuously. *kho laŋ ma-laŋ-ŋa-la ja btoŋ zer-rug*. = He asks for tea before he gets up. *ŋa laŋ-ŋa laŋ-ŋa bsam*. = I was thinking, should I get up. *kho la laŋ-loŋ ka mi-nug*. = He has no leisure to get up. *kho laŋ-laŋ-la ŋa yul-phe ko-ra gčig btaŋ de yoŋ 'en*. = Till he gets up, I will come taking round of the village. *kho mdun mdun- la sug 'dug*. = He-forward-forward-to-move-is. He is moving forward to forward.

བེ་ཏོ་སྤོ་མ་ལང་ཅེ་ལང་ཅེ་བཅོ་རུག།ལང།འཁྱུད་ཏ་མི་ནུག།། ང་ལང་ལང་ང་སྡད་དེ་ཆད་སོང་།། ཁོ་ལང་མ་ལང་ང་ལ་ཇ་བཏོང་ཟེར་རུག།། ང་ལང་ང་ལང་ང་བསམ།། ཁོ་ལ་ལང་ལོང་ཀ་མི་ནུག།། ཁོ་ལང་ལང་ལ་ང་ཡུལ་ཕེ་ཀོ་ར་གཅིག་བཏང་དེ་ཡོང་ཇེན།། ཁོ་མདུན་མདུན་ལ་སུག་འདུག།།

'grul-de 'grul-de čhad-soŋ. = I am tired for having walked continuously. *kho-'grul 'grul-la sdad-ta nag*. = He keeps on walking. *kho 'grul-len 'grul-len bal bkal-la nag*.= He spins wool, while walking.

འགྲུལ་དེ།འགྲུལ་དེ་ཆད་སོང་།། ཁོ་འགྲུལ།འགྲུལ་ལ་སྡད་ཏ་ནག།། ཁོ་འགྲུལ་ལེན།འགྲུལ་ལེན།བལ།བཀལ་ལ་ནག།།

9.9. Some verbs generally function as secondary verb to strengthen the function of the main verb. Some of these are: *btaŋ če.* = To give. *bor-če.* = To put, keep, leave. *bčo-če.* = To make, to do. *čha-če*= To go. *tshar-če* = To finish. *rgyab-če* = To hit. Example: *btaŋ btaŋ-če.* = To give away. *btaŋ bor-če.*= To give away. *bor btaŋ-če.* = To leave away. *btaŋ-če btaŋ-bor-če.*= To let the other give away. *lus čha-če btaŋ-bor-če.* = To allow to get left.

བཏང་བཏང་ཅེ།། བཏང་བོར་ཅེ།། བོར་བཏང་ཅེ།། བཏང་ཅེ་བཏང་བོར་ཅེ།།
ལུས་ཆ་ཅེ་བཏང་བོར་ཅེ།།

9.10. The word *laŋ-če* = To stand up functions slightly differently. *kho bud soŋ.* = He went. *kho laŋ bud soŋ.* = He went away (without telling). *ŋa gor soŋ.* = I got delayed. *ŋa gor laŋ bud soŋ.*= I got delayed.

ཁོ་བུད་སོང་།། ཁོ་ལང་བུད་སོང་།། ང་འགོར་སོང་།། ང་འགོར་ལང་བུད་སོང་།།

9.11. When a verb is repeated and the particle *'e* is placed between the two it becomes emphatic. *zer- 'e zer.* = You must say. *bčos- 'e bčos* = You must do. *soŋ-ŋe soŋ.* = You must go. *sdod-te sdod.* = You must stay.

ཟེར་འེ་ཟེར།། བཅོས་འེ་བཅོས།། སོང་ངེ་སོང་།། སྡོད་ཏེ་སྡོད།།

9.11. **Reporting Messages:** Here are given a few sentences commonly spoken while sending messages to the kinsmen with the travelers.

i. *sonam-la ŋe-si ŋa sleb sleb čha ma-čha- 'a sruŋ-de sdod zer-rug zer-de zer-btong.* = sonam-to by-me by me reach-reach go not-going wait-having stay, saying, say having, tell-give. "Tell Sonam, I was saying, "not going, to keep staying waiting till I reach".

བསོད་ནམས་ལ།ངེ་སི་ང་སླེབ་སླེབ་ཆ་མ་ཆ་འ་སྲུང་དེ་སྡོད།ཟེར་རུག་ཟེར་དེ་ཟེར་
བཏོང་།།

ii. The reporter will say, "*a-či si khyod-la zer-rug ŋa sleb bleb čha ma-čha- 'a sruŋ -de sdod zer-de zer-btoŋ.*" = "Sister-by you-to says I reach-reach go-not-going wait-having stay, say-having say-give." = Sister asks me to tell you, that till she reaches, not to go but to keep waiting.

ཨ་ཅེ་སི་ཁྱོད་ལ་ཟེར་རུག།ང་སྐྱེ་བ་སྐྱེ་བ་ཆ་མ་ཆ་འ་སྣང་དེ་སྟོད།ཟེར་དེ་ཟེར་བཏོང་།།

iii. "*ŋe-si sonam-la khaŋ-pa-la śog zer-rug zer-de zer-btoŋ.*" = By- me by sonam-to home-to come saying say-having say-give. "Sister says to tell you that she asks you to come home."

ང་སི་བསོད་ནམས་ལ་"ཁང་པ་ལ་ཤོག་ཟེར་རུག་ཟེར་དེ་ཟེར་བཏོང་།།

iv. *"a-či-si khyod-la khaŋ-pa-la śog zer-rug zer-de zer btoŋ zer-rug.* = sister-by you-to home-to come-saying say-having say-give saying. Sister asks me to tell you that she was asking you to come home.

ཨ་ཅེ་སི་ཁྱོད་ལ་ཁང་པ་ལ་ཤོག་ཟེར་རུག་ཟེར་དེ་ཟེར་བཏོང་ཟེར་རུག།།'

v. *ŋe si zer-rug zer-de zer ma-btaŋ.* = By-me by saying say-having say not-give. Don't tell that it was me who was telling.

ང་སི་"ཟེར་རུག་ཟེར་དེ་ཟེར་མ་བཏང་།།

vi. *ŋe si śog zer-rug zer-de zer čag.* = By-me by come saying say-having say-should have. = You should have said that I had asked him to come.

ང་སི་ཤོག་ཟེར་རུག་ཟེར་དེ་ཟེར་ཅག།།

10

Negation and Imperative

10.1. Particles of Negation: The negative particles function in the following ways.

i. Firstly there are prefixes which are prefixed before the verbs and the auxiliaries. These are *ma, mi* and *me. ma-čha* = Don't go. *ma-lab.* = Don't talk. *mi-yoŋ* = Will not come. *mi-zer.* = Will not say. *me-čha.* = Will not go. Here the negative particle '*m*' is used for second person present tense. '*mi*' and '*me*' are used for the first person in future tense.

ii, The following auxiliaries have their negative equivalents.

yod = *med. yin* = *man. 'dug* = *mi-nug. rag* = *me-rag. nag* = *ma-nag*

iii. The following auxiliaries take one of the above negative auxiliaries: *yin dro* = *man dro. yod-tro* = *med– tro. yod-kag* = *med kag. yin khag* = *man khag.*

iv. The following auxiliaries take a verb with negative prefix.

soŋ dog = *ma-soŋ dog. čha-śe-ka* = *mi-čha-śe-ka.*

v. *čha-čag* = *čha-če ma-nag.*

10.1.1. Present Tense: ŋe man. = It is not mine. *ŋa-man.* = It is not me. *ŋa-la med.* = I don't have.'i kho-ma-nag. = This is not him. *ri-'u 'i-ru mi-nug.* = The goat-lamb is not here. *ŋa-la zug me-rag.* = I don't feel pain.

ང་མན།། ང་ལ་མེད།། འི་ཁོ་མ་ནག།། རི་ཨུ་འི་རུ་མི་ནུག།། ང་ལ་ཟུག་མེ་རག།།

10.1.2. Past tense: *ma-yoŋ-ben.* = No-come-sign of past. I did not come. *khyod ma-yoŋ soŋ.* = You-not-come-went. You did not come. *khyod man-khag.* = You-not-might be. It might not have been you. *ŋa-la med-ten.* = I-to-not-sign of past. I did not have. *khyod-la mi-nug-pen* = You-to-not-is-was. You didn't have.

མ་ཡོང་པེན།། ཁྱོད་མ་ཡོང་སོང་།། ཁྱོད་མན་ཁག།། ང་ལ་མེད་ཧེན།། ཁྱོད་ལ་མི་ནུག་པེན།།

10.1.3. Future Tense: *ŋa mi-čha.* = I will not go. *ŋa čha-man.* = I don't want to go. *ŋa čha-'a med.* = I am not going. *kho-čha-'a ma-nag.* = He-going-not-is. He will not go. *bzhad-ma 'ang čha-'a med-kag.* = Other-also-going-not-will. Others are also not going.

ང་མི་ཆ།།ང་ཆ་མན།།ང་ཆ་འ་མེད།།ཁོ་ཆ་འ་མ་ནག།།བཞད་མ་འང་ཆ་འ་མེད་ཀག།།

10.1.4. Imperative: The particle '*m*' before a verb in imperative form turns it into negative form. *ma-čha* = don't go. *ma-yoŋ.* = Don't come. *ma-btaŋ.* = Don't give. *ma-yoŋ, ma-zer.* = Don't say not to come. *btaŋ ma-btaŋ-ŋa bor-btoŋ* = Keep it without giving. *di-riŋ tshag-pa ŋe ku- śu mthoŋ ma- myoŋ.* = Till today I have not seen apple.

མ་ཆ།། མ་ཡོང་།། མ་བཏང་།། མ་ཡོང་།མ་ཟེར།། བཏང་མ་བཏང་ང་བོར་བཏོང་།། དི་རིང་ཚག་པ་ངེ་ཀུ་ཤུ་མཐོང་མ་མྱོང་།

In the following sentences the verb is repeated and the negative particle *ma* and sometimes another additional particle *'e* alongwith it are placed in between the two verbs. Thus *ma-'grul.* = Don't walk. '*grul- ma-'grul.* = Don't walk. *'grul-le ma-'grul.* = Don't walk at all. *ma-'grul-'e ma-'grul.*= Don't walk at all. In the above four sentences the first sentence simply says not to walk, condition for one event. The second sentence prohibits from habitual walking like a doctor's advice to a patient. The last two sentences prohibit from walking.

མ་འགྲུལ།། འགྲུལ་མ་འགྲུལ།། འགྲུལ་འེ་མ་འགྲུལ།། མ་འགྲུལ་འེ་མ་འགྲུལ།།

10.1.5. Some more examples: *ma-soŋ mkhan.* = Those who have not gone. *mi-čha mkhan.* = Those who will not go. *ma-yoŋ mkhan.* = Those who have not come. *mi-yoŋ mkhan.* = Those who will not come. *za-če ma-bzos mkhan.*= Those who have not taken meal. *za-če mi-za mkhan.* = Those who will not take meal. *tham-phog gčig čha-'a čha-'a kho-'e log-de mig mi-lta.* = Turn-one-gone-gone-he-by-back-having-eye-not-look. Once gone, he will not look back. *kho de-ru med-če si ŋa-la hun med-ten.* = He-there-not-of-me-to-knowledge-not-had. I did not know that he was not there.

མ་སོང་མཁན།། མི་ཆ་མཁན།། མ་ཡོང་མཁན།། མི་ཡོང་མཁན།། ཟ་ཅེ་མ་བཟོས་མཁན།། ཟ་ཅེ་མི་ཟ་མཁན།། ཐམ་ཤོག་གཅིག་ཆ་འ་ཆ་འ་ཁོ་འི་ལོག་དེ་མིག་མི་ལྟ།། ཁོ་དེ་རུ་མེད་ཅེ་ཤི་ང་ལ་ཧྲུན་མེད་ཧྲེ་ན།།

10.2. The terms *med* and *man* are negative counterparts of the positive terms *yod* and *yin.*

ŋa-la khu-ru med. = I have no load. *kho-la rta yod.* = He has horse. *'i ku-lig ŋe man.* = This is not my lock. *'i g-yag ŋe yin.* = This is my yak.

ང་ལ་ཁུ་རུ་མེད།། ཁོ་ལ་རྟ་ཡོད།། འི་ཀུ་ལིག་ངེ་མན།། འི་གཡག་ངེ་ཡིན།།

There are some composite terms: *med-kag, man-khag, med-tro, man-dro.*

Sentences: *'i 'dsam-gliŋ-la med-kan-ne med-kan su- 'aŋ med-kag.* = In this world there is none who does not possess something. *mi-čha kham-med med-kag.* = One has to go, even if one has no desire. *a-ma man-na mi mi-šes, go-'a man-na yul ma-mthoŋ.* = He knows no man other than his mother; and knows no land other than the hearth. (One who does not meet other people and has not gone out of the area.). *mdaŋ di-riŋ kho 'i-ru med-kag.* = These days he is not here. *de-ne kho man-khag.* = Then it may not be him. *di-riŋ am-či yoŋ- če man.* =Today doctor is not coming./ will not.

མན།།མེད།། མེད་ཀག།། མན་ཁག།། མེད་ཏྲོ།། མན་ཏྲོ།། འི་འཛམ་གླིང་ལ་མེད་ཀན་ནེ་མེད་ཀན་སུ་འང་མེད་ཀག།། མི་ཆ་ཁམ་མེད།མེད་ཀག།། ཨ་མ་མན་ན་མི་མི་ཤེས།གོ་འ་མན་ན་ཡུལ་མ་མཐོང་།། མདང་དི་རིང་ཁོ་འི་རུ་མེད་ཀག།། དེ་ནེ་ཁོ་མན་ཁག།། དི་རིང་ཨམ་ཅི་ཡོང་ཅེ་མན།།

kho-la mi-šes-če med-kag. = For him there is nothing that he does not know. *tho-re ŋa-la yoŋ-če mi-čha.* = Tomorrow it will not be possible for me to come. *tho-re ŋa-la čha-če mi-yoŋ.* = Tomorrow it will not be possible for me to go. *tho-re ŋa-la yoŋ-če čha-če me-rag.* Tomorrow it will not be possible for me to come. *tho-re ŋa-la čha-če yoŋ-če me-rag.*= Tomorrow it will not be possible for me to go. *kho yoŋ ma-yoŋ-ŋa med-kag.* = He cannot do, but come. *čha-če kham-med-kan man-na.* = Perhaps he has no intention to go. *khyo-raŋ lam-la sdad ma-sdad-ta šog.* = You come without staying in the way.

ཁོ་ལ་མི་ཤེས་ཅེ་མེད་ཀག། ཐོ་རི་ང་ལ་ཡོང་ཅེ་མི་ཆ། ཐོ་རི་ང་ལ་ཆ་ཅེ་མི་ཡོང་། ཐོ་རི་ང་ལ་ཡོང་ཅེ་ཆ་ཅེ་མི་རག། ཐོ་རི་ང་ལ་ཆ་ཅེ་ཡོང་ཅེ་མི་རག། ཁོ་ཡོང་ མ་ཡོང་ང་མེད་ཀག། ཆ་ཅེ་ཁམ་མེད་ཀན་མན་ན། ཁྱོ་རང་ལམ་ལ་སྡོད་མ་སྡོད་ཏ་ཤོག།

A verb can be changed to negative in the following two ways: *mi-brjed-če bčos* and *brjed-če med-kan bčos.*= Make it unforgettable. Particle *mi* is placed before the verb. *brjed ma-brjed-ta khyoŋ.* = Bring without forgetting. *brjed-ta brjed-ta brjed-te čha-'a nag.*= If forgotten it is forgotten permanently. *Čha ma-čha med-kag.*= go- not-go not-is. Going or not going, there is no option. (He must have to go.)

མི་བརྗེད་ཅེ་བཅོས། བརྗེད་ཅེ་མེད་ཀན་བཅོས། བརྗེད་མ་བརྗེད་ཏ་ཁྱོང་། བརྗེད་ཏ་བརྗེད་ཏ་བརྗེད་ཏེ་ཆ་འ་ནག། ཆ་མ་ཆ་མེད་ཀག།

10.3. **Imperative** i. Verbs have uniformly an imperative form and they are fully understood in this sense without aid of any auxiliary. Thus: *rkos* = Dig. *ltos* = Look. *sdod* = Sit. *bčos.* = Do. *khyer* = Take away. *bor* = keep. *btoŋ* = give. *khyoŋ* = bring. *khur* = Carry. *yug* = Leave. The verbs *čha-če* and *yoŋ-če* change in the imperative to a new form as: *soŋ* = Go, and *šog* = Come.

ii. Some of such terms often get joined together and the statements become more explanative of the situation and emphatic. *btoŋ* is the most commonly used such word which is found joined with many such words. Ocassionaly some other verbs are also found fucntioing in the same manner. Example: We take two verbs *zer-če* = to say and *btaŋ-če* = to give. *zer* and *btoŋ* are their imperative forms. They can be used together with the same objective. *zer-btoŋ* = Speak out. *btoŋ-zer* = Say give (tell him to give).

yug-bor.	=	Leave it there.	*bor-btoŋ.*	=	Leave it there.
btoŋ-btoŋ	=	Give away.	*loŋ-šog.*	=	Come along.
ltos-btoŋ.	=	Have a look.	*sdod-bor.*	=	Stay here.
bor-šog	=	Come, leaving that there.	*khrid-khyoŋ.*	=	Bring (him) leading

རྐོས།། ལྟོས།། སྡོད།། བཏོང་།། བཙོས།། ཁྲོང་།། ཁུར།། ཡུག།། བཙོ་ཅེ།། ཟེར་ཅེ།། བཏང་ཅེ།། ཤོག།། ཡུག་བོར།། བོར་བཏོང་།། བཏོང་བཏོང་།། ལོང་ཤོག།། ལྟོས་བཏོང་།། སྡོད་བོར།། བོར་ཤོག།། ཁྲིད་ཁྲོང་།།

10.4. The term *ni* joined in a sentence at the end in imperative form in plural gives slightly an emphatic effect. *khyo-ža-raŋ 'grul btoŋ ni.* = You move on. *kharog la sdad-ta saŋ glu re btoŋ btoŋ ni.*= Silent-in-sitting-instead-song-some-give(vb)-give-ni(emphatic). Instead of keeping silent, sing some songs.

ཁྱོ་ཞ་རང་འགྲུལ་བཏོང་ནི།། ཁ་རོག་ལ་སྡད་ཏ་སང་གླུ་རེ་བཏོང་བཏོང་ནི།།

10.5. In order to emphasise a request the term *žo* is added at the end of the sentence. Thus: *śog- žo* = Must come. *ltos- žo.* = See. Be careful. *brjed ma-brjed-ta zer- žo.* = Must tell without forgetting.

ཤོག་ཞོ།། ལྟོས་ཞོ།།བརྗེད་མ་བརྗེད་ཏ་ཟེར་ཞོ།།

10.6. Particle 'm': The particle 'm' at the end of a sentence in imperative and also in the interrogative form lays emphasis. *laŋ ma-čha ma.* = Don't go away. *btaŋ-ŋ-med-ma.* = Are you not giving? *čha-'a yod ma.* = It is that you are going?

Some letters also take different additives. *sdod-čo. / sdod-to.* = Must stay. *zer-ro.* = Must say.

བཏང་ང་མེད་མ།། ཆ་འ་ཡོད་མ།། ལང་མ་ཆ་མ།། སྡོད་ཅོ།། སྡོད་ཏོ།། ཟེར་རོ།།

11

Adverbs

11.1. An adverb precedes the subject it qualifies. Examples: In the following sentence the adverb *mgyogs-pha* (fast) precedes the verb *rgyug* (run). *rta mgyogs-pha rgyug 'dug.* = Horse-fast-run-is. The horse is running fast. *tshos maŋ-po dmar-pho 'dug.* = Colour-much-red-is. The colour is much red. *čhar-pha maŋ-po yoŋ-soŋ.* = Rain-much-come-went. It rained much. *čhar-pha min-'dra maŋ-po yoŋ-soŋ.* = Rain-incomparable-much-come-went. It rained very much. *čhar-pha min-'dra žig-ka maŋ-po yoŋ-soŋ.* = Rain-incomparable one-much-come-went. There was exceedingly heavy rain.

རྟ་མགྱོགས་ཕ་རྒྱུག་འདུག།། ཚོས་མང་པོ་དམར་ཕོ་འདུག།། ཆར་ཕ་མང་པོ་ཡོང་སོང་།། ཆར་ཕ་མིན་འདྲ་མང་པོ་ཡོང་སོང་།། ཆར་ཕ་མིན་འདྲ་ཞིག་ཀ་མང་པོ་ཡོང་སོང་།།

11.2. Adverbs of Place: *'i-ru* = Here. *de-ru* = There. *ha-'i-ru* = There, at that place. *rtiŋ-la* = Afterwards. *mjug-la* = At the end. *rgyab-la* = On the back, behind. *rgyab-rgyab-la.* = Backwards. *'go-la* = At the beginning. *'i-ru-'aŋ med, de-ru-'aŋ med, ga-ru-'aŋ med, de-ne thaŋ-ke mthil-la ga-ru stor soŋ-khag.* = This-at-too-not, there-at-too-not, where-at-too-not, then-earth-of-under-to-where-in-lose-went-may. It is neither here, nor there, not to be seen anywhere, then where has it been lost, gone under the ground?

འི་རུ།། དེ་རུ།། ཧ་འི་རུ།། རྟིང་ལ།། མཇུག་ལ།། རྒྱབ་ལ།། རྒྱབ་རྒྱབ་ལ།། འགོ་ལ།། འི་རུ་འང་མེད།དེ་རུ་འང་མེད།ག་རུ་འང་མེད། དེ་ནེ་ཐང་ཀེ་ཐིལ་ལ། ག་རུ་སྟོར་སོང་ཁག།།

11.3. Quantity: *tsad-žig.* = A small measure. *tsad-ki-žig.* = In a small measure. *dsi-tag-žig.* = A small quantity. *maŋ-po.* = Much. *da-ruŋ.* = Still more. *'i-zam.* = This much. *de-zam.* = That much. *ga-zam* = How much. *tham-phog gčig.* =Once. *tshad-med* = Unlimited. *maŋ-čhe-'a* = Mostly. *maŋ-ñuŋ* = More or less. *da-ruŋ ta či tsha-rag, da-ruŋ a-tsig sruŋ* (şuŋ). = Still why hurry? Wait for a while. *kho-'e da-ruŋ-ta da-ruŋ btoŋ-lo.* = He-by-still-more-give-says. He asks to give him still more.

ཙད་ཞིག། ཙད་ཀི་ཞིག། ཛེ་ཏག་ཞིག། མང་པོ། ད་རུང་། འི་ཟམ། དེ་ཟམ། ག་ཟམ། ཐམ་ཕོག་གཅིག། ཚད་མེད།། མང་ཆེ་འ། མང་ཉུང་།། ད་རུང་ཏ་ཅི་ཚ་རག།ད་རུང་ཨ་ཙིག་སྲུང་།། ཁོ་འི་ད་རུང་ཏ་ད་རུང་བཏོང་ལོ།།

11.4. Manner: *'i-zug* = In this manner. *de-zug* = In that manner. *ga-zug* = How. *'o-zug* = In that way. *dal-la dal-la* = Slowly and slowly. *gaŋ-byuŋ* = However it comes; without caring. *tsug byuŋ-byuŋ.* = However it comes, without care.

འི་ཟུག།དེ་ཟུག། ག་ཟུག།འོ་ཟུག།དལ་ལ་དལ་ལ། གང་བྱུང་། ཙུག་བྱུང་"བྱུང་།

11.5. Time: i. *hrib-čig* = A moment. *ha-lam* = Some time or in some measure. *nam* = When. *nam-žig* = Sometime. *dad-saŋ* = Now. *de-bar-la* = During the period. *'i-dsa-na* = During this time. *de-dsa-na* = During that time. *gi-dsa-na* = During what time? *či-dsa-na* = During what time? *de-ne* = Then. *sŋon-la* = Earlier. *bar-bar-la* = Intermittently. *da-čig* = Just before. *de-'a med-ta-la* = At once. *a-tsig* =Slightly. *'gor-ži* = Delay. *naŋ-mo* = Some other day in future. *sŋa-mo* = Early, Morning. *phyi-mo* = Late. *hrib-čig-la ñi-ma 'thon-'ug, hrib-čig-la sprin-ne phag-la hib-čha-rug.* = The sun appears for a moment and then in a moment hides behind the clouds. *di-riŋ ŋa sa-kul-la čha-če la phyi-mo bud soŋ.* = Today I got late to school. *tsam-dsod-la* = At what time?

ཧྲིབ་ཅིག། ཧ་ལམ། ནམ། ནམ་ཞིག། དད་སང་། དེ་བར་ལ། འི་ཛ་ན། དེ་ཛ་ན། གི་ཛ་ན། ཅི་ཛ་ན། དེ་ནེ། སྔོན་ལ།། བར་བར་ལ། ད་ཅིག།དེ་འ་མེད་ཏ་ལ། ཨ་ཙིག། འགོར་ཞི། ནང་མོ། སྔ་མོ། ཕྱི་མོ། ཧྲིབ་ཅིག་ལ་ཉི་མ་འཐོན་འུག། ཧྲིབ་ཅིག་ལ་སྤྲིན་ནེ་ཕག་ལ་ཧིབ་ཆ་རུག།། དི་རིང་ང་ས་ཀུལ་ལ་ཆ་ཅེ་ལ་ཕྱི་མོ་བུད་སོང་།། ཙམ་ཛོད་ལ།།

ii. *žag-taŋ.* = Everyday. *di-riŋ.* = Today. *mdaŋ.* = Yesterday. *mdaŋ di riŋ* = These days. *di žag.* = The other day. *de di žag.* = The day before the other day. *tho-re.* = Tomorrow. *naŋ-ŋa.* = Day after tomorrow. *že.* = The fourth day. *dgu'i.*= The fifth day. *bču'i.* = The sixth day. *da-lo.* = This year. *na-niŋ.* = Last year. *naŋ-par.* = Next year. *saŋ- par.* = Next to next year. *lem.* = Now. *lem-ka.* = Just now. *lem-čig-la* = In a moment. *lem-ka-lem 'i-zam ḍha-ba ŋe khyod-la ga-ne khyoŋ-btaŋ-čag.* = At this moment from where can I get so much money for you?

ཞག་ཏང་། དེ་རིང་། མདང་། མདང་དེ་རིང་། དེ་ཞག། དེ་དེ་ཞག། ཐོ་རེ། ནང་ང་། ཞེ། དགུའི། བཙུའི། ད་ལོ། ན་ནིང་། ནང་པར། སང་པར། ལེམ། ལེམ་ཀ། ལེམ་ཅིག་ལ།། ལེམ་ཀ་ལེམ་འི་ཟམ་ཌྷ་བ་ངེ་ཁྱོད་ལ་ག་ནེ་ཁྱོང་བཏང་ཅག།

'i-dsad = this much, by this time. *de-dsad* = That much, by that time. *gi-dsad* = How much? By what time?

འི་ཛད། དེ་ཛད། གི་ཛད།

či-žig = Something. *či-žig -za-na.* = During sometime, during some event. *či-žig za-na-ŋa de-ru yod-ten.* = During certain event I was there.

ཅི་ཞིག།། ཅི་ཞིག་ཟ་ན།། ཅི་ཞིག་་ཟ་ན་ང་དེ་རུ་ཡོད་ཏེན།།

čaŋ: This is a term used before a negative auxiliary. *či-'ang* = What-also. *čaŋ ma-nag.* = It is not that. *ŋe čaŋ ma-bčos.* = I did not do. *ŋe čang mi-šes.* = I don't know. *'i-ru-ni čaŋ mi-nug.* = It is not here.

ཅང་།། ཅང་མ་ནག།། ငེ་ཅང་མི་ཤེས།། ངེ་ཅང་མ་བཅོས།། འི་རུ་ནི་ཅང་མི་ནུག།།

yin-tshad = Proper measure. *či yin-tshad (whatever it may be) rmur btang 'dug.* = He chews everything/whatever he gets. *gaŋ yin tshad la laŋ čha-rug.* = He goes anywhere (without caring).

ཅི་ཡིན་ཚད་རྨུར་བཏང་འདུག།། གང་ཡིན་ཚད་ལ་ལང་ཆ་རུག།།

12
Interrogative

12.1. Interrogative pronouns

12.1.1. The words of interrogative pronoun are: *su* = Who, *či* = What, *gaŋ* =Which. *či-la.* = Why. *su yoŋ 'dug.* = Who-come-is. Who is coming? *khyod-la či dgos.* = You-to what-want. What do you want? *khyo-'e khaŋ-pa gaŋ-de yin.* = You-of–house-which-one-is. Which is your house? *mug-zhug či-len gaŋ-len bčo-rug.* = Greedy-what-take-which-take-do-is. The greedy is looking, what to take and which one to take.

སུ།། ཅི།། གང་།། ཅི་ལ།། སུ་ཡོང་འདུག།། ཁྱོད་ལ་ཅི་དགོས།། ཁྱོ་འེ་ཁང་པ་གང་དེ་ཡིན།། ཁོ་སུག་ཞུག་། ཅི་ལེན།གང་ལེན།བཅོ་རུག།།

12.1.2. When interrogative terms are reduplicated they give a plural effect. *su-su.* = Who and who? *či-či* = What kinds? *tsug tsug.* = In what manners? *su-su-la či-či dgos-še yod si-rig-la 'dri btoŋ.* = Ask everybody who wants what. *lug gaŋ–gaŋ mi-nug.* = Which and which sheep is missing? *ma-mo se-bo de daŋ ra-ma khra-bo de mi-nug.* = The ash-coloured sheep and piebald goat are not there.

སུ་སུ།། ཅི་ཅི།། ཙུག་ཙུག།། སུ་སུ་ལ་ཅི་ཅི་དགོས་ཤེ་ཡོད་སི་རིག་ལ་འདྲི་བཏོང་།། ལུག་གང་གང་མི་ནུག།། མ་མོ་སེ་བོ་དེ་དང་ར་མ་ཁྲ་བོ་དེ་མི་ནུག།།

12.1.3. By placing the conjunctive particle *daŋ* in between the reduplicated interrogative pronoun it becomes a positive statement. It does not ask for answer. *či daŋ či mi-nug.* = What is not there? (=There are numerous things.) *su daŋ su yoŋ-de mi-nug.* = Who and who has not come? (There had come many kinds of people.) *či daŋ gaŋ za-čag.* = What and which one to eat? (It cannot be decided what and which one to eat.).

དང་།། ཅི་དང་ཅི་མི་ནུག།། སུ་དང་སུ་ཡོང་དེ་མི་ནུག།། ཅི་དང་གང་ཟ་ཅག།།

12.2. **Interrogative adverbials:** These are*: nam* = When, *ga-ru* = Where. *tsug* = How. *tsam* = How much, etc. *khyod-la dŋul tsam-yod.* = How many rupees do you have? (How much money do you have*?*) *khyod nam yoŋ.* = When did you come? *kho ga-ru 'dug.* = Where is he? *kho-'e tsug bčos-soŋ.* = How did he do?

ནམ། ག་རུ། ཙུག། ཁྱོད་ལ་དངུལ་ཙམ་ཡོད།། ཁྱོད་ནམ་ཡོང་།།
ཁོ་ག་རུ་འདུག།ཁོ་འི་ཙུག་བཅོས་སོང་།།

12.3.1. Many verbs are converted to interrogative form by reduplicating the end letter of the word alongwith the attached vowel sign. The following are verbs ending in the ten rjes-'jug.

log-če, laŋ-če, sdad-če, sñan-če, lab-če, rtsem-če, čha-če zer-če, sil-če, śes- śe. These can be used in both the forms with the additive letter and without additive. Thus in the first person: *log-ga? log-če-'a*? = Should I turn back?; *laŋ-ŋ? laŋ-če-'a*? = Should I stand up? *śes-śag-ga. śes-śe-'a.* = Can I recognize?

Second person *log-kan-na? log-gen-na*? = Will you return? *sdad-kan-na? sdad-ten-'a?* = Will you stay?

Third person: *lab-ben-na?*= Will he talk? *rtsem-men-na*? = Will he sew? The difference between the forms in the second and third persons is minor.

12.3.2. Sentences end with a helping verb. The ultimate letter of the end word in the sentence is reduplicated and then it transforms into interrogative. The helping verbs become: *yod-ta, yin-na, 'dug-ga,* etc. The letter *da* in *yod* and similarly in all cases becomes *ta*.

i. **Present.** *yoŋ 'dug*. = (He) is coming. *yoŋ 'dug-ga*? = Is he coming? *yoŋ-ŋa yod-ta.* = Are you coming? *yoŋ-ben-na.* = Did you come? *yoŋ-'en-na*? = Will you come? yo*ŋ-ŋa-nag-ga.* = Will he come? *yoŋ-čen-na.* = Will he come? *khyod de-ru yod-ta.* = Are you there? *čha-kan-na.* = Do you want to go? *yoŋ-kan na, yoŋ-ka-man.* = Whether you want to come or not? *yoŋ-če kham rag-ga me-rag.* = Coming-desire-do have- not have. Whether you are willing to come or not?

ང་ཡོང་ང་།། ང་ཡོང་ཅེ་འ།། ཡོང་འདུག་འ། ང་ཆ་ཅེ་འ།། ཁྱོད་དེ་རུ་ཡོད་ཏ།།
ཆ་ཀན་ན།། ཡོང་ཀན་ན།ཡོང་ཀ་མན།། ཡོང་ཅེ་ཁམ།རག་ག་མེ་རག།། ཡོང་འདུག།།
ཡོང་ང་ཡོད་ཏ།། ཡོང་བེན་ན།། ཡོང་ང་ནག་ག།། ཡོང་ཅེན་ན།།

ii. **Past**: *kho yoŋ soŋ-ŋa.* = Has he come? *kho yoŋ khag-ga.* = Has he come? *kho yoŋ-dog-ga.* = Has he come? *'dug-pen-na?* = Was he there? *kho laŋ ma-soŋ ŋa?* = Perhaps he has gone away, isn't it? *khyod da-ruŋ ma-soŋ-ma.* = You have still not gone, is it?

ཁོ་ཡོང་སོང་ང༎ ཁོ་ཡོང་ཁག་ག༎ ཁོ་ཡོང་དོག་ག༎ འདུག་པེན་ན༎ ཁོ་ལང་མ་སོང་ང༎ ཁྱོད་ད་རུང་མ་སོང་མ༎

iii. **Future**: *khyod tho-re yoŋ-ŋen-na.* = Will you come tomorrow? *kho tho-re yoŋ-ŋen-na.*= Will he come tomorrow? *kho tho-re yoŋ- čen-na. kho tho-re yoŋ-ŋa nag-ga. kho tho-re yoŋ-čag-ga.* = Will he come tomorrow? *kho tho-re yoŋ-ŋa yod-kag-ga.* = Is there any possibility that he will come tomorrow? *ŋa gčig-gčig čha khyud-ča-'a.* = Can I go alone? *nam šig yoŋ-čen-na.* = When may he come? *yoŋ-čen-na man.* = Whether he will come or not? *yoŋ-če čha-če yoŋ-ŋen-na.* = Will it be possible for me to come? *khyod yoŋ-laŋ man-ma.* = Is it that you are not coming? *tho-re brtan brtan 'sdad-če bčos-de yoŋ-ŋen-ma.* = Tomorrow will you make it sure to come for staying? *da ŋa nam yoŋ-če.*= Now when should I come ?

ཁྱོད་ཐོ་རེ་ཡོང་ངེན་ན༎ ཁོ་ཐོ་རེ་ཡོང་ངེན་ན༎ ཁོ་ཐོ་རེ་ཡོང་ཅེན་ན༎ ཁོ་ཐོ་རེ་ཡོང་ང་ནག་ག༎ ཁོ་ཐོ་རེ་ཡོང་ཅག་ག༎ ཁོ་ཐོ་རེ་ཡོང་ང་ཡོད་ཀག་ག༎ ང་གཅིག་གཅིག་ཆ་འཁྱུད་ཅ་འ༎ ནམ་ཤིག་ཡོང་ཅེན་ན༎ ཡོང་ཅེན་ན་མན༎ ཡོང་ཅེ་ཆ་ཅེ་ཡོང་ངེན་ན༎ ཁྱོད་ཡོང་ལང་མན་མ༎ ཐོ་རེ་བརྟན་བརྟན་སྡད་ཅེ་བཅོས་དེ་ཡོང་ངེན་མ༎ ད་ང་ནམ་ཡོང་ཅེ༎

12.4. The suffix *sa* after a verb indicates question mark. *sdad-sa* = Did you stay? *mthoŋ-sa.* = Did you see? *čhom-sa.* = Have you become ready? *bčos-sa.* =Did you do.?

སྡད་ས༎ མཐོང་ས༎ ཆོམ་ས༎ ཆོམ་ས༎ བཅོས་ས༎

12.5. The letter *ma* at the end of a positive statement asks for its confirmation. *bsod-nams yin ma.* = It is Sonam, are you? *khyod yoŋ -ma.* = You have come, is it? *kho čha-rug ma.*= He is going, is it? *'i naŋ khyo-'e yin ma.* = This is your room, is it?

ཁྱོད་ཡོང་།མ༎ ཁོ་ཆ་རུག།མ༎ འི་ནང་ཁྱོ་འེ་ཡིན།མ༎

12.6. Imperative, negative: Examples: *kho man-na su nag.*= If it is not he, who it could be otherwise? *khyod ma-čha-na ŋa laŋ čhen.* = If you don't want to go, I will go. *či bčo-čen-na, zer btaŋ-čen-na, bor btaŋ-če.* = What to do, should I say, or leave it? *de ma-na* (*de man-na*). = Otherwise. If not. *či-la man.* = Why not? *su-la man.* = To whom not? *gang- la man.* = To which not?

ཁོ་མན་ན་སུ་ནག།།   ཁྱོད་མ་ཆ་ན།ང་ལང་ཆེན།། ཅི་བཅོ་ཅེན་ན།ཟེར་བཏང་ཅེན་ན།བོར་བཏང་ཅེ།། དེ་མ་ན།དེ་མན་ན།། ཅི་ལ་མན།། སུ་ལ་མན།། གང་ལ་མན།།

13

Conjunctives

13.1.The common conjunctive particle is *daŋ* which means 'and'.

Sentences: *ŋa daŋ khyod.* = I and you. *lug daŋ ra-ma.* = Sheep and goats. *zlar daŋ ñima.* = The Moon and the Sun. *khab daŋ skud-pa.* = Needle and thread. *lug daŋ ra-ma daŋ g-yag daŋ.* = Sheep, goat and yak.

In literary practice in a sentence the conjunctive particle is added after each item in case the number of items are more than two. This practice is not followed always in colloquy.

ང་དང་ཁྱོད།། ལུག་དང་ར་མ།། ཟླར་དང་ཉི་མ།། ཁབ་དང་སྐུད་པ།། ལུག་དང་ར་མ་དང་གཡག་དང་།།

13.1.1. The term *daŋ* has some other usages. Here it means 'with'. *sman čhu-khol daŋ zo.* = Take medicine with boiled water. *le-na daŋ ral 'aŋ yoŋ-ŋa nag.* = Pashmina wool is also accompanied by goat's hair. *khyod-la či 'brel-la šiŋ-daŋ, khaŋ-pa bčo-laŋ med čaŋ med.* = What concern do you have with wood, you have not to construct house, or to do anything else.

སྨན།ཆུ་ཁོལ།དང་ཟོ།། ལེ་ན་དང་རལ་འང་ཡོང་ང་ནག།། ཁྱོད་ལ་ཅི་འབྲེལ་ལ། ཤིང་དང་།ཁང་པ་བཅོ་ལང་མེད།ཅང་མེད།།

3.1.2. When a pronoun word is repeated and the term *daŋ* is placed in the middle, the term means many. *su daŋ su mi-nug.*who-and-who-not-is. = There were many kinds of people. *ŋe khyo- 'e phyil-la či daŋ či ma-bčos.* = What did not I do for you? *ŋa-la či daŋ či med.* = What don't Ihave? (I have many things.).

སུ་དང་སུ་མི་ནུག།། ངེ་ཁྱོ་འེ་ཕྱིལ་ལ་ཅི་དང་ཅི་མ་བཅོས།། ང་ལ་ཅི་དང་ཅི་མེད།།

13.1.3. In the following proverb the term '*daŋ*' functions as a disjunctive.

so-med zas daŋ bral, nor-med gñen daŋ bral. = When one looses teeth one is deprived of food, when one becomes wealthless one is separated from one's relatives.

སོ་མེད་ཟས་དང་འབྲལ།ནོར་མེད་གཉེན་དང་འབྲལ།།

13.1.4. In the following sentences the term functions as an imperative. *hrib-čig šog daŋ.* = Come here for a moment. *zer btoŋ daŋ.* = J*ust s*peak out. *kho la ltos daŋ.* = Just look at him. *khyod loŋ btoŋ daŋ.* = You just stand up. *thaŋ-ka-la sdod btoŋ daŋ.* = You sit down.

ཧྲིབ་ཅིག་ཤོག་དང་།། ཟེར་བཏོང་དང་།། ཁོ་ལ་ལྟོས་དང་།། ཁྱོད་ལོང་བཏོང་དང་།། ཐང་ཀ་ལ་སྡོད་བཏོང་དང་།།

Sentences: *dge-paŋ zla re-re daŋ mčhod-ta nag.* = The deity Gepang is propitiated every month. *ŋa lo-daŋ mtsho mjal-la-la čha-'a yod.* = I go on pilgrimage to Riwalsar every year. *mi-daŋ dŋul gñis-gñis yoŋ-če rag.* = There comes two rupees in the share of each person. *yoŋ-ŋa čig-daŋ 'khrug-pa btaŋ-ŋa la zug-soŋ.* = As soon as he reached, he started querrelling. *khyi daŋ mi ga-ru 'dra-čen.* = What comparison is there between man and dog?

དགེ་པང་ཟླ་རེ་རེ་དང་མཆོད་ཏ་ནག།ང་ལོ་དང་མཚོ་མཇལ་ལ་ལ་ཆ་འ་ཡོད།།

མི་དང་དངུལ་གཉིས་གཉིས་ཡོང་ཅེ་རག།། ཡོང་ང་ཅིག་དང་།འཁྲུག་པ་བཏང་ང་ལ་ཟུག་སོང་།། ཁྱི་དང་མི་ག་རུ་འདྲ་ཅག།།

13.2. ***'aŋ:*** . A similar term is ***'aŋ.*** It means 'and' and 'also'. *'i-'aŋ btoŋ de 'aŋ btoŋ, či thob-thob si-rig btoŋ.*= Give this and also that, whatever you get, give everything. *'i-'aŋ mi-bčos de-'aŋ mi-bčos, de-ne či bčo-kan.* = You want to do neither this nor that, then what do you want to do? *'i pu-la de su-la-'aŋ gad ñan-laŋ med-kan žig 'dug.* = This straw shoe fits none.

འི་འང་བཏོང་དེ་འང་བཏོང་།ཅི་ཐོབ་ཐོབ་སི་རིག་བཏོང་།།འི་འང་མི་བཅོས།དེ་འང་མི་བཅོས།དེ་ནེ་ཅི་བཅོ་ཀན།། འི་པུ་ལ་དེ་སུ་ལ་འང་གད་ཉན་ལང་མེད་ཀན་ཞིག་འདུག།

This term ***'aŋ*** used repeatedly gives the sense of 'neither nor'. *ŋe su-la-'aŋ rgyal-la 'aŋ bčo-'a med, thu-'a 'aŋ bčo-'a med.* = I do, neither good, nor bad, to anybody. *su-la-'aŋ ŋe rgyal daŋ thu-'a bčo-'a med.* = I do not do good or bad to anybody.

དེ་སུ་ལ་འདང་ཀྱལ་ལ་འདང་བཙོ་འ་མེད།བྱུ་འ་འདང་བཙོ་འ་མེད།། སུ་ལ་འདང་དེ་ཀྱལ་དང་བྱུ་འ་བཙོ་འ་མེད།།

13.3. '*yaŋ*'means 'again'. *kho yaŋ yoŋ 'dug.* = He is coming again. *kho yaŋ yaŋ yoŋ 'dug* = He comes again and again. *tham-phog gčig yaŋ bčos btoŋ.* = Turn-one-again-do-give. Do it once again.

ཁོ་ཡང་ཡོང་འདུག།། ཁོ་ཡང་ཡང་།ཡོང་འདུག།།ཐམ་ཕོག་གཅིག་ཡང་བཙོས་བཏོང་།།

Sentences: *yoŋ-mkhan čha-mkhan thams-čad si mi 'un la ju bčo-'en si daŋ dgon-pa la phyag dpul-len čha-rug.* = Comer-goer-all-by-men-to-salute-doing-by-and -monastery-to-saluting-go-is. All those who are coming and going, are going by saluting the people and saluting by folded hands to the monastery. *tho tsog-se čig-gaŋ 'ang mi-šes-mkhan žig 'dug.* = Pillar-like-one-which-too-not-know-the one-a-is. He is like a pillar, knowing nothing.

ཡོང་མཁན་ཆ་མཁན་ཐམས་ཅད་སི་མི་འུན་ལ་ཛུ་བཙོ་འེན་སི་དང་དགོན་པ་ལ་ཕྱག་དཔུལ་ལེན་ཆ་རུག།། ཐོ་ཚོག་སེ་ཅིག་གང་འང་མི་ཤེས་མཁན་ཞིག་འདུག།།

či-la zer-na. = Because. *di-riŋ ŋa ba-zar-la čha mi-khyud, chi-la zer-na di-riŋ tshad-pa maŋ-po rag.* = Today-I-bazar-to-go-not-able, -why-say-if-today-warmth-much-is. Today I cannot go to bazaar because it is very hot.

ཅི་ལ་ཟེར་ན།། དེ་རིང་ང་བ་ཟར་ལ་ཆ་མི་འཁྱུད།ཅི་ལ་ཟེར་ན།དེ་རིང་ཚད་པ་མང་པོ་རག།།

13.4. Following are some particles used as disjunctives. *yaŋ-na ni. ya-na-ni.*= Either. *de-man-na. de-man-na-ni.* = Otherwise.

ཡང་ན་ནི།། ཡ་ན་ནི།། དེ་མན་ན།། དེ་མན་ན་ནི།

Examples: *yaŋ-na ni sdod btoŋ, yaŋ-na-ni loŋ soŋ.* = Either sit down or go away. *ya-na-ni sdod-btoŋ, de man-na loŋ soŋ-ni.* = Either sit down/stay here or go away. *ya-na-ni bsod-nams de man-na bkra-šis su la zer na-'aŋ gčig-gčig-la zer-čag.* = Either Sonam or Tashi, whoever it may be, we will ask to one of them.

ཡང་ན་ནི་སྡོད་བཏོང་།ཡང་ན་ནི་ལོང་སོང་།། ཡ་ན་ནི་སྡོད་བཏོང་།དེ་མན་ན།ལོང་སོང་ནི།། ཡ་ན་ནི་བསོད་ནམས།དེ་མན་ན་བཀྲ་ཤིས། སུ་ལ་ཟེར་ན་འང་། གཅིག་གཅིག་ལ་ཟེར་ཅག།

14

Particles

There are number of particles which are suffixed to a word or clause and they function to create variations in the meaning. Some of the important particles are given as follows:

14.1. mkhan and mkhan-pa

These two particles *mkhan* and *mkhan-pa* join with verbs and they form noun, indicating the action or the doer of that action. They are often used with the same meaning. But there is a slight distinction. We take for example the two verbs: *čha-če* = to go, *'bri-če* = to write. čha-če + mkhan = čha-mkhan. Goer. 'bri-če + mkhan = 'bri-mkhan. Writer/scribe. *ha-'i čha-mkhan su nag.* = Who is that, the one who is going? *yi-ge 'bri-mkhan su yin nag.* = Who is that, the one who is writing letter?

ཆ་ཅེ།། འབྲི་ཅེ།། མཁན།། ཧ་འི་ཆ་མཁན་སུ་ནག།། ཡི་གེ་འབྲི་མཁན་སུ་ཡིན་ནག།།

14.1.1. Here the two terms suffixed with *mkhan* indicate a person in an action. By suffixing the particle *–pa,* like *'bri-mkhan-pa,* also we get the same result, but is slightly more specific. Now we take two other verbs *mthung-če* = to drink, and *'gril-če* = to fall down. Then we ask two questions.

i. *'i mthung-mkhan su nag.* = Who is this who is drinking? /Who is this who has drunk this?

ii. *'i mthung-mkhan či nag.*= What is this which you are drinking? What is this that you drank?

iii. *'i 'gril-mkhan su nag.* = Who is this who is falling? Who is this who has fallen?

iv. *'i 'gril-mkhan či nag.* = What is this that is falling? What is this that has fallen?

Out of the above four the example numbers i and iii indicate a doer of an act or a person. Here one can add the particle *–pa.* This particle cannot be suffixed with the other two which indicate a thing or an article.

ཆ་མཁན།། འབྲི་མཁན།། མཐུང་མཁན་སུ་ནག།། འགྲིལ་མཁན་ཅི་ནག།།

Sentences: *kha-čig yoŋ-mkhan kha-čig čha-mkhan, su-'i šes-šag su yin su man.* = Some are coming, (are comers) some are going (are goers), who can recognize who the one is and who is not. *čig-gaŋ-'aŋ mi-šes-mkhan.* = Totally ignorant, knowing nothing. *ŋa bčo-mkhan kho gšig-mkhan.*= I am the creator and he the destroyer. *re-bag la čha-mkhan-pa da-ruŋ su-su 'dug.* = Who are more others going to Triloknath? *bo-mo glu bde-mo btang-mkhan-pa de šim-la ne nag.* = The girl who sings songs beautifully is from Shimla. *kho dran-'dra šes-mkhan su-'aŋ med.* = There is none knowledgeable equal to him.

ཁ་ཅིག་ཡོང་མཁན། ཁ་ཅིག་ཆ་མཁན། སུ་འི་ཤེས་ཤག་སུ་ཡིན་སུ་མན།། ཅིག་གང་འང་མི་ཤེས་མཁན།། ང་བཅོ་མཁན།ཁོ་གཤིག་མཁན།། རེ་བག་ལ་ཆ་མཁན་པ་དར་རུང་སུ་སུ་འདུག།། བོ་མོ་གླུ་བདེ་མོ་བཏང་མཁན་པ་དེ་ཤིམ་ལཱ་ནེ་ནག།། ཁོ་དྲན་འདྲ་ཤེས་མཁན་སུ་འང་མེད།།

Sentences: *soŋ-mkhan* (past) = One who has gone. *čha-mkhan* (present). = One who is going. *khrus-mkhan.*= Those who have taken bath, that which has been washed. *'i ku-šu-gun khrus-mkhan yin.* = These are apples which have been washed. *khrus bor-mkhan.* = That which has been washed.

སོང་མཁན།། ཆ་མཁན།། ཁྲུས་མཁན།། འི་ཀུ་ཤུ་གུན་ཁྲུས་མཁན་ཡིན།། ཁྲུས་བོར་མཁན།།

14.1.2. In the following examples the term *mkhan* appears to function like a particle of the past tense. *las-kha tshar-mkhan yin-če 'dug.* = Work-finsh-have-appears-is. The work appears to have finished. *khyo-'e kho-la rdung-mkhan yin-khag.* = You-by-he-to-beat-have-is-might. You might have beaten him. *'i pi-ši si di-riŋ yaŋ 'o-ma si-rig-ldag-mkhan yin-če 'dug.*= This cat appears to have licked the whole milk today again.

ལས་ཁ་ཆར་མཁན་ཡིན་ཅེ་འདུག།། ཁྱོ་འེ་ཁོ་ལ་རྫུང་མཁན་ཡིན་ཁག།། འི་ཕེ་ཤེ་སི་དེ་རིང་ཡང་འོ་མ་སི་རིག་ལྷག་མཁན་ཡིན་ཅེ་འདུག།།

kha: In the following examples the particle *kha* also appears to function like *mkhan*. Thus *zer kha/mkhan na ma zer mkhan su'i šes.* = Whether he told or not, who knows. *či laŋ soŋ kha/mkhan na.* = What might have happened? *da sleb kha/mkhan man na.* = Has he not arrived by now (It appears that now he has arrived).

ཟེར་ཁ་ན།མ་ཟེར་མཁན།སུ་འི་ཤེས།། ཅི་ལང་སོང་ཁ་ན།། ད་སླེབ་ཁ་མན་ན།།

14.2. ***kan***: This term functions in two ways. *kan* is an auxiliary expressing a wish, indicative of future tense. Thus *ŋa čha-kan.* = I want to go, or also, I will go. *ŋa yoŋ kan.* = I want to come/ I will come. *ŋe btaŋ-kan.* = I want to give./ I will give.

khyo-ye či bčo-kan. = What do you want to do?

khyod ga-ru čha-kan. = Where are you going?

kho-'e btaŋ-kan zer-rug. = He says he will give.

ང་ཆ་ཀན།། ང་ཡོང་ཀན།། ངེ་བཏང་ཀན།། ཁྱོ་འེ་བཏང་ཀན་ན།། ཁྱོ་འེ་ཅི་བཅོ་ཀན།། ཁྱོད་ག་རུ་ཆ་ཀན།། ཁོ་འེ་བཏང་ཀན་ཟེར་རུག།།

i. *kan* joined with some words expresses possessiveness. Like: *yod-kan* = Rich. *med-kan* = Poor. *gtsaŋ-kan* = Pauper, etc. *kha-čig yod-kan, kha-čig med-kan yod-kag; si-rig tsog-se med-kag.* = Some are possessed of, some are not possessed of: all are not similar. *yod-kan med-kan si-rig btaŋ-dog.* = He has given everything whatever he possessed.

ཁ་ཅིག།ཡོད་ཀན།ཁ་ཅིག།མེད་ཀན་ཡོད་ཀག།མི་སི་རིག་ཚོག་སེ་མེད་ཀག།། ཡོད་ཀན། མེད་ཀན་སི་རིག༣་བཏང་དོག།།

14.3. *Laŋ: i. laŋ-če* is a verb meaning to get up and to stand up. *kho laŋ 'dug.* = He-stand-is. He gets up or stands up. *kho da-rung ma-laŋ-ŋa 'dug.* = He-still-not-standing-is. He has not yet awakened.

ལང་ཅེ།། ཁོ་ལང་འདུག།། ཁོ་ད་རུང་མ་ལང་ང་འདུག།།

ii.The word *laŋ* joins with some verbs and functioning like an adverb indicates the purpose. Thus *čha-če* (to go) + *laŋ* = *čha-laŋ. ŋa žiŋ-ka la čha-laŋ yin či-re khur-laŋ ta med-ta.* = I-field-to go-for-is what-some-carry-for-if-not-if. I am going to the field, whether there is anything for carrying. It can be used with any verb. *tho-re ŋa ñuŋti la čha-laŋ yin.* = Tomorrow-I-Kullu-to-go-for-is. Tomorrow I have to go to Kullu.

ང་ཞིང་ཀ་ལ་ཆ་ལང་ཡིན།ཅི་རེ་ཁུར་ལང་མེད་ཏ།། ཐོ་རེ་ང་ཉུང་ཏི་ལ་ཆ་ལང་ཡིན།།

iv. It is found used before some verbs like *čha-če* and *btaŋ -če. loŋ–soŋ.* = Go away. Here it adds emphasis to the verb *soŋ* – imperative 'go'. But in the expression *loŋ btoŋ* = Get up **or** stand up, *laŋ* itself functions as verb and the second term *btoŋ* functions as a secondary verb to add force to the main verb *loŋ*. In this mmner *laŋ čha-če* means to go away and *laŋ btaŋ-če* means to stand up. *laŋ yoŋ če.* = To come up.

ལང་ཆ་ཅེ།། ལང་བཏང་ཅེ།། ལང་ཡོང་ཅེ།

14.4. *čan:* The particle '*čan*' is equivalent to Hindi 'wala', which means the one possessed of the quality of the term with which it is suffixed. The particle joined with a noun changes it into an adjective. *rin-čan.* = Costly. *ŋad-čan.* = Efficient. *so-de-čan.* = Lucky. *šad-čan.* = Powerful. *dab-čan.* = Haughty. *sems-čan.* = A living being. *ša-čan* = Healthy. *bčud-čan* = nutritious. *drin- čan* = kind. *sran (şan)-čan* = tolerant. *khag-čan* = Important. *las-kha khag-čan gya-ma sŋon-sŋon-la bčos btoŋ.*= Firstly finish the urgent works. *kho lo brgya soŋ-de mi-tshe sgaŋ-pa thob-de so-de-čan nag.* = He is lucky that he has lived hundred years, attaining complete human life.

རིན་ཅན། ངད་ཅན། སོ་དེ་ཅན། ཤད་ཅན། དབ་ཅན། སེམས་ཅན། ཤ་ཅན། བཅུད་ཅན། ཁག་ཅན།། ལས་ཁ་ཁག་ཅན་གྱ་མ་སྔོན་སྔོན་ལ་བཅོས་བཏོང་།། ཁོ་ལོ་བརྒྱ་སོང་དེ་མི་ཚེ་སྒང་པ་ཐོབ་མཁན་སོ་དེ་ཅན་ཡིན།།

14.5. *šan:* This is like the particle 'čan'. *šug-šan.* = Efficient, Fast. '*phel-šan, boŋ-šan* = expandable. *'i 'bras 'phel-šan 'dug.*= This rice has the quality of expanding./ This rice expands well.

ཕྱུག་ཤན།། པོང་ཤན།། འཕེལ་ཤན།། འི་འབྲས་འཕེལ་ཤན་འདུག།།

14.6. *le-ka:* This term indicates a moment of action or a point of time. *nyi-ma šar-le ka 'dug.* = The sun is about to appear. *las-kha zin-le ka la kho sleb soŋ.* = He reached, when the work was about to finish.

ཉི་མ་ཤར་ལེ་ཀ་འདུག།།ལས་ཁ་ཟིན་ལེ་ཀ་ལ་ཁོ་སླེབ་སོང་།།

14.7. *khyad:* 'worth'. *su la-'aŋ zer-khyad mi-nug.* = It is worthless to ask anybody. *khyo-raŋ yoŋ-khyad med-kag.* = It is not worth coming for you.

སུ་ལ་འང་ཟེར་ཁྱད་མི་ནུག།། ཁྱོ་རང་ཡོང་ཁྱད་མེད་ཀག།།

14.8. *ñan:* 'worth'. *kho la ni lag-pa thug-ñan med.*= It is not worth touching him (He is too sensitive). *kho-la zer-ñan med.* = It is not worth saying him (He reacts instantly).

ཁོ་ལ་ནི་ལག་པ་ཐུག་ཉན་མེད།། ཁོ་ལ་ཟེར་ཉན་མེད།།

14.9. *sa:* a place or space. *bor-sa.*= A place to keep a thing. *za-če za-sa.*= A place to eat meal. *ŋa-ža la sdad-sa med.* = We have no place to live. *khyod-la yoŋ-sa med.* = You are not allowed to come. *'i-ne čha-sa med.* = You cannot go from here. *'i-ne čha-sa mi-nug.* = There is no space to go through from here.

བོར་ས།། ཟ་ཅེ་ཟ་ས།། ང་ཞ་ལ་སྡད་ས་མེད།། ཁྱོད་ལ་ཡོང་ས་མེད།།འི་ནེ་ཆ་ས་མེད།། འི་ནེ་ཆ་ས་མི་ནུག།།

iii. It functions as a question mark. *sleb sa.* = Have you reached? *za-če bzos-sa* = Have you taken your meal?

སླེབ་ས།། ཟ་ཅེ་བཟོས་ས།།

14.10. ka. This particle is found used in the following manner

i. This is a part of a word.

tshur-ka. = This side. *čuŋ-ka.* = The red beaked

crow. *gnam-ka* = Sky. *lam-ka* = Path.

ཚུར་ཀ།། ཅུང་ཀ།། གནམ་ཀ།། ལམ་ཀ།།

ii. It functions as an emphatic. *kho-ka.* = Particularly he. *su-ka.* = Who particularly? *lem-ka.* = Just now. *kho-la men-tog dmar-pho ka dgos-lo.* = He says, he wants particularly the red flower.

ཁོ་ཀ།། སུ་ཀ།། ལེམ་ཀ།། ཁོ་ལ་མེན་ཏོག་དམར་པོ་ཀ་དགོས་ལོ།།

iii. In the following sentences it gives a different meaning. *tsher-ka ma tsher.* = Don't worry at all. *nam-ka čha-'en.* = When will he go? (Cannot say.). *ŋa yoŋ-ka ma-yoŋ.* = I didn't come at all. *yoŋ-ka man.*= I don't want to come/ I will not come. *čha-ka man.* = I don't want to go./ I will not go. *zer-ka man.* = I don't want to say./ I will not say.

ཚེར་ཀ་མ་ཚེར།། ནམ་ཀ་ཆ་འེན།། ང་ཡོང་ཀ་མ་ཡོང་།། ཡོང་ཀ་མན། ཆ་ཀ་མན།། ཟེར་ཀ་མན།།

14.11. *ki.* Words suffixed with the article *ki* are adjectival or adverbial. *nar-ki* = specially. *lug-ki.* = soft. *čab-ki* = silently. *tsad-ki* = slightly. *šug-ki* = quickly. *rtsad-ki 'thog-na 'gul čha-rug.* = It moves even by merely touching. *kho thug-ga la mdaŋ sŋa-mo ne-mad ne ŋa nar-ki soŋ-ben.* = He-meet-for-yesterday-morning-early-from-I-specially-went. I went yesterday early morning specially to meet him.

ནར་ཀི།། ལུག་ཀི།། ཅབ་ཀི།། ཙད་ཀི།། ཤུག་ཀི།། ཙད་ཀི་འཐོག་ན་འགུལ་ཆ་རུག།། ཁོ་ཐུག་ག་ལ་མདང་སྔ་མོ་ནེ་མད་ནེ་ང་ནར་ཀི་སོང་བེན།།

14.12. *go:* It implies necessity. *ŋa la čha-go med.*= Me-to-go-purpose-not. I don't need to go. *khyod la či zer-go rag.*= You-to-what-say-purpose-is. Why is it necessary for you to speak? *da ŋa-la sruŋ-go yoŋ-če med.* = Now-me-to-gurd-purpose-coming-not. Now I will not have to wait.

ང་ལ་ཆ་གོ་མེད།། ཁྱོད་ལ་ཅི་ཟེར་གོ་རག།། ད་ང་ལ་སྲུང་གོ་ཡོང་ཅེ་མེད།།

14.13 pa: This is part of some words.

i. *dud-pa* = smoke. *log-pa* = The outer garment, cloak of sheep skin worn over woolen cloak. *khog-pa.* =The bust.

དུད་པ།། ལོག་པ།། ཁོག་པ།།

ii. A word with the particle shows belongingness. *tshoŋ*= trade, tshoŋ-pa = trader. *thag-riŋ* = distance. *thag-riŋ-pa* = one belonging to the distant land. *las-med-pa* = The one without work, idle. *Gar-ža-pa* =One belonging to Garzha, Lahul.

ཚོང་། ཚོང་པ། ཐག་རིང་། ཐག་རིང་པ། ལས་མེད་པ། གར་ཞ་པ།

iii. The suffix '*pa'* with the following words lays emphasis to the statement. *yoŋ-ben-pa.* = In fact I came. *yin-nag-pa.* = In fact, it is. *btaŋ-ben-pa* = In fact I gave. *yoŋ-ŋa nag-pa.* = He will come certainly.

ཡོང་བེན་པ།། ཡིན་ནག་པ།། བཏང་བེན་པ།། ཡོང་ང་ནག་པ།།

14.14. *na.* The word means 'if'. *kho de-ru yod ka na.* = If he is there. *kho la šiŋ yod ka na med-kan.* = Whether he has wood or not? *kho ma yoŋ-na.* = If he does come. *kho yoŋ na ta či tshi-ri.* = If he comes then what worry? (there would be no worry.). *či bčo-'a yod ka-na yoŋ-laŋ ka me-rag.* = What-doing-might be-if-coming-same-not-is. What he might be doing, he is not still coming. *khyo-raŋ čha-na loŋ-soŋ.* = If you wish to go, you can go.

ཁོ་དེ་རུ་ཡོད་ཀ་ན།། ཁོ་ལ་ཤིང་ཡོད་ཀ་ན་མེད་ཀན།། ཁོ་མ་ཡོང་ན།། ཁོ་ཡོང་ན་ཏ་ཅི་ཚེ་རི།། ཅི་བཅོ་འ་ཡོད་ཀ་ན།ཡོང་ལང་ཀ་མེ་རག།། ཁྱོ་རང་ཆ་ན་ལོང་སོང་།།

14.15. *ta:*

i. It means 'if'. *yoŋ-na-ta.* = If he comes. *yod-na-ta.*= If there is. *kho sdad-na-ta.* = If he stays. *khyod yod-pa-na-ta čig-gaŋ- 'aŋ čha-če med-kag.* = You-were-if-a-which-too-going-not-would. There would have happened nothing, if you had been there. *'i-zug-la-ta ŋa-'aŋ yoŋ-če rag-pa* = This-manner-for-although-I-too-coming-wish. Although I also wanted to come.

ཡོང་ན་ཏ།། ཡོད་ན་ཏ།། ཁོ་སྡད་ན་ཏ།། ཁྱོད་ཡོད་པ་ན་ཏ་ཅིག་གང་འང་ཆ་ཅེ་མེད་ཀག།། འི་ཟུག་ལ་ཏ་ང་འང་ཡོང་ཅེ་རག་པ།།

ii. Here *ta* gives a little different meaning. *daŋ- śig kho-la naŋ-la-ta yoŋ-če btoŋ.*= For the time being-he-to-in-to-coming-give. Firstly let him come in. *kho-la zer-če-ta btoŋ.* = Let him say.

དང་ཤིག་ཁོ་ལ་ནང་ལ་ཏ་ཡོང་ཅེ་བཏོང་།། ཁོ་ལ་ཟེར་ཅེ་ཏ་བཏོང་།།

14.16 . *ma.*

i. It shows the place or the position. *gzur-ma.*= The one on the edge. *yog-ma* = The one below. *dgyen-ma.* = The one above. *sŋon-ma* = The former.

གཟུར་མ། ཡོག་མ། དགྱེན་མ་། སྔོན་མ།

ii. At the end of a sentence it functions as a mark of question. *khyod yoŋ-ben-ma.* = You have come, is it? *khyo-'e šes-ma.* = You know him, is it so? *čha-'a yod-ma.* = Is it that you are going?

ཁྱོད་ཡོང་བེན་མ།། ཁྱོ་འེ་ཤེས་མ།། ཆ་འ་ཡོད་མ།།

14.17. de : The term functions in three ways.

i. It is pronoun meaning 'that'. *de-mi su nag.* = Who is that man?

ii. It is an article equivalent to English 'the'. *gaŋ de.*= Which one? *'i mi de.* = This man. *ŋe bčos-mkhan de kho la 'thad-ta mi-nug.* = By me-do-having-the-he-to-like-is-not is. He does not like the one that I do.

The two forms are also found used together. Thus *de-de* = 'That one'. The first *de* is pronoun and the second one is particle. *de mi de/ mi de de.* = That-man-the/Man-that-the. That man.

དེ་མི་སུ་ནག།། གང་དེ།། འི་མི་དེ།། ངེ་བཅོས་མཁན་དེ་ཁོ་ལ་འཐད་ཏ་མི་ནུག།
དེ་དེ།། དེ་མི་དེ།། མི་དེ་དེ།།

iii. It functions as participle. *kho grul-de čha-rug.* = He-walk-having-go-is. He is going walking, on foot. *ŋa čha-če la čhom de yod.* = I-going-for-ready-having-is. I have got ready to go. *ŋa ni sdad de yod.* = I-for one-sit-having-is. I am sitting. *zer-de zer-de kha čhad-soŋ.* = Speak-having-speak-having-mouth-tire-went. I am (my mouth is) tired of saying again and again. This is a very common form of use of the term '*de*' with the verbs to show them in the participle form in all the tenses.

ཁོ་འགྲུལ་དེ་ཆ་རུག།། ང་ཆ་ཅེ་ལ་ཆོམ་དེ་ཡོད།། ང་ནི་སྡད་དེ་ཡོད། ཟེར་དེ་ཟེར་
དེ་ཁ་ཆད་སོང་།།

15
Interjections and Forms of Address

15.1. Interjection

Different forms of expressions of interjection are given as under:

15.1.1. **Prayer:** *bla-ma dkon-čog mkhyen.* = The Teacher, the Rare Excellent One knows! *dkon-čog gsum.* = The Three Rare Excellent Ones! *Gepaŋ mkhyen.* = Gepaŋ (a local deity of Lahul) knows!

བླ་མ་དཀོན་ཅོག་མཁྱེན།། དཀོན་ཅོག་གསུམ།། གེ་པང་མཁྱེན།།

15.1.2. **Wish**: *tshe-riŋ!* = Wish you long life! *bkra-šis šog!* = May come blessings upon you! *sñiŋ-ja.* = Love with kindness. *bče-pa.* = Expression of love.

ཚེ་རིང་། བཀྲ་ཤིས་ཤོག། སྙིང་ཇ། བཅེ་པ།

15.1.3. **Disgust or disapproval:**

a-kha-'a. = Oh, dirty! *a-ra-'a.* = Oh, pain! *a-tsha-'a.* = Oh, hot! Pricking pain. *a-čhu-'u.* = Oh, cold!

ཨ་ཁ་འ། ཨ་ར། ཨ་ཚ། ཨ་ཆུ།

15.1.4 Surprise

be-'e. = Oh! *A-be-'e.* = Oh! *a-ba-'a.* = Oh, my father! *a-ma-'a.* = Oh! my mother

བེ་འེ་། ཨ་བེ་འེ་། ཨ་བ་འ། ཨ་མ་འ།

15.1.5. Applause:

pho khyo-'a = Brave! *khram-pa* = Hard working!

dpa'a-bo = Hero! *pho khyo-'a yin khyod.* = You are brave!

ཕོ་ཁྲོ་ལ།། ཁྲམ་པ།། དཔའ་བོ།། ཕོ་ཁྲོ་ལ།ཡིན་ཁྲོད།།

15.1.6. These are some expressions of challenge or threat.

khyod šog-žo./ khyod šog daŋ. = You just come! *khyod soŋ žo.* = You just go! *khyod sdod-čo.* = You just wait. *khyod ŋo-tog yin-na.* = Are you really! y*in-na šog.* = If yes, come.

ཁྱོད་ཤོག་ཞོ།། ཁྱོད་ཤོག་དང་།། ཁྱོད་སོང་ཞོ།། ཁྱོད་སྡོད་ཅོ།། ཁྱོད་ངོ་ཏོག་ཡིན་ན།། ཡིན་ན་ཤོག།

15.1.7. Dispatching a bad spirit: *thos-skyol-lo.* = Go afar!

This expression is announced with loud noise, by all in the crowd, some of them whistling, after the prayers, ceremonial rites, etc. when the victuals are discarded or thrown away and the harmful spirits are departed away.

15.2. Addressial form

va. su-yin, va.= O, who are you! *a-'o. ŋa-yin.* = Yes. It is me. *ho-'o.* = O.K. *ka-sa-le* = Yes, Sir.

ཝ། སུ་ཡིན་ཝ། ཨ་འོ། ང་ཡིན། ཧོ་འོ། ཀ་ས་ལེ། བཀའ་གསལ་ལགས།།

15.3. Terms of greetings

In sTod there are two forms of saying greetings: Religious and Secular. In the religious form it is said *phyag-tsal-le* ('phyag-'tshal lags = I pay reverence), holding both the palms folded above the chest near the chin. This is done to all the religious objects like statues, temples, sacred books, etc. and the religious persons like the lamas, irrespective of whether he is elder or junior in age. *phyag-gyang,* long greeting, is paid by lying prostrate, then standing up and saluting thrice, by both palms folded over the head, forehead and the chest. He murmurs some mantra or the like in his mouth.

The term pronounced in the secular greeting is *Ju-lye*. This term is used by and for all the laymen including those of the Jo, class of the noble families, and the clans of the class. Here the customary etiquette is that a younger one has to say greetings first. Among the classes of the society the lower class has to initiate even though he may be senior in age from the other one. The method of paying greeting is that among the men the initiator lifts his right hand, his palm half curved inwards, and brings it near to over the right side of his forehead and says Ju-lye. Women have to follow a slightly more difficult exercise. She bends forward and opens the right hand palm similarly as done by the men and starting from her feet lifts up, both the palms together, and stands up and touching the middle of her forehead says Ju-lye. This is old custom. This gesture is often expressed in the conversations. When one solicits favour from someone, one says, *śa-be ju-ju rkaŋ-pa ne gyen-la.* Kindly, greetings, from the feet upwards. (So kind of you, greetings to you.)

rigs-'dsin śa-be ju-ju rkaŋ-pa ne gyen-la srib-gčig ŋa la ya-to bčos btoŋ daŋ. = Rigzin please help me for a while, I greet you from the feet upwards

རིགས་འཛིན་ཤ་བེ་ཛུ་ཛུ་རྐང་ནེ་གྱེན་ལ།། སྲིབ་གཅིག་ང་ལ་ཡ་ཏོ་བཅོས་བཏོང་དང་།།

16

Some More Features of the Language

Here are given some other features of the language: 1.Loan words. 2. Contraction of words and expressions into shorter forms and change in pronunciation. 3. Honorific Language. 4. Child Language. 5. Method of formation of new words.

16.1. Loan Words

sTodpa has but few loan words belonging to the family of Pahari/Hindi languages. These loan words are mostly names of articles of household use and common daily need. The following are some words borrowed and retained in original in the language.

tha-li (Hi. thālī) = plate. *ta-va* (Hi. ta-vā) = iron pan. *čim-ṭa* (Hi. čim-.tā) = pincer. *ča-ku* (Hi. čā-kū) = knife. *luṛ-ki* (Hi. lo-ṭā) = a pot. *di-ba* (Hi. dī-vā) = lamp. *di-ba-sa-li* (Hi. diya salāī) = matchbox. *ro-ṭi* (Hi. ro-ṭī) = cake. *ha-ṭi* (Hi. hāṭ) = shop. *ta-mag* (Hi.tambākū) = tobacco. *ka-.ti* (Ku. kāt) = shears. *ču-ti* (Hi.čoṭī)= tuft of hair. *ar-ši* = mirror. *saṛ-ka* (Urdu. saṛak) = road. *mun-ši* (Urdu. munšī)= teacher. *ra-ši* (Hi. rassī) = rope. *a-ḷu* (Hi. ālū) = potato. *sa-kul* (English) = School. *žu-li* (Hi. jholī)= Bag, carried on back. *kuṛ-ti* = Shirt. *ṭan-ṭa* = Botheration.

ཐ་ལི། ཏ་བ། ཅིམ་ཏ། ཅ་ཀུ། ལུཊ་ཀི། དི་བ། དི་བ་ས་ལི། རོ་ཏི། ཧ་ཏི། ཏ་མག། ཀ་ཏི།ཙུ་ཏི། ཨར་ཤི། སཊ་ཀ། མུན་ཤི། ར་ཤི། ཨ་ཊུ། ས་ཀུལ། ཞུ་ལི། ཀུར་ཏི། ཏན་ཏ།

ii. In the following cases names of the articles have been changed by adding the name of the metal i.e *lčags* = iron, of which it is made, prefixing with the old name of the article. *lčag- gyid* = three iron-legs of hearth, tripod; *-thab* = Iron hearth; - *ber* = Iron-bar, Lever; *-thag* = Iron rope, Iron chain; - *khyem* = Iron showel; - *dar* = Iron ladle; - *sgam* = Iron-box, etc.

16.2. Samples of some peculiar modern sentences: *mo-ṭar čha-rug.* = Motor is going/running. *sa-kul la sil-la la čha-'a yod.* = I go to school to study. *ŋa-la pa-ta med.* = I don't know. *mdaŋ-di-riŋ ba-sa tsam-zod-la yoŋ 'dug.* = At what time the bus comes these days? *ke-laŋ ne da-ṇa tshag-pa te-ksi la ki-ra-ya tsam phog-'dug.* = What is the fare for taxi from Kyelang to Manali? In these sentences the borrowed words are noun. Here the words used are motor, school, bus, taxi from English and kiraya (fare), pa-ta (= information) from Hindi.

མོ་ཊོར་ཆ་རུག། ས་ཀུལ་ལ་སིལ་ལ་ལ་ཆ་འ་ཡོད།། ང་ལ་པ་ཏ་མེད།། མདང་
དི་རིང་བ་ས་ཙམ་ཛོད་ལ་ཡོང་འདུག། ཀེ་ལང་ནེ་ད་ཎ་ཚག་པ་ཏེ་ཀ་སི་ལ་ཀི་ར་ཡ་ཙམ་
ཕོག་འདུག།

16.3. Changes in pronunciation

16.3.1. Variations are observed in the pronunciation of some words and expressions in the colloquy from that of the literary form.

i. Differentiation in pronunciation in respect of some compound letters like bya, kra, etc., of which some are contextual, have been discussed at appropriate places.

ii. In the following words the surmounted letters of the second part of the word is pronounced with its first part, which in literary language remains silent. In the following examples first colloquial and then literary form of the word has been given with its meaning. *mel-čeb* = *me –lčeb* (firefly) ñil-dab = gñis-ldab (two fold).

iii. In the following words the prefix of the second word is pronounced, which in literary language is silent. *rob-dag* = *ro-bdag* (a person handling the corpse). *lab-dag* = *lha-bdag,* Priest. *gyam-tsho* = rgya-mtsho. Sea.

མེལ་ཅེབ།། མེ་ལྕེབ།། ཉིལ་དབ།། གཉིས་ལྡབ།། རོ་བདག རོབ་དག།
ལྷ་བདག། ལྷབ་དག།།གྱམ་ཚོ།། རྒྱ་མཚོ།།

iv. In the following words a new letter is inserted between the two parts of a word.

rom-khaŋ = *ro-khaŋ* (corpse house, i.e. cemetery). *šir-zun* = *ši – mdsun* (pretend to be dead). *lur-pon.* = *glu – dpon* (song-officer). nam-za = *na-bds'a,* (Monks'dress).

The following are words in which the letter *la* has been inserted in between the two parts of the word:

čhul-tiŋ = Having excessive water like milk, soup, curry, etc. *čhul-phag* = splash, *čhul-rgyaŋ* = an eruption, *čhul-ti* = A child who is still held in laps.

རོ་ཁང་། ཤེ་མཛུན། སླུ་དཔོན། ཆུལ་ཏིང་། ཆུལ་ཕག། ཆུལ་རྒྱང་། ཆུལ་ཏི། ནམ་ཟ། ན་བཟའ།

16.3.2. In the following examples it is observed that some expressions have got contracted in colloquy. In the first is given the colloquial form and then the literary form.

dug-pen = ‘dug-pa-yin

si =‘is

chen = čha-‘en

ne = nas

mi-nug = min-‘dug

čha-čen = čha-če-yin

ŋe = ŋas

čaŋ = či-‘aŋ

འདུག་པེན།། འདུག་པ་ཡིན།། མི་ནུག།། མིན་འདུག།། སི།། འིས།། ཆ་ཅེན།། ཆ་ཅེ་ཡིན།། ཆེན།། ཆ་འེན།། ངེ་།། ངས།། ནེ།། ནས།། ཅང་།། ཅི་འང་།།

16.4. *Ya-ša'i skad,* Language of Love or Honorific Language In conversation with the persons belonging to the noble class a different set of vocabulary is used which is called *ya-ša'i skad,* language of love, known as honorific language. In this category come the members of the clans of Jo – a higher ranking class, members of the ecclesiastical class, sacred objects, images and a few celestial objects viz. the sun and the moon. The language is applied mostly for addressing the second person and to a small measure is used for the third person. It is not used in the first person.

Here are given words from colloquial. The first word is in *phal-skad* and the second in *ya-ša'i skad.*

16.4.1. Terms of kinship and parts of body

Noun

phal-skad	ya-ša’i skad.	phal-skad	ya-ša’i skad.
a-cho, elder brother	= *g'a-‘a.*	*a-ku,* uncle	= *a-‘u.*
no, younger brother	= *no-no.*	*gzugs,* body	= *sku.*

Pronouns

kho, he = *khoŋ.* *khyod,* you = nyo-raŋ.

ཨ་ཅོ། གའ་ལ། ཨ་ཀུ། ཨ་ཙུ། ནོ། ནོ་ནོ། གཟུགས། སྐུ། ཁོ། ཁོང་། ཁྱོད། ཉོ་རང་།

16.4.2. Kitchen items and furniture.

rtsam-pa, flour of parched grain = *žib. thug-pa*, gruel = *'jam. ko-re,* cup = *gdon-kyog. ta-'ir,* cake = *gdon-skyir. ja,* tea = *gsol-ja. thab-ka,* hearth = *gsol-thab. čhu, čhang,* water or beer = *skyem,* drink.

རྩམ་པ། ཞིབ། ཐུག་པ། འཇམ། ཀོ་རེ། གདོན་ཀྱོག། ཏ་འིར། གདོན་སྐྱིར། ཇ། གསོལ་ཇ། ཐབ་ཀ། གསོལ་ཐབ། ཆུ། ཆང་། སྐྱེམ།

16.4.3. Verbs.

šog, come, go = *skyod.* *'bod-če*, to call = *žu-če.*
bčo-če, to do = mdsad. *sdod,* sit = bžugs.
šes- še, to know = mkhyen. *lta-če,* to see = mjal-če.
zer-če, to say = mol. *nyal-če,* to sleep = gzims.
'thuŋ, drink = 'don, *lags,* Sir = le.
shi-če, to die = *'groŋ*, to give = *dpul-če.*
za-če, meal = *gtsaŋ-ma.* to wear away = *žol-če,*
to see = gzigs to go = *skyod-če*

ཤོག། སྐྱོད། འབོད་ཅེ། ཞུ་ཅེ། བཅོ་ཅེ། མཛད། སྡོད། བཞུགས། ཤེས་ཤེ། མཁྱེན། ལྟ་ཅེ། མཇལ་ཅེ། ཟེར་ཅེ། མོལ། ཉལ་ཅེ། གཟིམས། འཐུང་། འདོན། ལགས། ལེ། ཤི་ཅེ། འགྲོང་། བཏང་ཅེ། དཔུལ་ཅེ། ཟ་ཅེ། གཙང་མ།

In literary language such new words can be formed by combining two honorific terms or an honorific term with an ordinary word. The words have a class with which the generic honorific term like *sku* (body), *zhal* (face), *phyag* (hand), etc. are joined and words are formed, like:

phyag-las = work. *phyag-rgyas* = seal, gesture.

phyag-dpe. = book.

ཕྱག་རྒྱས། ཕྱག་ལས། ཕྱག་དཔེ།

Sentences: *ša-be ju-ju, rkaŋ-pa ne gyen-la, a-cho-'e thugs-rje-la ŋe le-kha sla-mo la grub-soŋ.* = Thank you, greetings. With your kindness, brother, my work was completed easily. *g'a-'a skyod-le.* = Brother, please come. *bžugs-le.*= Please sit. *gtsaŋ-ma 'don gsal-le.* = Please have meal. *da-ruŋ 'don-kyir gčig dpul-len le.* = Please, I offer one more cake. *gčig-gčig gsal-le, no-no-le.* = O, younger brother, please give me one. *ka-sa-le.* = Sir. *g'a-'a ño-rañ skyod-de thugs-rje čhe.* = Oh brother, you had been very kind to visit us. *'e-'e de-zug mol-čen-na.*= Oh, don't speak like this. *ñi-ma skyod-soŋ.* = The sun has set. *dslar šar-soñ* = The moon has risen.

ཨ་ཅོ་འི་།ཐུགས་རྗེ་ལ།ངེ་།ལེ་ཁ།སླ་མོ་ལ་།གྲུབ་སོང་།།
ག་འ། སྐྱོད་ལེ།བཞུགས་ལེ། གཙང་མ།འདོན་སྐྱལ་ལེ།།
ད་རུང་།འདོན་ཀྱིར་གཅིག། དཔུལ་ལེན་ལེ།། གཅིག་
གཅིག་གསལ་ལེ།ནོ་ནོ་ལེ།། ཀ་ས་ལེ།། ག་འ་ཉོ་རང་སྐྱོད་དེ་ཐུགས་རྗེ་ཆེ།།
འེ་དེ་ཟུག་མོལ་ཅེན་ན།། ཉི་མ་སྐྱོད་སོང་།།ཟླར་ཤར་སོང་།།

16.5. Child Language: There is a set of vocabulary which is used exclusively while speaking with children. These are used from the beginning and remain effective for two-three years. These are substitutes for the words of common use. These are forgotten as the child grows up. Then the actual learning of the language starts. These are formed by repetition of a letter or by joining two different letters. Words:

ka-ka = paper, book.	*ko-ko* = bowl.
ke-ke = cake.	*tu-tu* = water.
na-na = rice, parched grain.	*ča-ča* = mutton.
pa-ba = meal.	*ma-ma* = mother's milk
la-'u = hand.	*po-bo* = clothes.
a-čhu = cold.	*a-tshi* = hot.
čhi-čhi = dirty, urine.	*ta, ta-ti* = sleep.
a-kha = dirty, faeces.	*čog* = sit.
rtse-rtse = to stand up, dance.	*ti-su* = bathing.
hob = stand up.	*am* = to eat. *'o* = kiss
a-la,a-nu = beautiful	*a-ra* = Pain They are all in the form of noun.

ཀ་ཀ། གོ་གོ། ཀེ་ཀེ། ཧུ་ཧུ། ན་ན། ཙ་ཙ། པ་བ། མ་མ། ལ་ཟུ། པོ་བོ། ཨ་ཀུ། ཨ་ཆི། ཆེ་ཆེ། ཧ། ཧ་ཧི། ཨ་ཁ། ཅོག། ཅེ་ཅེ། ཧི་སུ། ཧོབ། ཨམ། ཨོ། ཨ་ལ། ཨ་ནུ། ཨ་ར།།

A simple verb is used with these words to make the meaning of the word understandable to the child. Thus: *hob bčos.* = stand-do. Stand up. *am-bčos*. = Eat up. *čog bčos*. = Sit down (cross legged).

ཧོབ་བཅོས།། ཨམ་བཅོས།། ཅོག་བཅོས།།

Kinship terms are more important for the children. Almost all the common terms of concern for the children are simple and they need no further simplification. Some of them are given below.

a-ba	=	father.	*a-ma*	=	mother.
me-me	=	grandfather.	*a-bi*	=	grandmother.
a-žaŋ	=	maternal uncle.	*a-ku*	=	uncle.
a-čo	=	eldest brother.	*no*	=	younger brother.
a-či	=	eldest sister.	*no-mo*	=	younger sister.

ཨ་བ། ཨ་མ། མེ་མེ། ཨ་བི། ཨ་ཞང་། ཨ་ཀུ། ཨ་ཅོ། ནོ། ཨ་ཅི། ནོ་མོ།

16.6. **Formation of New words: i.** We have seen in chapter 1 how some new words had been formed based on the experience of the society in the environment in which they have been living.

ii. Here are given two more methods of formation of new words as has been followed naturally in the society since early times.

a. Some limited number of words are formed by uniting primary words which may be found in the lexicons. But the secondary form may not be found in the lexicons and are local creations.

Examples: *čhu* + *mig* = water + eye = Water spring.

'bu + *riŋ-mo* = worm + long = Serpent. *thag-ra (ran-če)* + *'bu* = To spread the warp for weaving cloth, + worm. = spider. *ja*+*ro* = tea + corpse = Residual tea leaves left after straining tea. *rmog- śa* = helmet+ flesh = Mushroom. *a-ḍu*+ *snab- dsig* = potato + meshy like mucus = Root vegetable. taro. *mar*+*nag* = Ghee, butter+ black = Oil. *mar* + *srad-ma* = butter + pulse = The shining black pulse (Hindi = uḷad). *bag (+ phye)*+ *ša-tsi* = Wheat flour + meat = Cake cooked in oil. *bye-ma* + *lab-tsi* =

sand + leaves = butterfly. *mur-ti* = The place in the village from where the villagers collect water. *ri– bya* (= pronounced as *rib-ja*) = mountain+bird = Snow pheasant which lives in mountains higher than *srag-pa* (partridge) lives.

ཆུ་མིག། འབུ་རིང་མོ། ཐག་ར་འབུ། ཛ་རོ། སྨོག་ཤ། ཨ་ཊ་སྣབ་ཛིག།
མར་ནག། མར་སྲད་མ། བག་ཤ་ཅེ། བྲེ་མ་ལབ་ཅེ། སུར་ཧེ། རིབ་བྱ།།

b. sTopdpa has a unique method of formation of new words. A word, usually of two syllables, is first formed which usually is not found in the lexicons and then it is doubled. These words are generally based on sound, shape of an object, actions, feelings, views, etc. of the observer. Example:

zaŋ-zaŋ. = A guest doing too much alibis and refusing meal.

tshag-tshag. = Insistence by a host to the guest for meal.

da-ra du-re = A liquid thing like a thick soup.

dar-dar = rough. *nar-nar*= long.

tshen-tshen = tattered. *lhag-lhag.*= sparkling, shining.

dsiŋ-dsiŋ = giddiness. *dur-dur* = over riped.

lug-lug.= soft. *rkyaŋ-rkyaŋ*= thin and long.

ཟང་ཟང་། ཚག་ཚག། དར་དར། ནར་ནར།ཚེན་ཚེན། ལྷག་ལྷག། །ཛིང་ཛིང་།
ད་ར་དུ་རེ། ལུག་ལུག། རྐྱང་རྐྱང་།

The method has expanded further. Many words have two forms one for a smaller of a thing, etc. and the other one for the larger of the same kind. In some cases both the words also have their multiple forms.

Examples: We take the word *tsor-tsor* which means ‘a small thing of sharp edge, like stone. Its plural form is : t*sa-ra tso-re*. the word for such things of larger size is *zor-zor* and its plural form is *za-ra zo-re*.

i. *‘i rdo-‘a tsor-tsor de phaŋ-ŋa-la phoŋ btoŋ.* = Throw away this stone with sharp edges. ii. *‘i rdo-‘a tsa-ra tso-re de-‘un sdus-de chog-ki bčos-bor.* = Collect these edged-stones and keep making a heap. iii. *pha-loŋ zor-zor de zhiŋ-ke dkyl-la ‘dug.* = The big edged-boulder is situated in the middle of the field. iv. *ra-ma de pha-loŋ za-ra zo-re-‘un phag-la hib-de mthoŋ-ŋa med kag.* = The goat is not visible because it may be hidden behind the edged-boulders.

འི་རྡོ་འ་ཙོར་ཙོར་དེ་ཕང་ང་ལ་ཕོང་བརྡོང་།། འི་རྡོ་འ་ཙ་ར་ཙོ་རེ་དེ་འུན་སྣ་ས་དེ་ཙོག་གི་བཙོས་པོར།། ཕ་ལོང་ཟོར་ཟོར་དེ་ཞིང་ཀི་དཀྱི་ལ་ལ་འདུག།། ར་མ་དེ་ཕ་ལོང་ཟ་ར་ཟོ་རེ་དེ་འུན་ཕག་ལ་རྡིབ་"དེ་མཐོང་ང་མེད་ཀག།

Below are given some more similar words. Their plural form is given in the bracket.

i. *kor-kor* (*ka-ra ko-re*) = A small round pit, like a bowl.

ii. *gor-gor* (*ga-ra-go-re*) = A bigger round pit.

i. *tsoŋ tsoŋ* (*tsaŋ-ŋa tsoŋ-ŋe*) = A small peaked object like a bottle.

ii. *zoŋ zoŋ* (*zaŋ-ŋa zoŋ-ŋo*) = A larger peaked object, like a rock.

i. *čur čur* (*ča-ra ču-re*) = A small heap of grain, sand, etc.

ii. *byur byur* (*bya-ra byu-re*) = Heap like that of grain.

i. *kog-kog* (*ka-ga ko-go*) = A small crooked thing, like a small branch.

ii. *gog-gog* (*ga-ga go-ge*) = A bigger crooked thing like a log.

ཀོར་ཀོར།། ཀ་ར་ཀོ་རེ།། གོར་གོར།། ག་ར་གོ་རེ།། ཙོང་ཙོང།། ཙང་ང་ཙོང་ངོ་།། ཟོང་ཟོང་།། ཟང་ང་ཟོང་ངོ་།། ཅུར་ཅུར ཅར་ཅུ་རེ།། བྱུར་བྱུར།། བྱ་ར་བྱུ་རེ།། ཀོག་ཀོག།། ཀ་ག་ཀོ་འོ།། གོག་གོག།།ག་ག་གོ་འོ།།

Sentences: *pha-loŋ dsoŋ-dsoŋ žig kha-la dru-'u tog-tog žig 'dug. de mdo-la khyi tsel-tsel žig trog-trog soŋ-de sdad 'dug.* = Over the protruding rock there is a small ball of woollen thread. Near it is lying a small dog tightly crooked.

thab-ka gor-gor naŋ la lčags-gyid zoŋ zoŋ žig 'dug. = There is a high tripod in the deep hearth. *rdo-'a za-ra zo-re slaŋ de ñag-ra gyaŋ gyaŋ žig rgyab-laŋ yin.* = I have to construct a long fencing wall by raising conical slabs. *'i si gzur gčig zor zor la 'thon čha rug.* = One of its corners is protruding out. śiŋ *kyaŋ-ŋa kyoŋ-ŋe-re sgrug khyoŋ.* = Collect small branches of wood.

ཕ་ལོང་རྫོང་རྫོང་ཞིག་ཁ་ལ་དྲུ་འུ་ཏོག་ཏོག་ཞིག། དེ་མདོ་ལ་ཁྱི་ཙེལ་ཙེལ་ཞིག་ཏྲོག་ཏྲོག་སོང་དེ་སྡད་འདུག།། ཐབ་"གོར་གོར་ནང་ལ་ལྕགས་གྱིད་ཟོང་ཟོང་ཞིག་འདུག།། རྡོ་འ་ཟ་ར་ཟོ་རེ་སླང་དེ་ཉག་ར་གྱང་གྱང་ཞིག་རྒྱབ་ལང་ཡིན།། འི་སི་གཟུར་གཅིག་ཟོར་ཟོར་ལ་འཐོན་ཆ་ཅེ་འདུག།། ཤིང་ཀྱང་ང་ཀྱོང་ངེ་རེ་སྒྲུག་ཁྱོང་།།

17
Translation of Paragraphs

Below are given some compositions from the current usage:

17.1. Phrases

mgo čhod-če. = To be able to finish a task successfully. *kha-thug-sna-thug.* = Touching mouth and nose: very congested, like in a crowd. *yaŋ-pha bčo-če.* = To play joke. *bden čhe-čher.* = Posing as true: a false show. *lag-pa riŋ-mo.* = Long hands: habit of stealing. *mgo-skor btaŋ- če.* = To make head circle: to befool. *lag-pa yaŋ-mo.* = Having light hands: quick to strike. *rkaŋ-pa yaŋ-mo.* = Having light feet: fast in walking. *mdoŋ-phag nag-pho.* = Darkened face: to have angry look. *sna btuŋ-ŋun.* = Short nose: short tempered. *khu-ru med-ta-la khu-ru.* = Carrying a load, even it is not his load: self created problem. *lag-la theb-še med-kan.* = A person who cannot be handled easily: a smart person. *kha-tshan-te.* = Sharp mouth (= tongue): one who speaks harsh words. *kha-ti sna-ti.* = Water flowing from mouth and nose: a person in bad condition. *sna khur- če.* = To carry nose: to swear. *sems-ba lčin-te.* = Heavy heart: a person having unfavorable mind. *ma-'brel gu-'brel.* = Getting involved in matters not of one's concern. *tog mi-len bčo-če.*= To pounce upon. *khrag-mal* čhul-tob. = Drenched with blood. *mig rig-rig.*= Looking continuously. *han khyer-čha-če.* = To be astonished. *mal-zan mal-čhu.*= Meal and water in the bed. (The condition of an incapacitated person.). *kho-ba khrig-khrig khrig-la sdad-'dug.* = They are sitting in queue. *sbas-bśad* (= to tell secret) *ma-gyur.* = Don't boast. *'i-ru ni nyi-ma-la 'phrul bčo-čen.* = Here there appear ghosts even in the day. *rang-thog la bab-na mjug-dum 'ang hir-se-hir.* = If it comes on oneself even the tailless dances moving his hind part.

མགོ་ཆོད་ཅེ།། ཁ་ཐུག།སྣ་ཐུག།། ཡང་ཕ་བཅོ་ཅེ།། བདེན་ཆེ་ཆེར།། ལག་པ་རིང་མོ།། མགོ་སྐོར་བཏང་ཅེ།། ལག་པ་ཡང་མོ།། རྐང་པ་ཡང་མོ།། མདོང་ཕག་

ནག་ཡོ༎ སྣ་བཏུང་དུན༎ ཁུ་ཛུ་མེད་ཏ་ལ་ཁུ་ཛུ༎ ལག་ལ་ཐེབ་ཤེ་མེད་ཀན༎ ཁ་ཚན་ཏེ༎ ཁ་ཏེ་སྣ་ཏེ༎ སྣ་ཁུར་ཙེ༎ སེམས་པ་ལྷིན་ཏེ༎ མ་འབྲེལ་གྲུ་འབྲེལ༎ ཏོག་མི་ལེན་བཙོ་ཙེ༎ ཁྲག་མལ་ཆུལ་ཏོབ༎ མིག་རིག་རིག༎ ཏན་ཁྲེར་ཆ་ཙེ༎ མལ་ཟན་མལ་ཆུ༎ ཁོ་བ་ཁྲིག་ཁྲིག་ཁྲིག་ལ་བསྟོད་འདུག༎ འི་ཛུ་ནེ་ཉེ་མ་ལ་འཕྲུལ་བཙོ་ཙེ་ན༎ རང་ཡོག་ལ་བབ་ན་མཇུག་དུམ་འང་ཏེར་སེ་ཏེར༎

17.2. Proverbs and sayings

1. *za-na 'gag-če, 'grul-na gag-bub-če.* = To get obstructed in the throat while eating, and to get stumbled while walking. (A worthless person.)
2. *yon-bdag kha-žim, khyim-mtshes sna-žim.* = When a delicious food is cooked, owner gets the taste and the neighbor its smell.
3. *mi rgyal-la daŋ mthun-na gtam re-re daŋ dpe re-re. mi thu-'a daŋ thug-na sna re-re daŋ thu re-re.* = If one accompanies a noble person, one learns one lesson from him with each sentence. If one lives with a bad person, one receives insult from everybody.
4. *rta-rgan mi-rgan khyi-rgan gsum mi'i sñiŋ ma-sdug-na sdug-ge sdug.* = With an old horse, an old man, and an old dog, a person gets irritated even if one has no other trouble.
5. *rta-čhuŋ mi- čhuŋ khyi- čhuŋ gsum ni sñiŋ ma-rje-na rje-rje.* = A colt, a child and a pup, they look lovely even if one has no desire to love.
6. *gal gčig me mi-'bar, mi gčig gtam mi-lab.* = A single log cannot burn and a single man cannot talk. (A single person cannot do anything.)
7. *bu-lon maŋ-po so-ta-la mi-tsher, šig maŋ-po za-'a la mi-tshor.* = A person having large amount of debt for payment does not worry for borrowing more and a man habitual with tortures of lice, does not feel their excesses. The two are similar.
8. *mi-la skyes-tshul gčig, ši-tshul brgya.* = All the men are born in the same way, but they die in different ways.
9. *gčig-la gčig, gñis-la gñis.* = A person doing one work if he has been asked to do one, and doing two if he has been told to do so. (A person lacking ingenuity).

10. *lag-pas bčos, rkaŋ -pas bśigs.* = To construct with hands and destroy with feet. (Constructing on the one hand and destroying on the other at the same time. One doing a worthless task.)

11. *rta sa za-na khyi-la sro.* = If horse is eating grass, dog becomes angry. (One showing unnecessary concern in another's work).

12. *ba-lu bsad-de mi-khe, bkol-de khe.* = One will gain benefit not by killing the *ba-lu,* but by getting work done from him. (Work cannot be got done from others only by threatening, but one must know how to get work done from them. *ba-lu* is supposed to be a dwarf man, a spirit, found in the wild who can work continuously.).

13. *khal-pha brgya-la ma-mo gčig si lam bkag khyud-ta nag.* = One ewe can block the path of hundred rams.

14. *kha sgo-ru babs na ŋo-tsha khyim-la 'byuŋ.* = If the snow piles up equal to the door, shame fills in the room. It is sign of laziness not throwing the snow and allowing it to accumulate outside the house.

15. *lan-gchig bsdad ma śes na lan brgya laŋ-go yoŋ-ŋa nag.* = If one does not know at the first instance his proper place where to sit in a row, he has to get up again and again. (He will have to stand up with each new comer.)

16. *dgod-pa'i bo-mo-la yad med. bas ma-mo-la bžon med.* = A woman laughing continually has no respect: she is like a barren sheep bawing continuously.

17. *g-yag śus de rŋa-ma la 'khad-če.* = After completing skinning off a yak, to get stuck up at the tail. (To get stuck up at the end of the work after finishing large part of it.)

18. *khyim-mtshes la ba-glaŋ žig śi -na-'aŋ žag gsum sdug sruŋ -go yoŋ-ŋa nag. 'i ta mi nag.* = Even if a cattle dies in the neighbourhood, sorrow has to be observed at least for three days, after all this is a man.

19. *pho- žig 'grul-na rgyal. mo- žig 'dug-na rgyal.* = It is proper that a man should keep on going and a woman stay put, (economic division of work and environmental compulsion.).

20. *bsag-pa'i lo dgu. dgos-pa'i jag gčig.* = It takes nine years for amassing a thing, but the necessity will consume earning in a day. (It

takes long time for earning but the same can be consumed in a very short time.)

21. *ri la ši na bya-ro yin, luŋ-la ši-na ña-ro yin.* = If one dies up in the mountains it is like the corpse of a bird and if one dies in the low valley, it is like a dead fish. (There is none to take care of the dead body at both the places. They are fortunate who die at home. Men have to keep moving to earn livelihood.)

22. *čhug-na čhug-na mkhas-pa 'aŋ čhug, mkhas-pa čhug na bčos-thab med.* = If it comes to erring, even an expert can err; thus if an expert errs, there is no further remedy left.

23. *lto-la khur-na mi-'i nor yin, khog la khur-na raŋ nor yin.* = It is another's property if it is carried in the stomach, but if it is carried in the bust (heart) it is one's own property. (Everything should not be disclosed).

24. *mi-čhen la thu-lu'i spyod-pa.*= A grown up man showing the habit of *thulu* (= blanket of hides of sheep). (An elder person showing a mean behaviour.)

25. *gos phyed glan-ba yin, zas phyed tshod-ma yin.* = Half cloth is like a patch and half meal is like a curry. (Insufficient things are not much useful).

26. *khur-thag čhad-na khu-ru yaŋ.* = If the rope of the load breaks, the load becomes light. (For the load falls down. An easy way to get rid of the burden is to throw off the burden itself.)

27. *tshoŋ-la čha-na žag gčig, grogs la čha-na mi-tshe.* = The companionship in trade has life of one day, that of kinship lasts life long. (The companionship of the traders is temporary.)

28. *gson-na-'aŋ me, ši-na'aŋ me.* = Fire is necessary for sustaining the life as well as when one dies.

29. *lag-pa-gčig-'i zu-'u čhe-'a yod-na, čuŋ-ŋun yod-na, si-rig 'dran-'dra nag.* – Fingers of a hand, whether big or small, all are equal. (All the fingers feel pain equally.).

17.3. Paragraphs: Below are given some paragraphs as examples of compositions in modern colloquy.

17.3.1. i. Pa-pu sle-če. Knitting Socks: da-ruŋ ta ŋe pa-pu gsum man-na sle ma tshar. = So far I have been able to knit not more than three socks.

zoŋ gñis gsob ben. = I repaired two pairs. da-ruŋ zoŋ gñis so-ma the-rel la ma čhom-ma yod. = Two new pairs are yet unfinished. gčig gčig-'i si rkaŋ -rtse čhom de yod. = Legs of one pair have finished. tshom bčug-go man-na med. = Only designs have to be put in them. gčig-gčig la rtiŋ-pa sle-go yod. = Of the other pair the ankles remain to be knitted. gčig gčig bśig-go byuŋ. ya-ma ya-zug laŋ soŋ dog. = Of one pair, one side had to be dismantled because both sides became similar. sle-laŋ ta khur-khur-ra sdad-ta yod. = I constantly carry with me the work for knitting. sne-ma zin de yod-ten. bab-sa'i 'aŋ ma-tshaŋ- ŋa yod-ten. = I had exhausted the threads. I also did not have coloured threads of some colours for design.

པ་པུ་སླེ་ཅེ། ད་རུང་ཏ་དེ་པ་པུ་གསུམ་མན་ན་སླེ་མ་ཚར།། ཟོང་གཉིས་གསོབ་བེན།།
ད་རུང་ཟོང་གཉིས་སོ་མ་ཐེ་རེ་ལ་ལ་མ་ཆོམ་མ་ཡོད།། གཅིག་གཅིག་འི་སི་རྐང་རྩེ་
ཆོམ་དེ་ཡོད།། ཚོམ་བཅུག་གོ་མན་ན་མེད།། གཅིག་གཅིག་ལ་རྟིང་པ་སླེ་གོ་ཡོད།།
གཅིག་གཅིག་བཤིག་གོ་བྱུང་།ཡ་མ་ཡ་ཟུག་ལང་སོང་དོག།། སླེ་ལང་ཏ་ཁུར་
ཁུར་ར་སྡད་ཏ་ཡོད།། སྣེ་མ་ཟིན་དེ་ཡོད་ཏེན།བབ་ས་འི་འང་མ་ཚང་ང་ཡོད་ཏེན།།

17.3.2. ***Ka-ča 'dri-laŋ žig.* A Conversation:** *a-žaŋ ju-le. a-žaŋ khams-bzaŋ yod-ta. či bčo-'a yod.* = Uncle Julye, compliments. Uncle are you healthy? What are you doing?

ju-le stobs-rgyas. yod-ve, khya-ra khyo-re žig. khyod khams-bzaŋ. ñuŋ-ti ne nam yoŋ.= Julye, Tobge. Yes, I am so so. Are you healthy? When did you come from Kullu?

ŋa mdaŋ yoŋ ben. = I came yesterday.

lam-ka tsug 'dug. čhar-pha maŋ-po yoŋ-ŋa mi-nug-ga. žag kha- čig sdad-ten-na. de ne da-ruŋ ñuŋ-ti-'i ka-ča či 'dug.= How is the road? Is it not raining much? Will you stay for some days? Then what is more news about Kullu?

žag po bži lŋa sdad-ten bsam-ma rag.= I think I will stay for four-five days.

'o 'o, de ne khaŋ-pa ru śog a-'i. ja žig mthuŋ soŋ.= Yes, yes, then come to home. Have tea.

'o- 'o yoŋ - 'en . ja- 'un ta ob-rgyal ma-mdsad. ŋa 'i-zug-ka yoŋ- 'en. = Yes yes, I will come. Don't take trouble for tea. I will come by the way.

'e 'e či bar do. srib čig sdad čag. pe-ra re btaŋ čag. = Oh what trouble! We will stay for a while. We will have conversation.

'o 'o čha-če saŋ sŋon la ŋa brtan-brtan yoŋ 'en. a-žaŋ la a-me si rtags žig bkal 'dug. de 'aŋ skyal-go yod. de-ne a-žaŋ la skad dri rug zer lo. = Yes yes, I will come certainly before I go. Mother has sent you a present. I have to bring that also. Then she was conveying you her good wishes.

'o 'o. nan-than la a'a-'o thug-če ma-čha na brtan-po soŋ. lam-la ltos-de soŋ. lha-mo la-'aŋ skad-'dri rug zer-btoŋ. = Yes yes, if, by chance we are not able to meet go taking care of yourself. Be careful on the way. Pay compliments to Lhamo from me. *'o-'o de-ne khyo- ža-raŋ brtan-po sdod-ni.* = Yes, yes, take care of yourselves.

ཀ་ཙ་འདྲི་ཡང་ཞིག།། ཨ་ཞང་།ཧྲུ་ལེ།། ཨ་ཞང་།ཁམས་བཟང་ཡོད་ད།། ཙེ་བཙོ་འ་ ཡོད།། ཧྲུ་ལེ།སྐྱོབས་རྒྱས།།ཡོད་ལེ། ཁྲུ་ར་ཁྲོ་རེ་ཞིག།། ཁྲོད་ཁམས་བཟང་།། ཉུང་ཧྲེ་ནེ་ནམ་ཡོང་།། ང་མདང་ཡོང་པེན།། ལམ་ཀ་ཙུག་འདུག།། ཚར་ཕ་མང་པོ་ཡོང་ང་མི་ནུག་ག།། ཞག་ཁ་ཅིག་སྡད་ཧྲེན་ན།། དེ་ནེ་ད་རུང་ཉུང་ཧྲེ་འི་ཀ་ཙ་ཅིའདུག།། ཞག་པོ་བཞི་ལྷ་སྡད་ཧྲེན་བསམ་མ་རག།། འོ་འོ།དེ་ནེ་ཁང་པ་རུ་ཤོག།ཨ་འི།། ཇ་ཞིག་མཐུང་སོང་།། འོ་འོ།ཡོང་འེན།ཇ་འུན་ཏ་འོབ་རྒྱལ་མ་མཇོད།། ང་འི་ཟུག་ཀ་ ཡོང་འེན།། འེ་འེ།ཅི་བར་དོ།། སྲིབ་ཅིག་སྡད་ཙག།། པེ་ར་རེ་བཏང་ཙག།། འོ་འོ། ཆ་ཅེ་སང་སྔོན་ལ་ང་བརྟན་བརྟན་ཡོང་འེན།། ཨ་ཞང་ལ་ཨ་མེ་སི་རྟགས་ཞིག་བཀལ་ འདུག།། དེ་འང་སྐྱལ་གོ་ཡོད།།དེ་ནེ་ཨ་ཞང་ལ་སྐད་དྲི་རུག་ཟེར་ལོ།། འོ་འོ།ནན་ཐན་ ལ་ཨཱ་འོ་ཐུག་ཅེ་མ་ཆ་ན་བརྟན་པོ་སོང་།། ལམ་ལ་ལྟོས་དེ་སོང་།། ལྷ་མོ་ལ་འང་སྐད་ དྲི་རུག་ཟེར་བཏོང་།། འོ་འོ།དེ་ནེ་ཁྱོ་ཞ་རང་བརྟན་པོ་སྡོད་ནི།།

17.3.3. dGun-mjug-pa. Winter Migrants: de ne dpyid-ka mgyogs-pha śog. a-čo la skad dri-rug zer. = Then come early in the Spring. Say compliments to brother. 'o 'o khyo ža raŋ skyid-po bčos-de sdod-ni. = Yes, you keep enjoying yourselves. a-ma la ya-śa bčos. thug-pa bčos-de btoŋ. = Love mother. Serve her with thug-pa (soup, generally liquid soup of meat mixed with rtsampa). tsher ma-tsher-ra sdod-ni. = Stay without worrying. dpyid-ka ŋa mgyogs-pha yoŋ-če bčos-'en. = I will try to come early in the Spring.

དགུན་མཇུག་པ།། དེ་ནེ་དཔྱིད་ཀ་མགྱོགས་ཕ་ཤོག།། ཨ་ཙོ་ལ་སྐད་དྲི་ཙུག་ཟེར།། འོ་འོ། ཁྲོ་ཞ་རང་སྐྱིད་པོ་བཙོས་དེ་སྦོད་ནི།། ཨ་མ་ལ་ཡ་ཤ་བཙོས།། ཐུག་པ་བཙོས་དེ་བཏོང་།། ཆེར་མ་ཆེར་ར་སྦོད་ནི།། དཔྱིད་ཀ་ང་མགྱོགས་ཕ་ཡོང་ཙེ་བཙོས་འཇིན།།

17.3.4. *khyi-skor gčig-'i las-'grel.* Description of works done round the year:

17.3.4.1 dPyid-ka. Spring: sŋon-me ka-ča či bśad-čen. = What to talk of the former times? las-kha zin-laŋ ka yoŋ če man. = There used to be no end to work. za-loŋ mthuŋ-loŋ yoŋ-če man. = There was no time for eating and drinking. dpyid-ka ma śar ra la kha 'thon če btaŋ če phyil la žiŋ ka 'un la gog-thal g-yog- čen. = Before arrival of the Spring, ash is spread in the fields for melting the snow. de ne kha 'thon na rtiŋ la žiŋ ka la rdo-'a sgrug čen. = After the snow has melted pebbles and stones are removed from the fields. ra-ga ne lud bton de žiŋ ka la skyed čen. = Manures are taken out from the sheds and are carried to the fields. de ne bkram čen. = Then it is scattered. yang čhag-sa 'aŋ khyer-čen. = Then human wastes, collected in the toilets, are also taken out to the fields. mdso daŋ žiŋ rŋo čen. = Fields are ploughed with the pair of dso, cross-bred bullocks. mi gčig si sŋon-sŋon la sa bon g-yog čen. = One person spreads seeds before them. miŋ-ga gčig gčig si mdun ne mdso khrid ta nag. = One person leads the bullocks from the front. gčig gčig rgyab ne śol mñam-po sdad-ta nag. = One person follows from behind them holding the plough. bo mo drug bdun zam si tog-tse daŋ phul-ṭag rgyab-ba nag. = About six or seven women break the plods with hand hoes. kho-ba kha-čig khaŋ -pe mi nag. = Some of them are members of the family. kha-čig las-pha. kha čig be-mi yod kag. = Some of the others are invited on daily payment and some others are periodical workers. der- rgyag la žiŋ-rŋos-la dgun 'jug-pa mi-raŋ-'un leb khyoŋ-čen. = By the time of the ploughing the persons who had gone as winter migrants on foot reach from Kullu. rta-ba 'un rtiŋ la man-na leb-če man. = Those who have gone with the ponies reach later. de–ne kha čig yu-ra daŋ lam-ka daŋ zam-pa san-na la čha-čen. = Then some people go to reconstruct the water channels and repairing the paths and bridges. dbyar-ke phyil-la če-'a daŋ śiŋ sgrug-ga nag. = Then people collect wood and cattle droppings for the summer. ran-thag 'tag-čen. lug-rdsi tshe-ma rgyab-čen. čhu-re rgyab- čen. = Grains are milled. Turn of days of the shepherd for different households are fixed and turn of water for irrigation are also fixed.

ཁྲི་སྐོར་གཅིག་འི་ལས་འགྲེལ།། དཔྱིད་ཀ།། སྔོན་མི་ཀ་ཙ་ཅི་བཤད་ཅན།། ལས་ཁ་ཟིན་ལང་ཀ་ཡོང་ཅེ་མན།། ཟ་ལོང་མཐུང་ལོང་ཡོང་ཅེ་མན།། དཔྱིད་ཀ་མ་ཤར་ར་ལ་ཁ་འཐོན་ཅེ་བཏང་ཅེ་ཕྱིལ་ལ་ཞིང་ཀ་འུན་ལ་གོ་ག་ཐལ་གཡོག་ཅན།། དེ་ནེ་ཁ་འཐོན་ན་རྫིང་ལ་ཞིང་ཀ་ལ་རྡོ་འ་སྡུག་ཅན།། ར་ག་ནེ་ལུད་བརྡོན་དེ་ཞིང་ཀ་ལ་སྐྱེད་ཅན།། དེ་ནེ་བཀྲམ་ཅན།། ཡང་ཆག་ས་འང་ཁྲིར་ཅན།།མཛོ་དང་ཞིང་རྗོ་ཅན།། མི་གཅིག་སི་སྔོན་སྔོན་ལ་ས་བོན་གཡོག་ཅན།། མིང་ག་གཅིག་གཅིག་སི་མདུན་ནེ་མཛོ་ཁྲིད་ཏ་ནག།། གཅིག་གཅིག་ རྒྱབ་ནེ་ཤོལ་མཉམ་པོ་སྟུད་ཏ་ནག།། བོ་མོ་དྲུག་བདུན་ཟམ་སི་ཧོག་ཅེ་དང་ཞུལ་ཏྲག་རྒྱབ་བ་ནག།། ཕོ་བ་ཁ་ཅིག་ཁང་པེ་མི་ནག།། ཁ་ཅིག་ལས་ཕ།། ཁ་ཅིག་བེ་མི་ཡོད་ཀག།། དེར་གྲུག་ལ་ཞིང་རྗོས་ལ་དགུན་འཇུག་པ་མི་རང་འུན་ལེབ་ཁྱོང་ཅན།། རྟ་བ་འུན་རྫིང་ལ་མན་ན་ལེབ་ཅེ་མན།། དེ་ནེ་ཁ་ཅིག་ཡུ་ར་དང་ལམ་ཀ་དང་ཟམ་པ་སན་ན་ལ་ཆ་ཅེན།། དབྱར་ཀེ་ཕྱིལ་ལ་ཅེ་འ་དང་ཤིང་སྡུག་ག་ནག།། རན་ཐག་འདག་ཅན།། ལུག་ཛི་ཚེ་མ་རྒྱབ་ཅན།། ཆུ་རེ་རྒྱབ་ཅན།།

17.3.4.2. *dYar-ka.* Summer: *ču-re rim daŋ žiŋ-ka bču-čen.* = Fields are irrigated according to one's turn for water from community *yu-ra*, water channel. *yur-ma yur-čen.* = Weeding is done. *sa-yur daŋ phyi-yur gñis yod-kag.* = There are two weedings, early weeding and later weeding. *rta-ba 'un byaŋ-thaŋ la tshoŋ la čha- čen.* = Some people go with ponies to Jangthang for trading. *bra-bo pi-čen.*= Buckwheat is uprooted. *bra-bo rduŋ-čen.* = It is beaten. *rtsva rŋa-čen.* = Grass is mown. *rtsva skyed-čen.* = It is carried to home. *se-pen rtsig-čen.* = It is stacked. *nas daŋ gro rŋa-čen.* = Then Ne and wheat are harvested. *hi-ri rtsig-čen.* = They are stacked. *hi-ri skor-čen. bsam-pa baŋ-ŋa-la gyaŋ-čen.* = Then they are thrashed and the grains are stored.

དབྱར་ཀ།། ཆུ་རེ་རིམ་དང་ཞིང་ཀ་བཙུ་ཅན།། ཡུར་མ་ཡུར་ཅན།། ས་ཡུར་དང་ཕྱི་ཡུར་གཉིས་ཡོད་ཀག།། རྟ་བ་འུན་བྱང་ཐང་ལ་ཚོང་ལ་ཆ་ཅན།། བྲ་བོ་པི་ཅན།། བྲ་བོ་རྡུང་ཅན།། རྩྭ་རྔ་ཅན།། རྩྭ་སྐྱེད་ཅན།། སེ་པེན་སིག་ཅན།། ནས་དང་གྲོ་རྔ་ཅན།། ཧི་རི་རྩིགས་ཅན།། ཧི་རི་སྐོར་ཅན།། སམ་པ་བང་ང་ལ་གྱང་ཅན།།

17.3.4.3. sTon-ka, Autumn: žiŋ-ke las-kha-'un tshar-loŋ med-ta-la, dgun-ke bča-'a bčo-'a-la 'dsug- čen. = As soon as the works in the fields are finished, people start making arrangements for the winter. lug 'un sog la pab čen, bal grag-čen, bal dab-čen. = Sheep, goats and cattle are then put to grazing around the fields (instead of sending them to the mountains), sheep are sheared and the wool is carded. sog-ma rduŋ- ŋa-nag. = Straw of long wheat are beaten for making shoes. pu-la sle-'a nag. = Straw shoes are prepared. če-'a daŋ śiŋ sgrug-ga nag. = Cattle droppings and wood are collected. drun-dro ba-glaŋ phyil-la bč'a-'a bčo-go yoŋ-ŋa nag. = Arrangements for the cattle for the winter have to be made. ran-thag 'tag- čen. = Grains are milled. bo-mo kha-čig skor-ra-la, kha-čig re-bag la čha-'a nag. = Some women go for kora (circumambulation of Dril-bu Ri) and some to Rebag (Triloknath) for pilgrimage. kha-čig kha-čig mtsho-la čha-čen. = A few of them go to mTsho (Riwalsar in Mandi) for pilgrimage. khaŋ-pa-ru miŋ-ga kha-čig-re man na lus-śe man. = Only a few people are left at home. rta-ba 'un ñuŋ-ti ne dgun-rgyag la sam-pa khyoŋ-de skyal-de ñuŋ-ti la dgun-ka de-ru sdad-če-la log-de čha-čen. = The persons with the horses bring ration from Kullu and thereafter go back to stay there in the winter. de-ne de si rtiŋ-la dgun-'jug-la čha-kan-pa gun, ñuŋ-ti la čha-čen. = Then thereafter the winter migrants go to Kullu.

སྟོན་བཀ།།་ཀེ་ལས་ཁ་འུན་ཚར་ལོང་མེད་ཏ་ལ།དགུན་ཀེ་བཅའ་འ་བཅོ་འ་ལ་འཛུག་ཅེན།། ལུག་ འུན་སོག་ལ་པབ་ཅེན། བལ་གྲག་ཅེན།དེ་ནེ་དབ་ཅེན།། སོག་མ་རྡུང་ང་ནག།། ཕུ་ལ་སླེ་འ་ནག།། ཅེ་འ་དང་ཤིང་རུག་ག་ནག།། རྡུན་དྲོ་བ་གླང་ཕྱིལ་ལ་བཅའ་བཅོ་གོ་ཡོང་ང་ནག།། རན་ཐག་ཏག་ཅེན།། བོ་མོ་ཁ་ཅིག་སྐོར་ར་ལ།ཁ་ཅིག་རེ་བག་ལ་ཆ་འ་ནག།། ཁ་ཅིག་ཁ་ཅིག་རེ་མཚོ་ལ་ཆ་ཅེན།། ཁང་པ་རུ་མིང་ག་ཁ་ཅིག་རེ་མན་ན་ལུས་ཤེ་མན།། རྟ་བ་འུན་ཉུང་ཏི་ནེ་དགུན་རྒྱག་ལ་སམ་པ་ཁྱོང་དེ་སྐྱལ་དེ་ཉུང་ཏི་ལ་དགུན་ཀ་དེ་རུ་སྡད་ཅེ་ལ་ལོག་དེ་ཆ་ཅེན།། དེ་ནེ་དེ་སི་རྟིང་ལ་དགུན་འཇུག་ལ་ཆ་ཀན་པ་གུན།ཉུང་ཏི་ལ་ཆ་ཅེན།།

17.3.4.4. dgun-ka. Winter: dgun-ka su- čig-'aŋ čhon-la lus- śe man. = In the winter nobody is left idle. bal bkal- če daŋ tha-ga ran- če, tha-ga 'tag- če, ge-re ran- če se-ra bal daŋ ral-le las-kha maŋ-po yoŋ-čen. = Spinning of wool and spreading warp, weaving, and spreading the warp of threads of goat's wool, etc. are many kinds of works of wool and goat wool. lo gsar la mgron btaŋ čen, md'a rtse-čen.= In the festival of Losar, New

Year, feast is given to the villagers and the game of arrow is played. tam ba ri rgya btaŋ čen. = Tamba-rigya ceremony is celebrated. yaŋ mčhod-pa yoŋ- čen. = There is the big ceremony of mčhodpa, prayer. čhos sil-čen. = Sacred books are recited. pa-pu sle čen. = Socks are knitted. dgun ka dus bzaŋ daŋ 'dsom raŋ maŋ-po yoŋ- čen. = In the winter there are many sacred occasions and gatherings.

དགུན་ཀ།། དགུན་ཀ་སུ་ཅིག་འདང་ཆོན་ལ་ལུས་ཤེ་མན།། བལ་བཀལ་ཅེ། དང་ཐ་ག་རན་ཅེ།ཐ་ག་འཏག་ཅེ།གེ་རེ་རན་ཅེ།སེ་ར་བལ་དང་རལ་ལེ་ལས་ཁ་མང་པོ་ཡོང་ཅེན།། ལོ་གསར་ལ་མགྲོན་བཏང་ཅེན།མདའ་རྩེ་ཅེན།། ཏམ་བ་རི་རྒྱ་བཏང་ཅེན།། ཡང་མཆོད་པ་ཡོང་ཅེན།། ཆོས་སིལ་ཅེན།། པ་པུ་སླེ་ཅེན།།དགུན་ཀ་དུས་བཟང་དང་འཛོམ་རང་མང་པོ་ཡོང་ཅེན།།

17.4. The village of Tino: *ŋa-že yul-le min-la ti-no zer-čen.* = The name of our village is Tino. *'i-ru groŋ-pa ñi- śu saŋ thal-la yod.* = There are more than twenty households here. *ŋe khaŋ-pa yul-le dkyil žig la yod.* = My house is situated in about the middle of the village. *di-riŋ yul-pha tshaŋ-ma sa-kul-ru 'dsoms-de 'dug.* = Today all the villagers have gathered in the school. *tho-re groŋ-re mi-re yu-re las-kha la čha-čen zer-de grab btaŋ-soŋ.* = They have concluded after discussion that tomorrow one person from each household will go for the work of the canal. *yu-ra san-go yod-kag.* = Canal has to be repaired. *snaŋ-ŋa la zam-pe las-kha la čha-go yod-kag.* = Day after tomorrow we have to go for the work of the bridge.

ཏི་ནོ་ཡུལ།། ང་ཞེ་ཡུལ་ལེ་མིན་ལ་ཏི་ནོ་ཟེར་ཅེན།། འི་རུ་གྲོང་པ་ཉི་ཤུ་སང་ཐལ་ལ་ཡོད།། ངེ་ཁང་པ་ཡུལ་ལེ་དཀྱིལ་ཞིག་ལ་ཡོད།། དི་རིང་ཡུལ་ཕ་ཚང་མ་ས་ཀུལ་རུ་འཛོམས་དེ་འདུག།། ཐོ་རེ་གྲོང་རེ་མི་རེ་ཡུ་རེ་ལས་ཁ་ལ་ཆ་ཅེན་ཟེར་དེ་གྲབ་བཏང་སོང་།།ཡུ་ར་སན་གོ་ཡོད་ཀག།།སྣང་ང་ལ་ཟམ་པེ་ལས་ཁ་ལ་ཆ་གོ་ཡོད་ཀག།

17.5. mds'a-bo ŋo-śes. Friends and Acquaintances: ŋa- ža gñis-kod am-be yin. = We two are ambe, born in the same year. ŋa- ža gñis-kod-te lo 'dran-'dra yin. = We are of the same age. kho ŋa-že khyim-mtshes yin. = He is our neighbor. čuŋ-ŋun ne phal-la ŋa- ža ya-to yin. = We are companions since childhood. kho ŋe thams- čad saŋ ñe-mo mza'-bo zer-na mčhed-grogs zer na-'aŋ yin. = He is my closest friend. tshe-riŋ mtsho-ru zum mkhan ŋe mčhed spun yin. = Chhering is my friend who was made at Riwalsar (by lottery). ma-nu a-be rogs-po yin-nag. = Manu is companion (in travel with horses) of my father. čam-be gad-di čan-du ŋe a-be ŋo-śe nag. = Chandu Gaddi from Chamba is acquaintance of my father. kho-'e ŋa ža la lug btaŋ-ŋa yod. = He gives us sheep. ŋa že kho la 'bru daŋ rtsam-pa btaŋ- čen. = We give him grains and flours. ŋo- śes gčig byaŋ thaŋ ru yod. = One acquaintance is in Jangthang. a-ba lo-daŋ kho yod-sa ru tshoŋ la čha-a' yod.= Father goes there every year for trade. ŋa- že kho la nas daŋ tsam-pa khyer čen. = We take for him barley and sampa. a-nu byaŋ-thaŋ-ŋe braŋ-rogs nag.= A-nu is tent-companion to Jangthang.

མཟའ་པོ།ངོ་ཤེས།། ང་ཞ་གཉིས་ཀོད་ཨམ་བེ་ཡིན།། ང་ཞ་གཉིས་ཀོད་ཧེ་ལོ་འདྲན་འདྲ་ཡིན།། ཁོ་ང་ཞེ་ཁྲིམ་མཆོས་ཡིན།། ཙུང་དུན་ནེ་ཕལ་ལ་ང་ཞ་ཡ་ཧོ་ཡིན།། ཁོ་ངེ་ཐམས་ཅད་སང་ཉེ་མོ་མཟའ་པོ་ཟེར་ན་མཆེད་གྲོགས་ཟེར་ན་འངཡིན།། ཚེ་རིང་ མཚོ་རུ་ཟུམ་མཁན་ངེ་མཆེད་སྤུན་ཡིན།། མ་ནུ་ཨ་བེ་རོགས་པོ་ཡིན་ནག།། ཙམ་བེ་གད་དི་ཙན་དུ་ཨ་བེ་ངོ་ཤེས་ནོག།། ཁོ་འེ་ང་ཞ་ལ་ལུག་བཏང་ང་ཡོད།། ང་ཞེ་ཁོ་ལ་འབྲུ་དང་རྩམ་པ་བཏང་ཙེན།། ངོ་ཤེས་ཅིག་བྱང་ཐང་རུ་ཡོད།། ཨ་བ་ལོ་དང་ཁོ་ཡོད་ས་རུ་ཚོང་ལ་ཆ་འ་ཡོད།། ང་ཞེ་ཁོ་ལ་ནས་དང་རྩམ་པ་ཁྱེར་ཙེན།། ཨ་ནུ་བྱང་ཐང་ངེ་བྲང་རོགས་ནག།།

17.6 gñid slog-če. Sleeping: ŋa-la gñid rag. = I am feeling sleepy. ŋa-la gñid yoŋ-ŋa rag. = I am feeling sleepy. kho gñid la čha rug. = He is falling asleep. kho gñid slog 'dug. = He is sleeping. kho gñid la soŋ dog. kho la gñid thob dog. = He has fallen asleep. kho la gñid ka mi-nug. = He is not feeling sleepy. kho gñid bsad soŋ. = He has awakened. kho la gñid 'daŋ ma-'daŋ dog.= He has not yet become clear of the effect of the sleep. kho la gñid ŋoms dog. = He has slept to his satisfaction. kho gñid-snaŋ-la 'grul-la nag yaŋ slab-lo lab-ba nag. = He walks while in sleep and talks.

གཉིད་སློག་ཙེ། ང་ལ་གཉིད་རག།། ང་ལ་གཉིད་ཡོང་ང་རག།། ཁོ་གཉིད་ལ་ཆ་རུག།། ཁོ་གཉིད་སློག་ཙེ་འདུག།། ཁོ་གཉིད་ལ་སོང་དོག།། ཁོ་ལ་གཉིད་ཐོབ་དོག།། ཁོ་ལ་གཉིད་ཀ་མི་ནུག།། ཁོ་གཉིད་བསད་སོང་།། ཁོ་ལ་གཉིད་འདང་མ་འདང་དོག།། ཁོ་ལ་གཉིད་ངོམས་དོག།། ཁོ་གཉིད་སྣང་ལ་འགྲུལ་ལ་ན་ཡང་སླབ་ལོ་ལབ་བ་ནག།།

17.7. Below are given examples of some typical sentences from the common usage.

kho-'e las-kha tshar-tshar ŋa ṭaŋ ṭaŋ-la laŋ de sdad pen. = I kept standing impatiently till he finished his work. kho-ni hob 'gor-ra yod.= He makes much delay. ŋa graŋ-mo si tshiŋ-tshiŋ 'dar-ra rag.= I am shivering with cold. zug-si khyi khyir-khyir khor-rug. = The dog is circling frantically around itself due to pain. bo-mo de gon-če nar-nar nar-la drud-ten čha-rug. = The woman is going dragging her long cloak. luŋ-pho-'e śad-si ča-lag kha-čig phyir-phyir phyir-la bton khyer-rug, kha-čig naŋ-naŋ naŋ-la bčug khyoŋ 'dug. = The force of the wind is throwing some articles out and some others in. bag-thon la mi-daŋ-mi 'bu tsog-se žig-žig mog-mog bcho-rug. = Men have gathered in the marriage like the multitude of insects. khaŋ-pa ru soŋ-de lag-rkyaŋ rkaŋ- rkyaŋ- la sdad-čag. = We will sit at home in leisure spreading our hands and legs. yon-bdag si kho-la kha- śi kha nag btaŋ soŋ. = His master spoke to him much harsh words.

ཁོ་འི་ལས་ཁ་ཚར་ཚར་ང་ཏང་ཏང་ལ་ལང་དེ་སྡད་པེན།། ཁོ་ནི་ཧོབ་འགོར་ར་ཡོད།། ང་གྲང་མོ་སི་ཚིང་ཚིང་འདར་ར་རག། ཟུག་སི་ཁྱི་ཁྱིར་ཁྱིར་ཁོར་རུག། བོ་མོ་དེ་གོན་ཅེ་ནར་ནར།ནར་ལ་དྲུད་ཏེན་ཆ་རུག། ལུང་ཕོ་འི་ཤད་སི་ཅ་ལག་ཁ་ཅིག་ཕྱིར་ཕྱིར།ཕྱིར་ལ་བཏོན་ཁྱེར་རུག། ཁ་ཅིག་ནང་ནང་ནང་ལ་བཅུག་ཁྱོང་འདུག། བག་ཐོན་ལ་མི་དང་མི་འབུ་ཚོག་སེ་ཞིག་ཞིག།མོག་མོག།བཅོ་རུག། ཁང་པ་རུ་སོང་དེ་ལག་རྐྱང་རྐང་རྐྱང་ལ་སྡད་ཅག། ཡོན་བདག་སི་ཁོ་ལ་ཁ་ཤི་ཁ་ནག་བཏང་སོང་།།

17.8. *m Čhod-pa,* Prayers:

In sTod people say prayers at different occasions both in Buddhism and for the local deities in Lha Čhos. Here are given some samples.

17.8.1. Following is sample of a *lama'i mčhod-pa,* a short prayer of the lamas of the Dukpa Kagyud sect. This is one of the commonest of their prayers and is also used by the laymen.

rdor-rje čhaŋ čhen ti-lli na-ro daŋ

mar-pa mi-la sgam-po tha-tsha-pa

sna-phu-pa daŋ dpal-ldan 'brug-pa-yi

bk'a-brgyud bla-ma la mčhod-pa 'bul.

Pray to Vajradhara, Tilli, (Tili-pad, born in the beginning of tenth century CE.), Naropa (Naro-pad 956-1055), Marpa (1012-1097), Milarepa (1052-1154), Gampopa (1079-1161), Tha-tsha-pa and sNaphu-pa, the reverend teachers of the Dugpa Kagyud. Beginning from the origin, the list narrates the early lineage of the Teachers of the Dugpa Kagyud sect. The sect was founded in the end of the 12th century CE.

།།རྡོ་རྗེ་འཆང་ཆེན་ཏཻ་ལླི་ན་རོ་དང་། མར་པ་མི་ལ་སྒམ་པོ་ཐ་ཚ་པ།། སྣ་ཕུ་པ་དང་
དཔལ་ལྡན་འབྲུག་པ་ཡི། བཀའ་བརྒྱུད་བླ་མ་རྣམས་ལ་མཆོད་པ་འབུལ།།

17.8.2. The following two are *skye-bo'i mchhod-pa,* Prayers of Laymen. These are prayers of the priests of the folk religion pronounced at the time of worship of the local deities.

17.8.2.1. žag bzaŋ. skar bzaŋ. dkar dkyur rtag-tu. čhar čhu dus su. skyid-pa bkra-šis. mi daŋ drun-dro daŋ de-'i gdon-bgegs dgra yi-dwags thams-čad čhu-mjug la rtsal. re-'a la kha-rgyud ma-zad čig. sems-ba la bar-čhad ma mdsad. la-bas gži-bas bsam-pa'i don grub-če rtsal.

Translation: We pray, it is auspicious day and the stars are auspicious. We pray that, the white and sour materials, that is the snow and the buttermilk (therefore milk, curd and ghee), may keep on flowing incessantly; the rain water may continue coming from time to time. Bless us with happiness. The enemy spirits and those who bring diseases and obstructions to the human beings and the animals, we pray, may they be sent to the bank of the river. Grant us that the flow of snow does not end on the mountain slopes and let no hindrances be born in our mind. May the wishes of all those who are on the move and those stationary at home, be fulfilled!

ཞག་བཟང་།།སྐར་བཟང་།། དཀར་སྐྱུར་རྟག་ཏུ།། ཆར་ཆུ་དུས་སུ།།
སྐྱིད་པ་བཀྲ་ཤིས།། མི་དང་དྲུན་འགྲོ་དང་དེ་འི་གདོན་བགེགས་དགྲ་ཡི་དྭགས་ཐམས་
ཅད་ཆུ་མཇུག་ལ་སྩལ།། རེ་འ་ལ་ཁ་རྒྱུད་མ་ཟད་ཅིག།། སེམས་བ་ལ་བར་ཆད་མ་མཛད།།
ལ་བས་གཞི་བས་བསམ་པའི་དོན་གྲུབ་ཅེ་སྩལ།།།།

17.8.2.2. Below is another prayer of the same class as above. mčhod. yul -lha la mčhod. phye lha la mčhod. la-bas gži-bas bsam-pa'i don grub-čig. bas-pha bas-ru. gži-pha gži-ru khra-rogs kyi rtsal mdsad. brag-la čha-na them-pa. čhu-la čha-na zam-pa. phu-ru dkar-ma-čhad čig. mdo-ru dkyur ma-čhad čig. han-'dre gong-po thams-čad čhu-mjug la rtsal mdsad čig. lha klu gži-bdag thams-čad la bkal-mčhod rogs rtsal mdsad čig. mčhod.

(Here in the second sentence the readings are lha-be gži-be for the present rendering of la-bas gži-bas. In the next sentence the reading is bye-pha bye-ru, for the present rendering of bas-pha bas-ru.).

Translation: Adoration and offerings to the country gods! and the gods of Flour. May all the desires of those on the mountain pass (the family men on journey) and those stationed at home be fulfilled. May all those who are on the move and those stationed at home be present complete in number at their respective places. May we have steps to climb up the rocks and have bridges to cross rivers. May the perpetual stock of the white material, snow, at the interior of the valley never exhaust, and supply of the sour things (*buttermilk,* which is ordinarily sour, therefore, milk, curd, ghee, etc.) should never stop. Send all the evil spirits to the river bank. I make offerings to the gods (of the heaven), Nagas (of the nether world) and the gods of the manor (gods of the earth), the gods of the three regions, to all. Offerings!

མཆོད་ཡུལ་ལྷ་ལ་མཆོད།ཕྱེ་ལྷ་ལ་མཆོད།།

ལ་བས་གཞི་བས་བསམ་པའི་དོན་གྲུབ་ཅིག།

བས་ཕ་བས་རུ།། གཞི་ཕ་གཞི་རུ།། ཁྲ་རོགས་ཀི་སྐུ་ལ་མཇད།།

བྲག་ལ་ཆ་ན་ཐེམ་པ།། ཆུ་ལ་ཆ་ན་ཟམ་པ།།

ཕུ་རུ་དཀར་མ་ཆད་ཅིག།། མདོ་རུ་དཀྲུར་མ་ཆད་ཅིག།།

ཧན་དྲེ་གོང་པོ་ཐམས་ཅད་ཆུ་མཇུག་ལ་སྐུ་ལ་མཇད་ཅིག།།

ལྷ་ཀླུ་གཞི་བདག་ཐམས་ཅད་ལ་བཀལ་མཆོད་རོགས་སྐུ་ལ་མཇད་ཅིག།། མཆོད།།།།

17.8.3. Below is a small piece of a prayer on behalf of the *mdso*, bullocks, pronounced each day when during the days of ploughing the bullocks are freed of the harness of the yoke in the evening.

phyug-po'i rŋos-laŋ glaŋ-la mi-skyes šig. med-po'i sgo-khyi- žig-la mi-skyes šig. = May I not be born as a bullock in the household of a rich and as a watchdog at the door of a poor household. Life in both the births is difficult.

ཕྱུག་པོའི་རྔོས་ལང་གླང་ལ་མ་སྐྱེ་ཤིག།

མེད་པོའི་སྒོ་ཁྱི་ཞིག་ལ་མ་སྐྱེ་ཤིག།

17.9. bag-glu: Marriage Song

'brel-če = Here is a small piece of composition on the word 'brel-če, to join, from the local marriage song which is still in custom. It is reply by the bridal party from the side of bridegroom:

ལགས་སམ། ཕྱི་མས།
མི་འུ་རིགས་བཞི་ལ་འབྲེལ་གཏམ་རྣམ་པ་ལྔ་དོག།
སྔ་འབྲེལ་ཅང་མེད་ན་ད་འབྲེལ་ལག་ན་མཆིས།
དད་པའི་ལ་དང་པོ་ལ་སློབ་དཔོན་དམ་ཚིག་འབྲེལ།།
དམ་པ་ཆོས་སུ་འབྲེལ།།གཡུང་རུང་བོན་དུ་འབྲེལ།།
སྐྱེད་སྒོམ་གཉིས་སུ་འབྲེལ།།དཔོན་གཡོག་ལས་སུ་འབྲེལ།།
འདི་ཕྱི་གཉིསསུ་འབྲེལ།། ཁྱིམ་ཚེ་དུ་བ་འབྲེལ།།
གཉེན་དྲུང་ཤ་ཁྲག་འབྲེལ།།
སྔ་འབྲེལ་ཅང་མེད་ཀྱང་ད་འབྲེལ་ལག་ན་མཆིས།

lags-sam phyi-mas.

mi'u rigs bži-la 'brel-gtam rnam-pa lŋa dog,
sŋa-'brel čaŋ-med na, da–'brel lag-na mčhis.
dad-pa'i daŋ-po la, slob-dpon dam-tshig 'brel
dam-pa čhos-su 'brel, g-yuŋ-ruŋ bon-du 'brel
skyed-sgom gñis-su 'brel, dpon-g-yog las-su 'brel.
'di phyi gŋis-su 'brel, khyim-tshe du-ba 'brel.
gñen-druŋ śa-khrag 'brel.
sŋa 'brel čaŋ med kyaŋ, da 'brel lag na mčhis.
skyed-sgom gñis-su 'brel, dpon-g-yog las-su 'brel.

Translation: **Yes Sir, by the Outsiders.** (Answer by the bridal party of the bridegroom)

In the four classes (Brahmin, Rajput, Kshatriy and Labour.) of men, there are five kinds of relationship. Even if there was no former relationship, the present relationship is in our hand.

In the beginning of the Faith, Acharya, Professor, binds with the solemn vow. The excellence merges with the Doctrine; and Swastik, the sign of sacred cross, with Bon. The two kinds of meditation, skyed-rim and sgom-rim, merge together. The Officer and the servant are bound by work. The present and the future, the two, are connected. The neighbours are connected by smoke. The kinsmen are connected with flesh and blood. Even if there was no connection earlier, the present relationship is in our hand.

Vocabulary

Below are given explanations of some terms of sTodpa culture:

Ju-lye: This term Ju-lye, greetings, is current in sTod and a few other areas in Lahul, and in Zanskar, Ladak, Spiti and some parts of Kinnaur. There is no knowledge about its origin. But there appears a possible source of origin. Sung Yun, a Chinese Buddhist scholar, who was deputed to collect Buddhist books from India in 518 C.E. has a reference to such a term in his travelogue. He mentions the term Ju-lai from Khotan which is translated as Tathagata (Buddha), (Beal, 1869: 180).

ri-'a = ri-'a describes the whole region of mountainous slope rising behind the village from where the village draws benefits of all kinds. Here grows bushes, nutricious grass, medicinal plants, some groves of birchwood trees, etc. The villagers graze their sheep and cattle gather fuelwood, medicinal plants, etc. But there are only sparse forests there.

rtags = Present (literally= sign). People used to send small presents like one anna, a pair of socks, pula (straw shoes), etc. to their near ones with somebody going to some distant place like from Lahul to Kullu where their near ones lived, to be delivered to them. This is called rtags. Rtags skal-che. = To send rtags (present, gift, a memorial sign.)

skad-'dri-che: (=To ask news. In practice it means to ask welfare). Similarly people used to send message with the traverllers saying like 'Palmo la ŋe-si ska 'dri-rug zer' = Tell Palmo that I was asking about her welfare.

18

The Prodigal Son

ནོར་ལ་ཕང་མེད་བཙོ་མཁན་པ་ཏུ་ཨུ་དེ།

༡' མི་ཞིག་ལ་བུ་ཙ་གཉིས་ཡོད་ཀག་ལོ།། ཞག་གཅིག་ཁོ་བ་གཉིས་གོད་ནང་ནེ་སི་
བུ་ཙ་"ཆུང་ང་དེ་སི་ཁོ་རང་གི་ཨ་བ་ལ་ཟེར་རྡུག་ལོ།། ཨ་བ་ཇུ། ང་བན་ཁྲ་ལ་ཐོབ་
ལང་ནོར་ཅ་ལག་དང་ཞིང་ཁང་ང་རང་ཀ་ལ་བགོས་དེ་བཏོང་བཏོང་།།

༢' ཨ་བེ་སི་ཁོ་འི་བན་ཁྲ་སི་རིག་བགོས་དེ་ཁོ་ལ་བཏང་བཏང་སོང་།། དེ་ནེ་དེ་ཏུ་ཨུ་
དེ་"ཁོ་རང་གི་ནོར་ཐམས་ཅད་བསྡུས་དེ་ཁྱེར་དེ་ཡུལ་ཐག་རིང་ཞིག་ལ་ལང་བུད་
སོང་།།

༣' དེ་རུ་ཁོ་ཚེ་རི་མེད་ཏ་ལ་ཞག་ཕུད་ཏེན་བསྟད་སོང་།། ཞག་ཏ་ལམ་ཞིག་ལ་ཁོ་
འི་ནོར་གྱུ་མ་སི་རིག་ཟེན་ལང་བུད་སོང་།། ཁོ་གཙང་ཀན་ཐོན་སོང་དོག།། དེར་
གྱུག་ལ་དེ་ཡུལ་རུ་སྨུ་གེ་ཆེད་མོ་ཞིག་བྱུང་སོང་།།

༤' ཁོ་དེ་ཟན་གཅིག་གང་འང་མེད་ཀན་སོང་དེ་ཡོད་ཀག།། དེ་ནེ་ཁོ་དེ་རུ་མི་ཕྱུག་
པོ་ཞིག་ཡོད་ས་རུ་ལ་བོ་ལ་བསྟད་དོག།།

༥' ཞག་གཅིག་ཁོ་ཞིང་ཀ་རུ་ཕག་ཚོ་འ་ལ་བཀལ་དོག།། དེ་རུ་ཕག་གུན་
གྲོད་པ་འགྲང་འགྲང་ཆག་ཟ་ཙེ་མཐོང་ང་ཅིག་དང་ཁོ་ལ་རློ་བསམ་ཞིག་བྱུང་སོ
ང་།། ང་ལ་འི་ཚོག་སེ་གྲོད་པ་འགྲང་འགྲང་ཟ་ལང་སུ་འི་བཏང་ཅག།། སུ་འི་སི་
འང་བཏང་ང་མ་ནག།།

༦' དེ་ནེ་ཁོ་ལ་ཁང་པེ་ཡི་ཧྲུ་ཡོང་སོང་།། ཁོ་ལ་ཨ་བ་དྲན་སོང་།། བསམ་སོང་།།
ང་ཨ་བ་ལ་འི་ཟམ་ཟ་ཙེ་མང་པོ་ཡོང་ཅེན།། ལ་བོ་ཙམ་ཡོད་ཀན་ཐམས་ཅད་གྲོད་

པ་འགྲང་འགྲང་ཟ་འ་ཡོད།། དེ་ནེ་འང་ལྷག་མ་ལུས་ཤེན།། ང་འི་རྟུ་ལྟོག་རི་ལ་ལུས་དེ་ཤེ་ཙེ་ལ་ཐུག་དེ་རག།

༧་ དེ་ནེ་ཁོ་འི་བསམ་སོང་།། ང་ལེམ་ཀ་ལོག་དེ་ཁང་པ་ལ་ཆེན།། ངེ་ཨ་བ་ལ་ཟེར་རེན། ཨ་བ་ཧྲུ།། ང་ཁྱོད་ཡོད་ས་རྟུ་ཡོད་ཟན། ངེ་དགོན་ཅོག་ལ་བློ་བསམ་མ་བཏང་བེན།། དེ་ཟན་ངེ་ལ་ཡོག་བཙོས་ཁག།། དང་ཁྱོ་འི་བུ་ཙ་ཟེར་ཁོ་འ་མེད།། ང་ཡང་ལོག་དེ་ཡོང་དེ་ཡོད།། ང་ལ་ཁྱོ་རང་གི་ལ་བོ་ཅོག་སེ་བཙོས་དེ་འཁོར་ན་འང་འགྲིག།

༨་ དེ་ནེ་ཁོ་ལང་དེ་དེ་འ་མེད་ཏ་ལ་ཁོ་རང་གི་ཁང་པ་ལ་ལྟོས་དེ་ཆོམ་སོང་།། ཁང་པ་རྟུ་སླེབ་མ་སླེབ་བ་ལ་ཐག་རིང་ནེ་སེ་ཁང་པ་ལ་ལྟོས་དེ་བལྟོས་སོང་།། ཨ་བ་ཕྱི་ཏ་རྟུ་སྡོད་དེ་ཡོད་ཙེ་མཐོང་འདུག། ཁོ་ཡོང་ཙེ་མཐོང་ང་ཅིག་དང་ཨ་བ་ཤུག་ལང་དེ་ཐག་རིང་ནེ་ཁོ་ལ་ཐུག་ག་ལ་ཡོང་སོང་།། ཁོ་ལ་ཟུམ་དེ་ཁོ་ལ་འོལ་རྫིལ་བཏང་སོང་།།

༩་ དེ་ནེ་ཁོ་འི་སྔོན་ལ་བསམ་མཁན་ཅོག་སེ་སི་རིག་ཁོ་རང་གི་ཨ་བ་ལ་ཟེར་ར་ཅིག་དང་རྗེང་མཇུག་ལ་ཟེར་སོང་།། ང་ཁྱོའི་བུ་ཙ་ཟེར་ཁོ་འ་མེད།།

༡༠་ དེ་ནེ་ཨ་བེ་སི་ཁོ་རང་གི་ལ་བོ་ཙུན་ནང་ནེ་གཅིག་གཅིག་ལ་ཟེར་དེ་བཏང་སོང་།། ངེ་འི་ཏུ་ཙུ་ནང་ལ་ཁྱེར།། ཁོ་ལ་ཐམས་ཅད་སང་བདེ་མོ་ཡོད་ཀན་གོས་ལག་དེ་བཏོང་།། ཡང་ཁོ་ལ་ལག་པ་ལ་སྐད་ལང་གསུར་དུབ་དང་རྐང་པ་ལ་གོན་ལང་ཀབ་ཤ་འང་བཏོང་།། དེ་ནེ་ཨ་བེ་སི་ཟེར་སོང་གྲུལ་ཨྰ་འོ་ཟ་ཙེ་ཟོ་འེན།ཡང་ད་ཙུ་ལབ་བེན། ཙེ་ལ་ཟེར་ན་ང་ལ་ཁྱོད་ཤེ་ཡུལ་ནེ་ལོག་དེ་ཡོང་བསྡད་མཁན་ཅོག་སེ་ཚོར་ར་རག།། ཁྱོད་གསོན་པོ་ལ་ལོག་དེ་ཡོང་སོང་།། སྟོར་སོང་དེ་ཡོད་ཧེན།། ད་ཡང་ལོག་དེ་ཐོབ་སོང་།། དེ་ནེ་ཁོ་བ་སྐྱིད་པོ་བཙོས་དེ་བསྡད་ཙེ་བཙོས་སོང་།།

༡༡་ དེ་ཟན་ཁོ་འི་ཨ་ཅོ་ཞིང་ཀ་ནེ་ཡོང་ང་ཡོད་ཀག།། ཁང་པེ་མདུན་དེ་རྟུ་སླེབ་བ་ཅིག་དང་ཁོ་ལ་ནང་རྟུ་རྩེ་ཙེ་དང་གླུ་བཏང་ཙེ་སྐད་ཚོར་སོང་།། ཁོ་འི་ལ་བོ་ཞིག་ལ་བོས་དེ་དྲིས་སོང་།། འི་ཙེ་ཡིན་ནག།། ལ་བོ་སི་ཕཤད་སོང་ཁྱོ་རང་

ཀི་ནོ་ཡོང་དེ་འདུག། ཨ་བེ་སི་ཁོ་ལ་མགྲོན་བཏང་འདུག། ཅི་ལ་ཟེར་ན་ཁོ་
གསོན་པོ་ལ་ལོག་དེ་ཡོང་ཁག། དེ་ལ་ཨ་ཙོ་མ་འཐད་སོང་།། ཁོ་ལ་ཁང་པེ་
ནང་དུ་ཆ་ཅེ་ཁམ་ཞིག་མ་བྱུང་སོང་།།

༡༢་ དེ་ནེ་ཁོ་འི་ཨ་བ་ཕྱི་ཏ་ལ་འཐོན་དེ་ཁོ་བཙོལ་ལ་ལ་ཟུག་སོང་།། ཁོ་འི་སི་ཨ་བ་
ལ་ལན་ལ་ཟེར་སོང་།། ང་ལ་ལྷོས་ང་ལོ་འི་ཟམ་ནེ་སི་ཕལ་ལ་ཁྱོ་འི་ལ་བོ་བཙོ་འ་
ཡོད།། ཡང་ཁྱོ་རང་"ཀི་ཟེར་མཁན་སི་རིག་ངེ་བཙོ་འ་ཡོད།། དེ་ནེ་འདང་དི་རིང་
ཚག་པ་ནམ་ཞིག་འདང་ཁྱོའི་སི་ང་ལ་།ང་རང་ཀི་ཡ་ཧོ་ཙུན་མཉམ་པོ་སྡད་དེ་སྡུད་
ཅེ་ཞིག་བཙོ་ཅེ་ཕྱིལ་ལ་ལུ་ཙུ་ཞིག་འདང་བཏང་མ་སྒོང་།།

༡༣་ ཁྱོ་འི་འི་བུ་ཙ་དོན་མེད་སི་ནེ་ཏུ་ཙུ་དོན་མེད་ཙུན་མཉམ་པོ་སྡད་དེ་ཁྱོ་རང་ཀི་ནོར་
ཙ་ལག་གྲུ་མ་སི་རིག་ཕང་མེད་ལ་ཟེན་ཅེ་བཏང་སོང་།། དེ་ནེ་འདང་ཁོ་ཡོང་ལོང་
མེད་དེ་ཁོ་འི་ཕྱིལ་ལ་ཁྱོ་འི་སི་སྐྱིད་པོ་བཙོས་དེ་མགྲོན་བཏང་སོང་།། ཨ་བེ་
སི་ཁོ་ལ་ཟེར་སོང་།། བུ་ཙ་ཁྱོད་ཙབ་ཙ་རེ་ང་མཉམ་པོ་སྡད་ཏ་ནག། ང་ལ་ཅི་
ཡོད་ཀན་སི་རིག་ཁྱོ་འི་ནག། དེ་ནེ་འདང་ང་ལ་བགའ་རི་རག་ཅི་ལ་ཟེར་ན་ཁྱོའི་
ནོ་ཤི་སོང་མཁན་ཅོག་སེ་ཡོད་ཧེན།། ཁོ་ཡང་གསོན་པོ་ལ་ལོག་དེ་སླེབ་སོང་།།
སྟོར་སོང་དེ་ཡོད་ཧེན་ཡང་ལོག་དེ་ཐོབ་སོང་།།

Transliteration and Translation: The Prodigal Son

nor-la phaŋ-med bčo-mkhan ṭu-‘u-de.

1. mi-žig-la bu-tsa gñis yod-kag-lo. žag-gčig kho-ba gñis-kod naŋ-ne bu-tsa čhuŋ-ŋa-de-si kho-raŋ-ki a-ba-la zer-rug lo. a-ba ju. ŋe ban-ṭha-la thob-laŋ nor ča-lag daŋ žiŋ-khaŋ ŋa-raŋ-ka-la bgos-de btoŋ btoŋ.

   It is told that a man had two sons. One day, among the two, the younger son asked his father, oh kind father, give me my share of ornaments, articles and the propertys dividing to me.

2. a-be-si kho-‘e ban-ṭha si-rig bgos-de kho-la btaŋ btaŋ soŋ. de-ne de ṭu-‘u de kho-raŋ-ki nor thams-čad bsdus-de khur-de yul thag-riŋ žig-la laŋ bud soŋ.

The father dividing the property gave him all his share. Then the boy collecting all his property went carrying them to a far off village.

3. de-ru kho tshi-ri med-ta-la žag pud-ten bsdad soŋ. žag ha-lam žig-la kho-'e nor gya-ma si-rig zin laŋ-bud soŋ. kho gtsaŋ-kan thon-soŋ dog. der-gyag-la de yul-ru mu-ge čhed-mo žig byuŋ-soŋ.

   There he lived without worry, spending the days. After some days he exhausted all his property. He became a pauper. By the time there occurred a big draught in the area.

4. kho de-za-na gcig gaŋ-'aŋ med-kan soŋ-de yod-kag. de-ne kho de-ru mi phyug-po žig yod-sa-ru la-bo-la bsdad-dog.

   At that time he possessed nothing. Then he became a servant of a rich man.

5. žag gcig kho žiŋ-ka-ru phag tso-'a-la bkal-dog. de-ru phag-gun grod-pa 'graŋ-'graŋ čag za-če mthoŋ-ŋa čig daŋ kho-la blo(g)-bsam žig byuŋ-soŋ. ŋa-la 'i tsog-se grod-pa 'graŋ-'graŋ za-laŋ su-'i btaŋ čag. su-'i si-'aŋ btaŋ-ŋa ma-nag.

   One day he was sent to graze the hogs to the field. Looking at the hogs there eating the grains to their full, a thought arose to him. Who will give me meal like this to my full. Nobody will give me.

6. de-ne kho-la khaŋ-pe yi-tu yoŋ-soŋ. kho-la a-ba dran soŋ. bsam-soŋ. ŋe a-ba-la 'i-zam za-če maŋ-po yoŋ-čen, la-bo tsam yod-kan thams-cad grod-pa 'graŋ-'graŋ za-'a yod. de-ne 'aŋ lhag-ma lus- šen. ŋa 'i-ru ltog-ri-la lus-de ši-če-la thug-de rag.

   Then he remembered his home. He remembered his father. He thought, my father owned so much food that, there could be any number of servants, all ate to their full. Still there used to be left surplus. Here I am left in hunger and am nearing to the death.

7. de-ne kho-'e bsam soŋ. ŋa lem-ka log-de khaŋ-pa la čhen. ŋe a-ba-la zer-ren. a-ba ju. ŋa khyod yod-sa-ru yod-za-na. ŋe dkong-čog la blo(g)-bsam ma-btaŋ-ben. de-za-na ŋe la-yog bčos-khag. da ŋa khyo-'e bu-tsa zer kho-'a med. ŋa yaŋ log-de yoŋ-de yod. ŋa-la khyo-raŋ-ki la-bo tsog-se bcos-de 'bor-na-'aŋ 'grig.

   Then he thought. I will go back to home just now. I will tell my father. Oh kind father, during the time when I was with you, I did not remember the god. At that time I committed sin. Now I am not worth calling your son. I have come back. It will be alright even if you keep me as your servant.

8. de-ne kho laŋ-de de-'a med-ta la kho-raŋ-ki khaŋ-pa la ltos de chom-soŋ. khaŋ-pa-ru sleb ma-sleb-ba la thag-riŋ ne si khaŋ-pa la ltos-de bltos-soŋ. a-ba phyi-ta-ru sdad-de yod-če mthoŋ 'dug. kho yoŋ-če mthoŋ-ŋa čig daŋ a-ba śug laŋ-de thag-riŋ ne kho-la thug-ga-la yoŋ soŋ. kho-la zum-de kho-la 'ol-hril btaŋ soŋ.

   Then immediately he stood up and started going towards his home. Before reaching home he looked from distant towards his home. He saw his father sitting outside. As soon as he saw him coming his father stood up at once and came from distant to meet him. Holding his son he embraced him.

9. de-ne kho-'e sŋon-la bsam-mkhan tsog-se si-rig kho-raŋ-ki a-ba-la zer-ra-čig daŋ rtiŋ-mjug-la zer-soŋ. ŋa khyo-'e bu-tsa zer kho-'a med.

   Then after saying whatever he had thought earlier, at the end he said, now I am not worth to be called your son.

10. de-ne a-be si kho-raŋ-ki la-bo-'un naŋ-ne gcig gcig-la zer-de btaŋ soŋ. ŋe 'i ṭu-'u naŋ-la khyer. kho-la thams-čad saŋ bde-mo yod-kan gos-lag de btoŋ. yaŋ kho-la lag-pa-la skad-laŋ gsur-dub daŋ rkaŋ-pa-la gon-laŋ kab-śa btoŋ. de-ne a-be si zer-soŋ grul a'a-'o za-ce zo-'en yaŋ da-'u lab-ben. či-la zer-na ŋa-la khyod ši-yul ne log-de yoŋ sdad-mkhan tsog-se tshor-ra rag. khyod gson-po la log de yoŋ soŋ. stor-soŋ de yod-ten. da yaŋ log-de thob soŋ. de-ne kho-ba skyid-po bcos-de bsdad-ce bcos-soŋ.

    Then the father called one of his servants and told him, take this my son in. Give him the best suit. Then give him finger-ring and shoes. Then the father said, let us go, we will have meal and we will talk together. Because, I feel like that you have come live from the land of death. You have come back live. I had lost you. Now I have found you again. Then they arranged to live happily.

11. de za-na kho-'e a-čo žiŋ-ka ne yoŋ-ŋa yod-kag. khaŋ-pe mdun-de-ru sleb-ba čig daŋ kho-la naŋ-ru rtse-če daŋ glu btaŋ-če skad tshor soŋ. kho-'e la-bo žig-la bos-de dris-soŋ. 'i či yin-nag. la-bo-si bšad soŋ khyo-raŋ-ki no yoŋ-de 'dug. a-be-si kho-la mgron btaŋ 'dug. či-

la zer-na kho gson-po la log-de yoŋ-khag. de-la a-čo ma-'thad soŋ. kho-la khaŋ-pe naŋ-ru čha-če kham-žig ma-byuŋ soŋ.

At that time his elder brother was coming from the field. As soon as he reached in front of his home he heard sound of dancing and singing inside. He called a servant and asked him, what is this. The servant told, your younger brother has come. Father is giving him feast because he has come live. The elder brother was not pleased on this. He did not like to go in..

12. de-ne kho-'e a-ba phyi-ta la 'thon-de kho bčol-la-la zug soŋ. kho-'e si a-ba la lan-la zer-soŋ. ŋa-la ltos ŋa lo 'i-zam ne si phal-la khyo-'e la-bo bčo-'a yod. yaŋ khyo-raŋ ki zer-mkhan si-rig ŋe bčo-'a yod. de-ne 'aŋ di-riŋ tshag-pa nam-žig 'aŋ khyo-'e si ŋa-la. ŋa-raŋ-ki ya-to-'un mñam-po sdad-de sdud-če žig bčo-če phyil-la lu-'u žig 'aŋ ma-btaŋ myoŋ.

    Then his father came out and began entreating him. He told his father. Look at me I have been serving you for so many years. I do all whatever you say to do. Even then till today you never gave even a lamb for sitting and feasting with my friends.

13. khyo-'e 'i bu-tsa don-med-si ni ṭu-u don-med 'un mñam-po sdad-de khyo-raŋ-ki nor ča-lag gya-ma si-rig phaŋ-med-la zin-če btaŋ soŋ. de-ne 'aŋ kho yoŋ-loŋ med-de kho-'e phyil-la khyo-'e si skyid-po bčos-de mgron btaŋ soŋ. a-be si kho-la zer soŋ. bu-tsa khyod čab-ča-re ŋa mñam-po sdad-ta-nag. ŋa-la či yod-kan si-rig khyo-'e nag. de-ne 'aŋ ŋa-la bg'a-ris rag či-la zer-na khyo-'e no ši soŋ mkhan tsog-se yod-ten. kho yaŋ gson-po log-de sleb soŋ. stor soŋ-de yod-ten. yaŋ log-de thob soŋ.

    Your worthless son wasted all your wealth in the company of worthless boys. Even then as soon as he came you arranged a feast for him for making pleasure. The father told him. Oh my son, you live always with me. Whatever I own all is yours. Still I am happy because your younger brother was like as if he had been dead. He came again live. He had been lost, we have found him again.

Note: This story has been taken from the Grierson's Linguistic Survey of India which was got translated in every language included in the survey but sTodpa language was not included in the Survey.

19
Vocabulary: Verbs

Transliteration and Meaning

Note on Pronunciation: All compound letters with the consonants s and r should be pronounced as voiced retroflex fricative *ş* **.** Examples:

sran-če = şan-če, srung-če = şung-če, sprad-če = şad-če. About the other words wherever they have some deviation in voice from the lexical norms are shown in bracket.

kakug-če = to bend, branch of tree; turn, a herd of sheep going in wrong direction. **kum-če** = to reduce in size gradually (in knitting sweater). **kog-če** = to snatch. **krum-če** (ṭum) = to prune, a tree. **bkag-če** = to block, obstruct. **bkad-če** = to hang, on a nail. **bkab-če** = to cover, with a lid. **bkar-če** = to put in confinement. **bkal-če** = 1. To spin, wool; 2. to send, a message; 3. to place a thing on something, (kho'e khu-ru mgo'e kha la bkal-de kher-rug. = He carries load on his head.). **bkog-če** = 1. To snatch. 2. To peel off, **dkri-če** (şi-če) = wind (thod şi-če = wind turban). **dkrug-če**. (şug-če) = to shake, stir. **dkrog-če** (şog-če) = to drive away, birds. **bkram-če** (ṭam-če) = to spread in arranged manner. **bkral-če** (ṭal- če) = to split, tear. **bkri-če** (ṭi-če) = to reduce, meal from plate. **bkrol-če** (ṭol-če) = to loosen, open a knot. **'kyiŋ-če** = to bind; tether. **rku–če** = to steal. **rkod-če**. = to dig. **rkyaŋ-če** = to stretch. **skaŋ-če** = to fill. **skad-če** = entrust (las-pha la las-kha skad-če = to entrust work to a worker.). **skam-če** = to dry up. **skar-če** = to weigh. **skuŋ-če** = to put, keep in a pit.

skud-če = to smear, **skul-če** = to shake. **skon-če** = to dress, put on clothes on another person, thing. **skor-če** = 1. to encircle (by boundary wall). 2. tr. to spin. **skol-če** = to boil. **skyag-če** = to spend, expend. **skyal-če** = to conduct, carry a thing and deliver. carry and deliver a thing at some distant place. (khaŋ-pa ne zhiŋ-ka ru za- če skyal-če. = to carry, meal from home and deliver at the field).

skyi-če = to borrow; lend. **skyil-če** = to gather water in a vessel, pool. **skyug-če** = to vomit. **skye-če** = to give birth, concieve; be born, to sprout. **skyed-če** = to carry. **skyel-če** = to fell by pushing. **kyog-če** = to weild, to engage hand, in a work. **skyod-če, hon.** = to come, go. **skyon-če** = to put astride upon a thing (rta'i kha la **skyon-če** = to put, a man on a horse). **skyob-če**= to protect. **skyor-če** = to block (light, view). **skraŋ-če** (şaŋ-če) = to get swelled.

kha

khaŋ-če = to get filled. **khog-če** = to cough. **khoŋ-če** = to become shriveled (by cold). **khyag-če** = to freeze. **khyam-če** = to roam, wander; move aimlessly. **khyil-če** = to get accumulated, water in pond. **khyug-če** = to move, move in wavering manner, like the feeling of moving pain in the arm. **khyus-śe** = to get melted, ghee in natural heat. **khyed-če** = to suffice (ration for a week). **khyob-če**= to be numbed by cold. **khyor-če** = to stagger (a drunkard). **khrab- če** = to argue. **khrel-če** = to mock at (a person wearing unmatched clothes). **khrod-če** =t. to suit. 2. to get hit at target. **khros-śe** = to re-erupt, a wound. **mkhyen-če,** hon. = to know. **mkhraŋ-če** = to become straight, stand erect. **'khad-če** = to get stuck up with something (wood log with a rock in the river). **'khar-če** = to get stuck up, by road block, be encircled. **'khun-če** = to make short and low voice of agony (by a serious patient). **'khur-če** = to carry. '**khor-če** = to turn around, roam, travel. '**khol-če** = to get boiled. **'khyer-če** = to carry, take away. **'khyoŋ-če** = to bring. **'khrig-če**= to become cloudy. **'khrid-če** = to lead. **'khril-če** =to wind, coil round. Like two serpents together. **'khrug-če** = to quarrel **'khrud-če** = to bathe, wash (utensils).

ga

gad-če = to be fit, dress to a person, plug in a hole. **gam-če** = to eat dry (a spoonful) (rtsam-pa gam- če). **guŋ-če** = to sink, (dam-pag la guŋ-če = to merge in the mud). **gur-če** = to bear, tolerate. **go-če** = to understand. **gom-če** = to cross over a thing. **gos-śe** = to get smeared (ŋe gos-lag la tshos gos-soŋ= My clothes have caught colour). **graŋ-če** = to become cold. **grog-če** = get suddenly frightened. **glu-če** = to allure, (ṭu-'u glu- če = to look after a child). **dgar-če** = to confine (lug dgar-če = to put sheep in the pen). **dgod-če** = to laugh. **dgos-śe** = to be in necessity. **bgod-če** = to divide. **bgon-če** = to put on, wear, to dress. **'gag-če** = to get choked (food in throat). **'gab-če**

= to cover, bird over its eggs. **'gar-če** = to put to confinement. **'gug-če** = to wait. **'gul-če** = to get stirred. **'gog-če** = to get peeled. **'gor-če** = to get delayed. **'gyur-če** = to get changed. **'gyel-če** = to fall. **'gyes-śe** = to be split up, be cleaved. **'gyog-če** = be quick, be earlier than the stipulated time, (kho saŋ ŋa 'gyog = I am faster/earlier than him). **'graŋ-śe** = to be satiated. **'grad-če** = to scratch. **'gred-če** = to slip. **'gral-če** = to be torn. **'grig-če** = to suit, agree, suffice. **'grim-če** = to get sold. **'gril-če** = to fall. **'grub-če** = to be complete, finish, a task. **'grul-če** – to walk. **'groŋ-če,** hon. = to die, be no more.. **'grol-če** = to become loosened. **rgal-če** = to ford river, cross pass. **rgas-śe** = to grow old. **rgyag-če** = to become fattened, be healthy; to get spent. **rgyaŋ-če** = fill in. **rgyab-če** = to hit, do. **rgyal-če** = to win; recover (from sickness). **rgyug-če** = 1. To run 2. flow, water. **rgyud-če** = to put thread through needle's eye (khab-la skud-pa rgyud- če). **sgar-če** = to dry up (water in curry on the hearth). **sgom-če** = to meditate. **sgyur-če** = to change, transform, turn. **sgrig- če** = to arrange. **sgrug-če** = to pick. **sgrog-če,** (rog-če), = recitation of scriptures.

ŋa:

ŋu-če = to weep. **ŋom-če** = to be satiated (from thirst). **rŋa-če** = to mow. **rŋo-če** (Lex. rmo) = to plough. **rŋod-če** = parch (nas yos rŋod-če = parch barley grain).

ča

čag-če = to wash, clothes (gos-lag čag-če = wash clothes). **čar-če** = winnow. **gčar-če** = to stick to wall, a paper. **bčag-če** = to break. **bčad-če** = to cut. **bčab-če** = to become attached with someone. **bču-če** = 1. To irrigate 2. take out water with laddle. **bčug-če** = to put in. **bčun-če** = to allure. **bčus-če** = to screw, wind. **bčer-če** = to squeeze. **bčo-če** = to do (las-kha bčo-če = to do work, to work). **bčom-če** = to pillage, conquer. **bčol-če** = 1. to entreat, request 2. give a thing for safe-keeping. l**čog-če =** to cover (lab-si daŋ mgo lčog-če = to cover, head with towel). **lčeb-če = to** embrace (čhu la čeb-če = to embrace water, i.e. river, i.e. to commit suicide by jumping into river).

čha

čha-če = to go. **čhug-če** = to be dented (zaŋ-bu čhug-de 'dug= the kettle is dented). **čhud-če** = to have space enough for insertion of a thing;

(‘i naŋ ru miŋ-ga lŋa čhud-če ‘dug = Five persons can be accommodated in this room). **čhub-če** = to land (birds, aeroplane). **čhom-če** = to be ready for going (khyod mñam-po ŋa-‘aŋ čhom-kan= I also want to come with you). **mčhoŋ-če** = to jump. **mčhod-če** hon. = to propitiate, worship; to offer prayers and small pieces or drops of articles placed for consumption like čhaŋ, arag, food items, to the deities, before starting eating or drinking. **‘čhag-če** = 1. to be broken. 2. be born, to bear fruit. **‘čhags-če** = to be founded, settle. **‘čhad-če** = be cut off. **‘čham-če** = 1. To be in accord. 2. dance (religious) (bag čham-če= do mask dance). **‘čhol-če** = to be shaken, water in a half filled pitcher.

ja

mjal-če hon. = to see, meet (zlar mjal-če = have view of the moon). **‘jab-če** = to sneak, lie in wait. ‘jar- **če** = to get stuck. **‘jig-če** (žig) = to be destroyed, go out of order. **‘jigs-če** = to fear. **‘jib--če** = to suck. **‘jug-če** (žug) = to enter, get in. **‘jur-če** (žur) = to chop, branches of a tree, snatch. **‘jus-če** (žu) = to take hold of, hold a branch for remaining suspended. **‘jog-če** (žog) = to make plain, a plank with aisle, hew. **rjed-če** (žed) = to forget. **ljon-če** = to be capable of doing a thing, know how to do a thing (ŋa-la pa-pu sle-če ljon-na med. = I don’t know how to knit socks).

ña

ñag-če = sawing. **ñan-če** = to lend ear to, listen. **ñal-če** = to sleep. **ñug-če** = to fumble (śug čan-da la ñug ‘dug = at once fumbles in the pocket); to gropc. **ñul-če** = searching around, sheep amid boulders for grass. **ño-če** = to purchase. **gñal-če** = to put to sleep. **mñaŋ-če =** to taste. **mñed-če** = to rub, to tan. **sñan-če** = to be able to do a thing (dad-saŋ bsan ñan-če mi-nug = It cannot be repaired presently). **sñid-če** = to whither, fade. **sñel-če** = to lie along, the wall, lean on. **sñod-če** = to feed by putting meal in mouth. **sñom-če** = to make level, smoothen.

ta

tel-če = to reach. **to-če** = to happen (čaŋ mi-to = does not matter). **gtad-če** = to deliver with care, entrust. **gtub-če** = to cut. **gtum-če** = wrap. **gtul-če** = to crush, grind. **btaŋ-če** = to give. **btab-če** = to put in (seed in field) (thug-pa la pu-ḷu tab- če = to put noodles in gruel). **btiŋ-če** = to spread, mat. **‘tag-če** = to grind, spice; to mill (ran-thag ‘tag-če = to mill flour); weave (tha-ga ‘tag-če= weave). **rten-če** = to uphold, support. **rtol-če** = to prick open, a blister; pierce. **lta-če** = to see. **ltag-če** = to lift. **ltab-če** = to fold. **ltam-če, hon.** = to be born. **ltem-če** = to become brimmed. **stan-če** = to show, exhibit. **stig-če** = to plug. **stug-če** = to sew, with hand; to lit fire. **sten-če** = to lean against. **ston-če** = 1. To show; 2. bring out, expel. **stor-če** = be lost, have lost.

tha

thag-če = to become ready for going (ŋa mñam-po čha-če la si-rig thag de ‘dug = All have become ready to go with me). 2. get elevated, increased, wages. 3. be able to carry a load; (‘i khu-ru ŋe thag khyud-če rag = I can carry this load). **tham-če** = to hold. **thar-če** = to cross successfully (‘i zam-pa la ṭu-‘u ‘un thar-če mi-nug= children cannot cross this bridge). **thal-če** = to exceed. **thim-če** = to get absorbed. **thug-če** = to meet, come to contact. **thub-če** = to be able to do. **theb-śe** = to be sufficient to reach from one point to another, by thread, rope. **thob- če** = to find, get. **mthaŋ-če** = to become clear, sky. **mthud-če** = tr. to join, two ends of thread. **mthun-če** = to agree. **mthoŋ-če** = to be seen. **‘thad-če** = to be pleased, be happy. **‘thab-če** (ṭhab) = to quarrel, argue. **‘thig-če** = to drip, to fall in drops. **‘thuŋ-če** = to drink. **‘thul-če** = to make ball of thread. **‘then-če** = to pull. **‘thog-če** = to touch. **‘thon-če** = to go out, come out.

da

dag-če = to become clean, after washing. **dar-če** = to get spread, expand. **dib-če** = to crumble down, a roof. **dur-če** = 1. to compete; 2. overripe while cooking. **dogs-če** = to keep safe. **dom-če** = to be busy (ŋe lag-pa dom-de rag= I am busy).

rdar-če = to sharpen. **rduŋ-če** = to beat. **rdol-če** = to come out, break forth from, burst out. **ldag-če** = to lick. **ldab-če =** 1. To knock, to throw; 2. card wool. **ldir-če** = to thunder (‘brug ldir-ra rag. = The dragon is thundering (shaking?) i.e. the cloud is thundering.

sdad-če = to sit. **sdam-če** = to bind. **sdug-če** = get burned, clothes. **sdud-če** = to collect. **sdeb-če** = exchange, change.

drags- če = to bind, load (khu-ru drags-če = to bind load). **dran- če** = to remember (a-ma dran-če= A child remembering mother after separation). **dras-śe** = to cut, cloths.

bdab-če = to measure. **bdug-če** = to take incense, (bdug-rdsas bdug-če = to take incense). ‘daŋ-**če** = to be cleared of an effect like that of anger or drink, etc. ŋa ra/sro ‘daŋ-de rag. = I am clear of the effect of intoxication/ anger. **‘dar-śe** = to tremble, with fear, cold. **‘dig-če** = to become choked. **‘dus-śe** = to gather, assemble. **‘ded- če** = to drive. **‘don-če, hon.** = to eat, drink. **‘dra-če** = to be similar. **‘dral-če** = to get torn, be separated. **‘dri-če** = to ask. **‘drud-če** = to draw, pull along, drag. **‘dre-če** = to get mixed. **‘dros-śe** = become warm.

na

na-če = to become sick. **nan-če** = to press, to add. **nub-če** = set, to sink, merge (kha-la nub čha-’a rag = My feet are merging in the snow). **nog-če** = to be harmed, spiritually. **non-če** = overtake. **nor-če** = to make mistake, faulter. **gnod-če** = to harm. **mnum-če** = to smell. **snam-če** hon. = to take, hold; to die down, (mčhod-me snam soŋ.- the prayer lamp has dimmed). **snol-če** = to grapple, fight. **mnam-če, hon.** = to go dim. mčhod-me mnam-soŋ = The prayer lamp has died out.

pa

pab-če = to bring down. **pi-če** = to uproot. Plants, grass. **pir-če** = to crush (to separate seed from dry pod by pressing between the fingers, without damaging the grains). **pil- če** = to rub slowly. **puŋ-če** = to heap up. **pud-če** = to let loose. **‘pul-če hon.** = to offer (mčhod-me pul-če= to light prayer lamp).

dpe-če = to open, sort, separate. **dpag-če** = to measure. **dpuŋ-če** = to heap up.

spag-če = to dip, a crumb of cake in curry. **spar-če** = to stretch for throwing, a stone; light fire like lamp; excite an animal for sacrifice. **spug-če** = to make hole. **spub-če** = to lay or spread tent. **spel-če** = to add to mix. **spo-če** = spill, pour out. **spog-če** = to put down, load.

sprad-če (şad-če) = to send off, depart. **spriŋ-če (şiŋ)** = to hand over, convey, give, deliver. **sprug-če (şug-če)** = to shake.

pha

phaŋ-če = to throw, cast. **phan-če** = to benefit; to suit, medicine. **phebs-če, hon.** = to come, go. **phyid-če** (fid-če) = to be affected by chilblains. Potato becoming affected by frost; wipe off, to clean.

'pham-če = to be defeated. (pham-če btaŋ-če = defeat). **'phar-če** = to increase, cost. **'phud-če** = blow, pipe. 2. light fire, in the hearth. **'phur-če** = to fly. **'phul-če** = to push. **'phel-če** = to expand, spread. **'phog-če** = to be hit. **'phrad-če** = to meet unexpectedly, calf with mother. **'phrod-če** = to be fired, matchlock; hit the mark.

ba

ba-rim-če = to wipe. **bir-če** = to be scattered, seed from a pod. **bil-če** = to cat, consume. **bud-če** = to get loosened, separated. **ber-če** = to twinging pain, feel wavering pain on a wound. **ba-run-če** = to sprout.

byis-če (byis) = to get uprooted, hair from head. **bro-če** = to taste (tsha bro-'a-rag= salt tastes proper). **dbye-če** = to get opened. **'bag-če** = to put in mouth to taste, (kha-la 'bag-če 'aŋ ma-thob= I did not get even for putting in my mouth, for tasting.). **'bab-če** = to move down. **'bar-če** = to bloom (men-tog 'bar-dog= the flower has blossomed); get burned (me 'bar-rug.= The fire is burning). **'bug-če** = to get hole made. **'bub-če** = to stumble (ga-ga 'bub-**če** = stumble.). **'bur-če** = to sprout. **'bo-če** = to be spilled out. **'bog-če** = to be uprooted, teeth. **'bod-če** = to call. **'bor-če** = to leave, keep, place. **'bos-śe** = swell, spill out. **'byuŋ-če** = to become, to be. **'byor-če** = to gain, own, find. **'bral-če** = to get separated. **'brag-če** = to cut, hair; shear wool. **'brad-če** = to scratch.

'brab-če = to pluck, leaves from a plant. **'bri-če** = to be reduced, lessened, decrease. 2. write. ' **'bru-če** = to dig, burrow. **'brug-če** = get dispersed (seeds from pods), fall. **'bred-če** = to slip. **'brel-če** = to get mixed, come together. **'bres-če** = to cut cloths by the tailor. '**brog-če** = to be surprised, be suddenly frightened. **sbaŋ-če** = to soak, be soaked, be drenched. **sbas-če** = hide. **sbyaŋ- če** = to study, learn, practice. bčo-'en bčo-'en sbyaŋ čh-'a nag. = As you keep on doing, you become trained.

ma

mig-če = to swallow. **mun-če** = 1. To get dimmed, a lamp. 2. become unconscious. **med- če** = not to have. **mol-če** hon.= to say. **mer-če** = to settle down, the thick matter in a liquid mixture. **myaŋ-če** = to taste, for salt. **myoŋ-če** = experience trouble. **dmod-če** = to curse. **rmug-če** = 1. to bark (dog); 2. bite (by dog). **rmur-če** = to gnaw. **smyo-če** = to become insane, mad.

tsa

tsum-če = to close (mig tsum-če = close eyes). **tsem-če** = to sew. **tso-če** = to graze. **tsog-če** = to prick, hit with a pointed object like stone block. **tsoŋ-če** = to sell. **tsod-če** = cook, die with colour.

gtsir- če = to squeeze. **gtsug-če** = prick, needle; plant. **btsag-če** = to sieve. **btsal-če** = to search. **rtsi-če** = count. **rtsig-če** = to construct. **rtsis-če** = to twinging sensation in teeth after eating a strong sour thing. **rtse-če** = play, dance. **rtsom-če** = to compose. **srtsal-če** hon. = to give, take.

tsha

tshaŋ-če = to be complete in number. **tshad-če** = to be complete in measure or number. **'tshar-če** = 1. to be finished (las-kha 'tshar-soŋ= the work has been finished; 2. grow (mi 'tshar-**če** la **či** 'gor-śen = It takes no time for a man to be grown up.). **tshal-če** = to cough when the throat gets choked while drinking water, etc. **tshig-če** = to get burned, get roasted. **tshugs-**śe = 1. To take roots, to survive a plant; 2. Settle down. t**shur-če** = to sneak. **tsher-če**. = worry. t**shod-če** = to guess. **tshor-če** = 1. hear, be heard. (ŋa-la tshor-ra me-rag = It is not heard to me.); 2. feel (ŋa-la tshan-te tshor-ra rag = I feel hot); 3. taste (ŋa la khan-te tshor-ra rag= I taste bitter). **tshos-**śe = to get cooked; to become ripe, fruit.

dsa

mdsad- če, hon.= to do. **'dsag-če** = 1. To ascend. 2. leak, seep. 3. get pricked, thorn. **'dsim-če**, hon. = to sleep. **'dsir-če** = to drip. **'dsis-če** = to crush, trample, mix.

'dsug-če = to begin, start. **'dsum-če** = to hold, (ŋe lag-pa sran-to ṭe[ṣan-ṭe] 'dsum.= Hold my hand fast). **'dsem-če** = to hesitate. **'dsel-če** = to get unseamed. **'dsom-če** = to assemble. **'dsol-če** = to sneak away. **rdsi-če** = to knead. **rdse-če** = tuck up, fold up (pyjama). **rdsogs-če** = to get exhausted, be finished (stock of grain).

ža

žag-če = to get torn, paper. **žaŋ-če hon.** = to build, to do, construct. **žar- če** = to become blind. **žu-če hon.** = to request. **žug-če** = 1. to enter; 2. hon. to sit**. žud-če** = to twist, the thread to make two fold, or more. **žub-če** = to get dented. **žus-če** = to get digested (za-če **ž**us soŋ.= The food has digested); to melt down (kha žus-soŋ. = The snow has melted). **žed -če (rjed)** = to forget.

žen-če = to get attached to, get adhered to, (smell), (gos-lag là smanne dri-ma žen-de rag. = The clothe has caught smell of medicine). **žig-če ('jig)** = to be destroyed, go out of order. **žo-če** = to milk cow. žog-**če ('jog)** = to make plain, a plank with aisle, hew. **žod-če** = to remember. **žon-če** = to ride, mount. **gžar-če** = to shave. **gžur-če** = to chop (bu-ṭa žur btaŋ soŋ.= the tree has been cleared of branches). **'žog-če** = to cut, hew.

za

za-če = eat. **zag-če** = to get pricked, thorn, needle. (khab zag-ga rag. = I feel needle pricking). **zab-če** = be decorated, (No-no di-riŋ min-'dra zab de 'dug= Today No-no is very much decorated, with new clothes, etc.). **zin-če** = to get finished, be exhausted, stock of grain. **zer-če** = say. **gzigs-če,** hon. = see. **zim-če** hon. = sleep. gz**ir-če** = to aim at. **'zad-če** = to get exhausted, get finished.

ya

yags-če = to be overjoyed. **yaŋs-če** = to become light after pain, agony. **yan-če** = to lose. **yar-če** = to get scattererd, dispersed, as grains while parching popcorn. **yal-če** = to fade away (flower, smell). **yin-če** = to be. **yib-če** = to hide oneself (kho buṭe phag-la yib-de 'dug = he is hiding behind the tree). **yug-če** = leave. **yur-če** = to weed. **yoŋ-če** = come. **yod-če** = to have, be. **g-yar-če** = to lend. **g-yo-če** = stir (zan, porridge with a stick). **g-yog-če** = sprinkle, spread, water.

ra

rag-če = to tag with. **raŋ-če** = to become cold, the body; to become numbed. **rad-če** = to spread, a sheet in the air, in sun. **ran-če** = 1. To arrive the proper time (da dus ran soŋ. = now the time has arrived); 2. spread the warp for weaving (tha-ga ran-če). **rab-če** = to be suited. **ras-če** = beg. **rig--če** = to arrange. **rid-če** = to become weak. **rib-če** = to get behind. get covered, (ñi-ma gaŋ-ke 'phag la rib-soŋ. = The sun has hidden behind the ridge). **ril-če** = to trample, in crowd. **rug-če** = to gather, pick up, to collect. **rud-če** = to knead, mix. **rub-če** = to flock together. **rum-če** = to prepare mixture (paste); bra-kur rum-**če** = to prepare paste for leavening for making buckwheat cake. **rul-če** = to be rotten. **rog-če** = to boil oil, ghee, for frying. **rlog-če** = to turn over, overthrow. **ro-če** = to become intoxicated. (ra ro-če = get intoxicated).

la

laŋ-če = to get up, rise, stand up. **lab-če** = to talk. **lam-če** = to be willing, work, (kho ma-laŋ-ga las-kha bčo-če lam-ma ma-nag.= He is lazy, has no will to work).

lug-če = to pour, serve, tea, čhaŋ. **lud-če** = to overflow. **lus-śe** = to be left behind (rgyab-la lus-śe = be left behind). **len-če** = to take, take hold of. **leb-če** = to reach. **lem-če** = to yeast (zho lem- če= yeast milk for curd).

lo = said. **log-če** = intr. To return, turn back; get turned aside, tilt.. **lom-če** = to have liking for a thing to eat, (kho tshod-ma lom-ma ma-nag. = He does not like vegetables.)

śa

śag-če = to tear, paper, (kha-śag-če = to make way through snow). **śar-če** = to rise (sun). **śi-če** = die, be dead. **śub-če** = to speak in secret. **śus-če** = to remove cover, skin, to peel, bark. **śes-śe** = to know. **śoŋ-če** = to have room, capacity, ‘i-kya-phe naŋ-la ‘i-zam ča-be rtsam-pa śoŋ-če/čhud-če mi-nug. = This much tsam-pa cannot be filled in this skin-bag. **śor-če** = 1. To flee. 2. get fallen from hand. **śos-če** = leave remainder (meal). **gśad-če** = to comb. **gśin-če** = to get digested. **gśer-če** = to borrow, but not to be returned or paid back. **bśam-če** = to arrange. **bśad-če** = to tell, explain. **bśal-če** = 1. To wash, utensils, 2. pay debt, 3. have loose motion. **bśig-če** = to destroy, demolish. **bśum-če** = to weep, sob. **śog** = imperative: come.

sa

siŋ-če = to let the pure liquid come up and the thick matter settle down, like purifying muddy water. **sil-če** = to read, to study. **su-če** = to shake, salt tea. **sug-če** = to move slightly, while sitting. **suŋ-če** = to be rotten, curry, etc. **sun-če** = to be bored, annoyed, (ŋa-raŋ čig-čig sdad-de sun čha-‘a rag.= sitting alone, I am getting bored). **sub-če** = to cover, under blanket. **se-če** = to touch, (‘i ča-lag ‘un-la se ma-se’a bor. = don’t touch these articles). **sed-če** = to sort, assort, (wool by hand for carding). **soŋ** = imperative: go. **sod-če** = to request, ask, a child demanding something again and again. **sob-če** = to repair, socks.

srag-če = to burn, roast a cake in fire. **sraŋ-če** = to straighten; get swelled up, bulgeed. **sran-če** = ot bear, to suffer. **sral-če** = to rear. **sri-če** = to save, retain. **srim-če** = to twist, a thread. **sril-če** = to roll, a thread ball. **srug-če** = to shake, a tree. **sruŋ-če** = to wait; to keep guard. **srub-če** = to hook (khab srub-če = to bind two ends of a cloth with safety-pin). **srul-če** = to mix, a small quantity of flour in a liquid, (thug-pa la tsam-pa srul-če. = to mix rtsam-pa in thug-pa.). **sred-če** = to mix. **srod-če** = warm up with heat, sun, fire.

slaŋ-če = to cause to rise, arouse. **slad-če** = to add, mix. **slan-če** = to stick, touch, like hot water bottle with body. **slab-če** = to teach. **slam-če** = to fry. **sliŋ-če** = make float. **slug-če** = pour, serve, tea, čhaŋ. **sle-če** = to knit. **sleb-če** = reach. **slog-če** = tr. to turn over, to spill, let turn back, send back. (ko-re slog-soŋ = the cup has been turned over, and spilled). **sloŋ-če** = to search. **slob-če** = to learn, study, to practice.

gsaŋ-če = to do a thing secretly, conceal. **gsal-če** = to remove. ('i ča-lag 'un sol-bor. = have these articles removed of cover.)

bsag-če = to accumulate, collect. **bsad-če** = to kill, (me bsad-če = put off fire.). **bsan-če** = to repair **bsam-če** = to think.

gso-če = to enliven, nourish, refresh; enliven a dying fire in the hearth. **gson-če** —= to be alive, to live.

ha

hug-če = to let the slumbering fire kindle; get kindled. **hud-če** = to lose, *da-ba si-rig hud-dog.* = He has lost all his money.) **hol-če** = to loosen, belt. **lhag-če** = flourish, crop. shine. **lhug-če** = get loosened. **lhem-če** = to shine.

hrul-če = (i) To add a thing in a liquid like tsampa in tea and shake; (ii) drive, a vehicle.

a

ab-če = to stammer. **aor-če** = to pour water into mouth for drinking from a pot without touching it.

Verbs

ཀུག་ཅེ། ཀུམ་ཅེ། ཀོག་ཅེ། ཀྲུམ་ཅེ། བཀག་ཅེ། བཀད་ཅེ། བཀབ་ཅེ། བཀར་ཅེ། བཀལ་ཅེ། བཀོག་ཅེ། དཀྲི་ཅེ། དཀྲུག་ཅེ། དཀྲོག་ཅེ། བཀྲམ་ཅེ། བཀྲལ་ཅེ། བཀྲི་ཅེ། བཀྲོལ་ཅེ། འཀྲིང་ཅེ། རྐུ་ཅེ། རྐོད་ཅེ། རྐྱང་ཅེ། སྐང་ཅེ། སྐད་ཅེ། སྐམ་ཅེ། སྐར་ཅེ། སྐུང་ཅེ། སྐུད་ཅེ། སྐུལ་ཅེ། སྐོན་ཅེ། སྐོར་་ཅེ། སྐོལ་ཅེ། སྐྱུག་ཅེ། སྐྱལ་ཅེ། སྐྱི་ཅེ། སྐྱིལ་ཅེ། སྐྱུག་ཅེ། སྐྱེ་ཅེ། སྐྱེད་ཅེ། སྐྱེལ་ཅེ། སྐྱོག་ཅེ། སྐྱོད་ཅེ། སྐྱོན་ཅེ། སྐྱོབ་ཅེ། སྐྱོར་ཅེ། སྐྲང་ཅེ།

ཁང་ཅེ། ཁོག་ཅེ། ཁོང་ཅེ། ཁྱུག་ཅེ། ཁྱུམ་ཅེ། ཁྱིལ་ཅེ། ཁྲུག་ཅེ། ཁྲུས་ཤེ། ཁྱེད་ཅེ། ཁྱོབ་ཅེ། ཁྱོར་ཅེ། ཁྲབ་ཅེ། ཁྲིལ་ཅེ། ཁྲོད་ཅེ། ཁྲོས་ཤེ། མཁྱེན་ཅེ། མཁྲང་ཅེ། འཁད་ཅེ། འཁར་ཅེ། འཁྱུན་ཅེ། འཁྱུར་ཅེ། འཁོར་ཅེ། འཁོལ་ཅེ། འཁྱེར་ཅེ། འཁྱོང་ཅེ། འཁྲིག་ཅེ། འཁྲིད་ཅེ། འཁྲིལ་ཅེ། འཁྲུག་ཅེ། འཁྲུད་ཅེ།

གད་ཅེ། གམ་ཅེ། གུང་ཅེ། གུར་ཅེ། གོ་ཅེ། གོམ་ཅེ། གོས་ཤེ། གྲང་ཅེ། གྲོག་ཅེ། གླུ་ཅེ། དགར་ཅེ། དགོད་ཅེ། དགོས་ཤེ། བགོད་ཅེ། བགོན་ཅེ། འགག་ཅེ། འགབ་ཅེ། འགར་ཅེ། འགུག་ཅེ། འགུལ་ཅེ། འགོག་ཅེ། འགོར་ཅེ། འགྱུར་ཅེ། འགྱེལ་ཅེ། འགྱེས་ཤེ། འགྱོག་ཅེ། འགྲང་ཤེ། འགྲད་ཅེ། འགྲེད་ཅེ། འགྲལ་ཅེ། འགྲིག་ཅེ། འགྲིམ་ཅེ། འགྲིལ་ཅེ། འགྲུབ་ཅེ།། འགྲུལ་ཅེ། འགྲོང་ཅེ།། འགྲོལ་ཅེ། རྒལ་ཅེ། རྒས་ཤེ། རྒྱག་ཅེ།། རྒྱང་ཅེ། རྒྱབ་ཅེ། རྒྱལ་ཅེ།། རྒྱུག་ཅེ།། རྒྱུད་ཅེ།། སྒར་ཅེ། སྒོམ་ཅེ། སྒྱུར་ཅེ། སྒྲིག་ཅེ། སྒྲུག་ཅེ། སྒྲོག་ཅེ།

ངུ་ཅེ། ངོམ་ཅེ། རྔ་ཅེ། རྔོ་ཅེ། རྔོད་ཅེ།

ཅག་ཅེ། ཅར་ཅེ། གཅར་ཅེ། བཅག་ཅེ། བཅད་ཅེ། བཅབ་ཅེ། བཙུ་ཅེ། བཙུག་ཅེ། བཙུན་ཅེ། བཙུས་་ཅེ། བཅེར་ཅེ། བཅོ་ཅེ། བཅོམ་ཅེ། བཅོལ་ཅེ། ལྕོག་ཅེ། ལྕེབ་ཅེ།

ཆ་ཅེ། ཆུག་ཅེ། ཆུད་ཅེ། ཆུབ་ཅེ། ཆོམ་ཅེ། མཆོང་ཅེ། མཆོད་ཅེ། འཆག་ཅེ། འཆགས་ཅེ། འཆད་ཅེ། འཆམ་ཅེ། འཆོལ་ཅེ།

མཇལ་ཅེ། འཇབ་ཅེ། འཇར་ཅེ། འཇིག་ཅེ། འཇིགས་ཅེ། འཇིབ་ཅེ། འཇུག་ཅེ། འཇུར་ཅེ། འཇུས་་ཅེ། འཇོག་ཅེ།། རྗེད་ཅེ། ལྗོན་ཅེ།

ཉག་ཚེ། ཉན་ཚེ། ཉལ་ཚེ། ཉུག་ཚེ།། ཉུལ་ཚེ།། ཉོ་ཚེ། གཉལ་ཚེ། མཉང་ཚེ། མཉེད་ཚེ། སྙན་ཚེ། སྙིད་ཚེ། སྙིལ་ཚེ། སྙོད་ཚེ། བསྙོམ་ཚེ།'

ཏིལ་ཚེ། ཏོ་ཚེ། གཏད་ཚེ། གཏུབ་ཚེ། གཏུམ་ཚེ། གཏུལ་ཚེ། བཏངཚེ། བཏབ་ཚེ། བཏིང་ཚེ། འཏག་ཚེ། རྟེན་ཚེ། རྟོལ་ཚེ། ལྟ་ཚེ། ལྟག་ཚེ། ལྟབ་ཚེ། ལྟམ་ཚེ། ལྟེམ་ཚེ། སྟན་ཚེ། སྟིག་ཚེ། སྟུག་ཚེ། སྟེན་ཚེ། སྟོན་ཚེ། སྟོར་ཚེ།

ཐག་ཚེ། ཐམ་ཚེ། ཐར་ཚེ། ཐལ་ཚེ། ཐིམ་ཚེ། ཐུག་ཚེ། ཐུབ་ཚེ། ཐེབ་ཤེ། ཐོབ་ཚེ། མཐང་ཚེ། མཐུད་ཚེ། མཐུན་ཚེ། མཐོང་ཚེ། འཐད་ཚེ། འཐབ་ཚེ། འཐིག་ཚེ། འཐུངཚེ། འཐུལ་ཚེ། འཐེན་ཚེ། འཐོག་ཚེ། འཐོན་ཚེ།

དག་ཚེ། དར་ཚེ། དིབ་ཚེ། དུར་ཚེ། དོགས་ཚེ། དོམ་ཚེ། རྡར་ཚེ། རྡུང་ཚེ། རྡོལ་ཚེ། ལྡག་ཚེ། ལྡབ་ཚེ། ལྡིར་ཚེ། སྡད་ཚེ། སྡམ་ཚེ། སྡུག་ཚེ། སྡུད་ཚེ། སྡེབ་ཚེ། དྲགས་ཚེ། དྲན་ཚེ། དྲས་ཤེ། བདབ་ཚེ། བདུག་ཚེ། འདར་ཤེ། འདིག་ཚེ། འདུས་ཚེ། འདེད་ཚེ། འདོན་ཚེ།

འདང་ཚེ། འདར་ཤེ། འདིག་ཚེ། འདུས་ཤེ། འདེད་ཚེ། འདོན་ཚེ། འདྲ་ཚེ། འདྲལ་ཚེ། འདྲི་ཚེ། འདྲུད་ཚེ། འདྲེ་ཚེ། འདྲོས་ཤེ།

ན་ཚེ། ནན་ཚེ། ནུབ་ཚེ། ནོག་ཚེ། ནོན་ཚེ། ནོར་ཚེ། གནོད་ཚེ། མནུམ་ཚེ། སྣམ་ཚེ། སྣོལ་ཚེ། མནམ་ཚེ།

པབ་ཚེ། པི་ཚེ། པིར་ཚེ། པིལ་ཚེ། པུད་ཚེ། འཔུལ་ཚེ། དཔེ་ཚེ། དཔག་ཚེ། དཔུང་ཚེ། སྤག''ཚེ། སྤར་ཚེ། སྤུག་ཚེ། སྤུབ་ཚེ། སྤེལ་ཚེ། སྤོ་ཚེ། སྤོག་ཚེ། སྤྲད་ཚེ། སྤྲིང་ཚེ། སྤྲུག་ཚེ།

ཕང་ཚེ། ཕནཚེ། ཕེབས་ཚེ། ཕྱེད་ཚེ། འཕམ་ཚེ། འཕར་ཚེ། འཕུད་ཚེ། འཕུར་ཚེ། འཕུལ་ཚེ། འཕེལ་ཚེ། འཕོག་ཚེ། འཕྲད་ཚེ། འཕྲོད་ཚེ།

བ་རིམ་ཚེ། བེར་ཚེ། བེལ་ཚེ། བུད་ཚེ། བེར་ཚེ། བ་རྟུན་ཚེ། བྱིས་ཚེ། བྲོ་ཚེ། དབྱེ་ཚེ། འབག་ཚེ། འབབ་ཚེ། འབར་ཚེ། འབུག་ཚེ། འབུབ་ཚེ འབུར་ཚེ། འབོ་ཚེ། འབོག་ཚེ། འབུར་ཚེ། འབོད་ཚེ། འབོར་ཚེ། འབོས་ཤེ། འབྱུང་ཚེ། འབྱོར་ཚེ།

འབྲལ་ཅེ། འབྲག་ཅེ། འབྲད་ཅེ། འབྲབ་ཅེ། འབྲི་ཅེ། འབྲུ་ཅེ། འབྲུག་ཅེ། འབྲིད་ཅེ། འབྲེལ་་ཅེ། འབྲེས་ཅེ། འབྲོག་ཅེ། སྦྲང་ཅེ། སྦྲས་ཅེ། སྦྲུང་ཅེ།

མིག་ཅེ། སྨུན་་ཅེ། མེད་ཅེ། མེར་ཅེ། མོལ་ཅེ། སྨྱུང་ཅེ། སྨྱོང་ཅེ། དམོད་ཅེ། སྨུག་ཅེ། སྨུར་ཅེ། སྨྱོ་ཅེ། དམོད་ཅེ། སྨུག་ཅེ། སྨུར་ཅེ། སྨྱོ་ཅེ།

ཙུམ་ཅེ། ཙེམ་ཅེ། ཙོ་ཅེ། ཙོག་ཅེ། ཙོང་ཅེ། ཙོད་ཅེ། གཙེར་ཅེ། གཙུག་ཅེ། བཙག་ཅེ། བཙལ་ཅེ། རྩེ་ཅེ། རྩེག་ཅེ། རྩེས་ཅེ། རྩེ་ཅེ། རྩོམ་ཅེ། སྩལ་ཅེ།

ཚང་ཅེ། ཚད་ཅེ། ཚར་ཅེ། ཚལ་ཅེ། ཚེག་ཅེ། ཚུགས་ཤེ། ཚུར་ཅེ། ཚེར་ཅེ། ཚོད་ཅེ། ཚོར་ཅེ། ཚོས་ཤེ།

མཛད་ཅེ། འཛག་ཅེ། འཛེམ་ཅེ། འཛེར་ཅེ། འཛེས་ཅེ། འཛུག་ཅེ། འཛུམ་ཅེ། འཛེམ་ཅེ། འཛེལ་ཅེ། འཛོམ་ཅེ། འཛོལ་ཅེ། རྫི་ཅེ། རྫེ་ཅེ། རྫོགས་ཅེ།

ཞག་ཅེ། ཞང་ཅེ། ཞར་ཅེ། ཞིག་ཅེ། ཞུ་ཅེ། ཞུག་ཅེ། ཞུད་ཅེ། ཞུབ་ཅེ། ཞུར་ཅེ། ཞུས་ཅེ། ཞེད་ཅེ། ཞེན་ཅེ། ཞོ་ཅེ། ཞོག་ཅེ། ཞོད་ཅེ། ཞོན་ཅེ། གཞར་ཅེ། གཞུར་ཅེ། འཞོག་ཅེ།

ཟ་ཅེ། ཟག་ཅེ། ཟབ་ཅེ། ཟིན་ཅེ། ཟིམ་་ཅེ། ཟེར་ཅེ། གཟིགས་ཅེ། གཟེར་ཅེ། འཟད་ཅེ

ཡགས་ཅེ། ཡངས་ཅེ། ཡན་ཅེ། ཡར་ཅེ། ཡལ་ཅེ། ཡིན་ཅེ། ཡིབ་ཅེ། ཡུག་ཅེ། ཡུར་ཅེ། ཡོང་ཅེ། ཡོད་ཅེ། གཡར་ཅེ། གཡོ་ཅེ། གཡོག་ཅེ།

རག་ཅེ། རང་ཅེ། རད་ཅེ། རན་ཅེ། རབ་ཅེ། རས་ཅེ། རིག་ཅེ། རིད་ཅེ། རིབ་ཅེ། རིལ་ཅེ། རུག་ཅེ། རུད་ཅེ། རུབ་ཅེ། རུམ་ཅེ། རུལ་ཅེ། རོ་ཅེ། རོག་ཅེ། རློག་ཅེ།

ལང་ཅེ། ལབ་ཅེ། ལམ་ཅེ། ལུག་ཅེ། ལུད་ཅེ། ལུས་ཤེ། ལེན་ཅེ། ལེབ་ཅེ། ལེམ་ཅེ། ལོ། ལོག་ཅེ། ལོམ་་ཅེ།

ཞག་ཅེ། ཞར་ཅེ། ཞི་ཅེ། ཞུབ་ཅེ། ཞུས་ཅེ། ཞེས་ཞེ། ཞོང་ཅེ། ཞོར་ཅེ། ཞོས་ཅེ། གཞད་ཅེ། གཞིན་ཅེ། གཞིར་ཅེ། བཞམ་ཅེ། བཞད་ཅེ། བཞལ་ཅེ། བཞིག་ཅེ། བཞུམ་ཅེ། ཞོག།

སིང་ཅེ། སིལ་ཅེ། སུ་ཅེ། སུག་ཅེ། སུང་ཅེ། སུན་ཅེ། སུབ་ཅེ། སེ་ཅེ། སེད་ཅེ། སོང་། སོད་ཅེ། སོབ་ཅེ། སྲག་ཅེ། སྲང་ཅེ། སྲན་ཅེ། སྲལ་ཅེ། སྲི་ཅེ། སྲིམ་ཅེ། སྲིལ་ཅེ། སྲུག་ཅེ། སྲུང་ཅེ། སྲུབ་ཅེ། སྲུལ་ཅེ། སྲེད་ཅེ། སྲོད་ཅེ།

སླང་ཅེ། སླད་ཅེ། སླན་ཅེ། སླབ་ཅེ། སླམ་ཅེ། སླིང་ཅེ། སླུག་ཅེ། སླེ་ཅེ། སླེབ་ཅེ། སློག་ཅེ། སློང་ཅེ། སློབ་ཅེ། གསང་ཅེ། གསལ་ཅེ། བསག་ཅེ། བསད་ཅེ། བསནཅེ། བསམ་ཅེ། གསོ་ཅེ། གསོན་ཅེ།

ཧུག་ཅེ། ཧོལ་ཅེ། ལྷགཅེ།་ལྷུག་ཅེ། ལྷེམ་ཅེ། ཧུལ་ཅེ། ཨབ་ཅེ། ཨོར་ཅེ།

Bibliography

English Language

Agrawala, V.S. 1953. *India as Known to Panini,* Lucknow University, Lucknow.

Banerji, R.D. 1919. *The Origin of the Bengali Script,* University of Calcutta, Calcutta.

Beal, Samuel. 1869. *Travels of Fah-Hian and Sung-Yun, Buddhist Pilgrims,* reprinted Asian Educational Services, New Delhi, 1993.

Dani, A.H. 1963. *Indian Palaeography*, Clarendon, Oxford.

Das, Saratchandra. 1915. *An Introduction to the Grammar of the Tibetan Language*, Motilal Banarsidas, Delhi, reprinted, 1972.

Deambi, B.K. Kaul. 1982. *Corpus of Sarda Inscriptions of Kashmir,* Agam Kala Prakashan, Delhi.

Francke, A.H. 1911-12. The Tibetan Alphabet, in *Epigraphica Indica*, Vol. XI, 1911-12 (pp. 266-272).

Grierson, G.A. 1908. *Linguistic Survey of India,* Vol. III, Tibeto-Burman Family, Part I, reprinted 1967, Motilal Banarsidass, Delhi.

Jaeschke, H.A. Morav. Missionary. 1865. *A Short Practical Grammar of the Tibetan Language with special reference to the spoken dialects,* Kyelang in Brit. Lahoul.

Jaeschke, H.A. 1883. *Tibetan Grammar,* Ed. by H. Wenzel, Second Edition, Trubner, London.

Jaeschke, H.A. 1883. A Tibetan-English Dictionary, with special reference to the prevailing dialects, third reprint 1958, Routledge & Kegan Paul, London.

Kaushal, Sanyukta.1976. *Ladakhi Reader,* Central Institute of Indian Languages, Mysore.

Koul, Omkar N. 2009. *Modern Hindi Grammar,* Indian Institute of Language Studies, Rohini, Delhi.

Obermiller, E. (Tr.). 1932. *The History of Buddhism in India and Tibet, by Bu-ston*, Sri Satguru Publications, Delhi, reprinted, 1986.

Richardson, H.E. 1985. *A Corpus of Early Tibetan Inscriptions,* Royal Asiatic Society.

Roerich, G.N. (Tr.).1949. *The Blue Annals,* Motilal Banarsidass, Delhi, reprinted, 1976.

Roerich, George De. 1934. The Tibetan Dialect of Lahul, *Tibetica I, Journal of Urusvati Himalayan Research Institute,* Vol. III of the Roerich Museum, Naggar (Kullu) and New York.

Sachau, Edward, C. 2002. *Alberuni's India,* Rupa and Co. New Delhi, reprinted.

Upadhyay, Jiwan. 1998. *Development of Sarda Script,* Ed. by T.P. Verma, Ramanand Vidya Bhawan, New Delhi.

Vogel, J.Ph. 1911. *Antiquities of Chamba,* Vol. I, Archaeological Survey of India, reprinted, 1984.

Vostrikov, A.I. 1970. *Tibetan Historical Literature*, Translated by Harish Chandra Gupta, Indian Studies, Past and Present, Calcutta.

Wangdu, Pasang and Hildegard Diemberger (Trans.). 2000. *dBa'-bzhed, The Royal Narrative Concerning the Bringing of the Buddha's Doctrine to Tibet*, Verlag der Osterreichischen Akademie der Wwissenschanften, Wien.

Hindi

Ojha, Gaurishankar Hirachand. 1918. *The Palaeography of India, Bhartiya Prachin Lipimala,* Motilal Banarsidass, reprinted, 2011.

Sankrityayan, Rahul.1948. *Tibbat me baudh dharma,* Kitab Mahal, Allahabad, reprinted, 1979.

Tobdan. 1990. *Bhoti Parichaya – Vyakaran evam Anuvad* (Itroduction to Bhoti: Grammar and Translation), Sonam Lamo, V. Tinno, Lahul & Spiti, H.P.

Bhoti

The Fifth Dalai Lama (rGyal-dbang nga-pa chhen-po). 1981. reprinted, Gangs-chan yul-gyi sa-la spyod-pa'i mtho-ris kyi rgyal-glon gtso-bor brjod-pa'i deb-ther, Dharamsala, H.P.

Sonam Gyalthsan (bSod-nams rGyal-tshan) : 1973. *rGyal-rabs gsal-ba'i me-long*, reprinted, distributed by Tibetan Bonpo Monastic Centre, Ochghat, Solan, H.P.

Nawang Dagpa (nGag-dbang grags-pa). 1996. *mNgaris rgyal-rabs,* Tholing gtsug-lag khang –lo-gchig stong 'khor ba'i rjes dran-mdsad sgo-'i go-sgrig tshogs-chhung gis dpar-skrun, Dharamsala, reprinted.